Numb. III.] THE [August 12, 1786.

PITTSBURGH GAZETTE

Price Six-Pence.] SATURDAY, August 12, 1786. [Vol. I.

Foreign Intelligence.

HAGUE, April 18.

WE are assured that the emperor of Morocco has offered their high mightinesses the exclusive privilege of the port of Larache, for the trade of the inhabitants of the United Provinces.

PARIS, April 18.

We have just now an express arrived from Pera, which mentions a dangerous insurrection at Constantinople, that raged so much as to occasion all the gates and avenues of the city to be shut up, and no person suffered to pass but under proper restriction; all the ambassadors had shut themselves up in their hotels; the French consul at Pera despatched this news.

MADRID, April 4.

For some weeks past two Americans have been at this place, who were presented to his majesty and the royal family on Tuesday last. They are a Mr Barclay, consul general of the United States, at l'Orient, and an officer named Franks. They are going to Morocco, to negociate a peace with the emperor of Barbary and the states of America. Two other Americans have been here these two months, one of them an officer by the name of Randal. They have set off from Barcelona for Algiers, with a view to effect a conciliation between that power & the United States.

NAPLES, (italy) March 15.

A few days since an occurence took place in this city, shocking to human nature, though it happily had not its full effect. A young man of quality being violently enamoured of a girl of inferior rank, determined to marry her. The marquis of ——— took measures to prevent so disadvantageous an alliance, which so irritated the son that he took the horrid resolution of depriving the author of his existence of life, and for that purpose bribed a servant to put some poison into a bottle of the wine which the marquis was accustomed to drink. Upon taking a glass of the wine, the marquis and a friend who was at dinner with him observed, that it had a very particular taste: and a physician being sent for, he found it to be impregnated with poison. Medicines for counteracting the poison were administered with success; but the precipitate flight of the youth convinced the unhappy father of a truth more painful than the effects of the poison.

March 18. His Sicilian majesty's deputy has had several conferences with the dey of Algiers; but according to the dispatches received, nothing has yet been concluded upon, and indeed there are not much hopes of success; notwithstanding which, the deputy expressed himself with all the force and energy that belongs to a polished nation when treating with a country of pirates:—he answered the dey, "that before the king his master would consent to pay the odious tribute which he dared to demand under the name of presents, he would use all the force of his country, not only to defend his subjects against the piracies of the Algerines, but to force him to make compensation for the damage done by the corsairs."

LONDON, April 27.

According to the accounts at the Bullion Office it appears, that there has been remitted from America in specie, that is, dollars of silver, since the conclusion of the late peace, upwards of one million two hundred and sixty thousand pounds sterling. This is one proof that America is not in a despicable situation, or sunk to such a degree as has been industriously circulated, in order to depreciate the value of a commercial connection with them.

During the late war, Mr Fox, a merchant of Falmouth, had a share in a ship, which the other owners determined to fit out as a letter of marque, very much against the opinion and inclination of Mr Fox, who was of the society of Quakers. The ship had the luck to take two French merchantmen; and the share of the prize money due to Mr. Fox amounted to the sum of 1500l. At the close of the war Mr. Fox sent his son to Paris with the 1500l. which he faithfully repaid to the owners of the ships taken. The young gentleman, to discover the owners of the vessels, was obliged to advertise them in the Paris Gazette. In consequence of this advertisement, he received a letter from a small village near Nismes, in the province of Languedoc, acquainting him, that a society of Quakers was established in that remote part of France, consisting of about 100 families. That they were so much struck with this true instance of generosity in one of their sect, that they were very desirous to open a correspondence with their friends in England. Since this accident, a count of Marsilliac, who is one of the heads of the society, has been in London to pay his friends there a visit, and is returned highly pleased with his reception. The society of French Quakers has subsisted in their present residence more than a century, without maintaining a correspondence with any other society. They are supposed to be a remnant of the ancient Albigenses, against whom several persecuting crusades were instituted in the reign of Philip the second, towards the close of the twelfth century. The count de Marsilliac was a captain of horse before he became a Quaker.

Copy of a letter from lord George Gordon, to the marquis of Carmarthen, one of his majesty's principal secretaries of state, &c. &c.

My Lord,

Mr. TUFFTS, an American gentleman, now in London, is possessed of undeniable intelligence, that John Adams, esquire, (who is received by the king as ambassador from the United States of America) has his salary paid him quarterly by the compte d'Adhemar, the French ambassador. I thought it my duty to acquaint your lordship with Mr. Tuffts's communication to me, for the immediate information of his majesty's council and government, that you may beware of Mr. Adams.

"I have the honor to be, &c.

"Ten o'clock, Saturday night, Welbeck street." G. GORDON.

The Marquis of Carmarthen's answer addressed to the right honorable lord George Gordon, Welbeck street, and subscribed "Carmarthen."

Monday night, May 1, 1786.

"LORD CARMARTHEN presents his compliments to lord George Gordon and returns his lordship thanks for the note received from him yesterday.

"Right Hon. Lord George Gordon."

May 3.

SIR,

"Having seen in your paper of this day, a copy of a letter, &c. signed G. Gordon, asserting that I was possessed of undeniable intelligence, that John Adams, esquire, has his salary paid him quarterly by the compte d'Adhemar, the French ambassador: please to inform your readers of the true state of the case, which is as follows:

"I had the honor of being introduced by an acquaintance, by mere accident, to lord George Gordon, in Bond-street. We stept into the Blenheim coffee house, where, in the course of conversation, I happened to mention that I heard from a gentleman, whose name I have mentioned to the parties, that the American ambassador, as he heard, was paid through the French ambassador.

"Without any further authority the above publication appeared. I leave the world to judge how far his lordship's conduct is consistent with propriety.

I am, sir, your humble servant,

May 3, 1786. S. TUFFTS."

Doctor Priestly has lately found that water is essential to the production of inflammable air, and that charcoal and iron when intensely hot have so strong an affinity to water, that they will attract it in the midst of the greatest fire, and even through the pores of a glass retort. This discovery, it is thought, will be of great importance in the several branches of chemistry.

Extract of a letter from the Hague, April 11.

"The report prevails again here, that in the first sittings of the states of Holland, the command of the garrison of this city will be offered to the prince stadtholder, and it is assured that the stadtholderian family will certainly not fail to be here by the 15th of May next, the day of the annual review of the burghers. This festival would certainly not take place without the presence of his serene highness, who is in some measure the object of it, as first citizen of the city, and to whom the military honors of the citizens are rendered exclusively on that day.

"The citizens of Wyck in the province of Utrecht, shew the firmest countenance, and brave openly the severest resolutions of the states. There is not the least appearance that the other provinces (Gueldres alone perhaps excepted) will grant any of their troops to that of Utrecht, to make the burghers submit; now the province of Utrecht has not a sufficient number of regiments, any more than that of Gueldres, for such an undertaking; therefore, it is naturally concluded that the citizens will probably attain their ends, and that, finally, the regulations of the regency will pass in the affirmative on the 20th of October next."

May 7. The most authentic accounts from Dublin, by the last packet, inform us, that there is at present a greater prospect of an union between Great Britain and Ireland, than has appeared in any former period; the most distinguished patriots having given the strongest assurance to government, that they are ready to meet in any impartial plan for a lasting alliance between the two islands in the most cordial manner. An event most devoutly to be wished, as it is only by an union between the sister islands that the species of the one can become the interest of the other, and that the riches and strength of either kingdom can become the property of both.

DUBLIN, *April 21*

A curious trial will come on next month before the parliament of Limoges, in France. An adventurer of the masculine gender, who travelled through most parts of the kingdom, sometimes as a lady, and sometimes as a gentleman, had long made a practice of forming matrimonial connexions with either sex. He had a carriage and suit agreeable to the pretensions of a person of quality; and managed his designs so artfully, either in a male or female character, that several of both sexes have become dupes to his art. He always made it a practice to decamp early the morning after the ceremony was performed, and carried with him the most valuable portable articles that were to be found.

A letter received yesterday by a gentleman of this city from London, on whose authenticity we have every reason to rely, contains the following very important intelligence: That Mr. Pitt and a nobleman of this kingdom, now in London, have had of late several conferences touching the affairs of Ireland, the result of which is a determination, as soon as the British parliament rise, to resume the business of a [illegible] of the Irish privy council are to be in London in July next: The British minister being determined, says the letter writer, to carry this, his favorite measures through the Irish houses, *let it cost what it will.*

ON NEGROES.
A FRAGMENT.

——WHEN Tom, an' please your honor, got to the shop, there was nobody in it, but a poor negro girl, with a bunch of white feathers slightly tied to the end of a long cane, flapping away flies—not killing them.

'Tis a pretty picture! said my uncle Toby— She had suffered persecution, Trim, and had learnt mercy—

—She was good, an' please your honor, from nature, as well as from hardships; and there are circumstances in the story of that poor, friendless slut, which would melt a heart of stone, said Trim; and, some dismal winter's evening, when your honor is in the humor, they shall be told you, with the rest of Trim's story, for it makes a part of it—

Then do not forget, Trim, said my uncle Toby.

A negro has a soul, an' please your honor, said the corporal—doubtingly.

I am not much versed, corporal, quoth my uncle Toby, in things of this kind; but I suppose God would not leave him without one, any more than thee or me—

—It would be putting one sadly over the head of another, quoth the corporal—

—It would so, said my uncle Toby.

Why, then, an' please your honor, is a black wench to be used worse than a white one?

I can give no reason, said my uncle Toby—

—Only, cried the corporal, shaking his head, because she has no one to stand up for her.—

'Tis that very thing, quoth my uncle Toby, which recommends her to protection, and her brethren with her—'Tis the fortune of war which has put the whip into our hands now—where it may be hereafter, Heaven knows! but be it where it will, the brave, Trim, will not use it unkindly.

God forbid, said the corporal.—Amen, responded my uncle Toby, laying his hand upon his heart.

STERNE.

THE OLDEST ISSUE OF THE PITTSBURGH GAZETTE

PITTSBURGH'S POST-GAZETTE

"The First Newspaper West of The Alleghenies"

J. CUTLER ANDREWS

BOSTON
CHAPMAN & GRIMES
Mount Vernon Press

JOHNSON REPRINT CORPORATION   JOHNSON REPRINT COMPANY LTD.
111 Fifth Avenue, New York, N.Y. 10003   Berkeley Square House, London, W1X6BA

SERIES IN AMERICAN STUDIES

Editor-in-Chief: Joseph J. Kwiat

PROGRAM IN AMERICAN STUDIES
UNIVERSITY OF MINNESOTA

TO

ARTHUR M. SCHLESINGER

TEACHER AND FRIEND

PREFACE

Writing the history of a newspaper is something of an experiment—not on account of the novelty of the task, for already several histories of individual newspapers have appeared. It is rather the "stuff" of which a newspaper is made that presents the real problem. A newspaper is first of all a transmitter of news. But it is more than that. It is also one of the most important of the agencies that are continuously working to shape the attitudes of the public mind upon questions of the day. A half century ago, Lord Bryce, an outstanding foreign critic of the American scene, noted in his *American Commonwealth* that the press, particularly the newspaper press, was at that time the chief determinant of public opinion in the United States. Only a few months ago, at a meeting of the American Historical Association, a leading American historian expressed the view that the contemporary newspaper was "a factor of increasing importance in evaluating the patterns in the public mind. Other agencies for expression of public opinion may have declined in importance. The newspaper has not." On the other hand, there is no denying the fact that the newspaper itself is to a large degree what its readers want it to be, and so it takes something of its color from the ideas of the great mass of its constituency. For that reason it is difficult, if not well nigh impossible, to divorce the history of this newspaper—any newspaper —from the life of its times.

The following pages seek to portray the contribution that the *Pittsburgh Gazette* under its various names has made to the history of the Pittsburgh district and of the country at large. It is particularly fitting that a history of the paper should appear this year, at the time of the sesqui-centennial anniversary of the paper's founding. Throughout the last century and a half, Pittsburgh has stood figuratively at the crossroads of the nation watching the western migration sweep by and taking an active part in laying the foundations of industrial America. All of this and much more is depicted by the issues of the *Gazette*, which have run without interruption through the period.

v

To assemble all of the extant issues of the paper was in itself
no small task. A majority of them were to be found in libraries in
and around Pittsburgh, but a respectable number were located in
miscellaneous libraries from Boston to Chicago. Many issues have
been preserved only by the sheerest good fortune. Sometime in
the year 1877 or 1878 Horace Hayden, rector of one of the churches
in Brownsville, Pennsylvania, chanced upon a sheaf of old newspapers protruding from a neighboring ash bin. Upon examination
they proved to be a more or less continuous file of the *Pittsburgh
Gazette* for the years 1793 and 1794, which had been removed from
an attic in the home of one of the original settlers in Brownsville,
Jacob Bowman. Hayden rescued the precious issues and later put
them up for public sale in Philadelphia, where they were purchased
by Senator George T. Oliver and consigned to their ultimate home,
the Carnegie Library of Pittsburgh. The writer was so fortunate
as to discover also a considerable number of issues still in the
hands of private families in the locality.

Facts pertaining to the subject were drawn from a variety of
sources. Interesting and important information was discovered
in other Pittsburgh newspapers, in the private papers of John
Scull, Neville B. Craig, Nelson P. Reed, and Charles M. Bregg;
in memoirs, histories of Pittsburgh, local county histories, mono-
graphs treating of the local history of the region, and works of a
more general nature. Those who are interested in a more detailed
treatment of the early period are referred to the author's doctoral
dissertation, "A History of the *Pittsburgh Gazette*, 1786–1861," on
file in the Widener Library, Harvard University.

The writer desires to express here his indebtedness to those
who have notably assisted in the preparation of this volume: to
Professor Arthur M. Schlesinger of Harvard University, who carefully supervised this work in its early stages; to Mr. Oliver J.
Keller, present editor of the *Post-Gazette*, whose interest in the
project is gratefully acknowledged; to Dr. Solon J. Buck, Director
of Publications for the National Archives, who as director of the
Western Pennsylvania Historical Survey was kind enough to offer

many scholarly criticisms; to Miss Rose Demarest and others of the Carnegie Library staff, who gave assistance freely at every turn; to the staff of the Historical Society of Western Pennsylvania, whose newspaper collection was always readily available; to Mrs. Charles M. Bregg, Mr. Neville Craig Davison, Mrs. William Lecky, Mr. Joseph Mitchell, Mrs. Alfred Reed, and Mr. John I. Scull, for the loan of valuable newspaper and manuscript materials; to Mr. Warren Christman, Mr. Walter Christy, Mr. William De Beck, Mr. Charles Doyle, Mr. Pierce Egan, Mr. Robert Ginter, Mr. Glendinning Keeble, Mr. John McKirdy, Mr. McCready Huston, Mr. William Martin, Mr. Augustus K. Oliver, Mr. George S. Oliver, and Mr. George Seibel for many enlightening comments and suggestions. Dr. Austin Wright and Dr. Lester M. Beattie of the faculty of the Carnegie Institute of Technology and Mrs. Norman H. Dawes read and criticized selected chapters. Special mention should be made of my secretary, Miss Mary Jo Hauser, who extended invaluable aid in the preparation of the manuscript. The illustrated half titles for the various parts of the book have been designed and executed by Miss Edith Berthold, of Detroit. I cannot conclude without stating the debt I owe to my father, who first directed my attention to the fascination that the study of American history has for those who cherish the memory of the past.

J. CUTLER ANDREWS.

Carnegie Institute of Technology
Pittsburgh, August 1, 1936

CONTENTS

ILLUSTRATIONS

THE PIONEER

PITTSBURGH'S POST-GAZETTE

CHAPTER I

THE PRESS IN THE WILDERNESS

One afternoon late in the autumn of 1785 a certain George Kimzer was driving his team and wagon along the weary mountain road west of Chambersburg, Pennsylvania. In the course of his journey over hills and around precipitous curves, he was overtaken by another wagon carrying Samuel Walker and his family westward. The travelers exchanged the time of day. How far was Kimzer going? "To Fort Pitt," he replied. Stowed away under his wagon top was a printing press that he had brought all the way from Philadelphia. It was consigned to two young printers, John Scull and Joseph Hall, who were anxious to put it to work, explained Kimzer as he clucked warningly to his horses. The wagon wheels started rolling again, and in due time the first press west of the Allegheny Mountains was in the hands of its owners.

In 1785 the "Gateway to the West" was not much more than a collection of huts around Fort Pitt. Yet there was among its citizenry an active-minded young lawyer named Hugh Henry Brackenridge, Princeton-trained and not without some journalistic experience. Brackenridge had been influential in procuring the press for Scull and Hall; probably it was also he who suggested that it might be used to put out a public gazette, or newspaper. At any rate, on July 29, 1786, the two young men gathered together what information and advertising they could find and struck off the initial number of the first newspaper to be published west of the mountains, the *Pittsburgh Gazette*.

Scull, apparently the moving figure of the enterprise, sprang from a family of substance in eastern Pennsylvania. Nicholas Scull, the first of the line in America, was a Quaker and an intimate friend of William Penn. Nicholas Scull the second was surveyor-general of the Pennsylvania colony for a time and a respected friend of Benjamin Franklin. One of his sons, Jasper, moved to Reading. There his son, John Scull, was born sometime during

1

1765. Not much can be learned of John's boyhood days. An old Pittsburgh tradition has it that he was known around town as the "handsome young man with the white hat." Tall, of upright bearing, with his hair combed neatly back over his forehead, he well answered the flattering description. He was very nearsighted, but that did not prevent him from greeting his friends with a pleasant nod as he chanced to pass them on the street.

One and all, they must have crowded eagerly into the printing office on Water Street the day the press arrived. There they beheld a small wooden hand machine, fashioned by Adam Ramage, perhaps the most celebrated of the early American press-makers, and purchased from Andrew Brown, proprietor of the *Philadelphia Federal Gazette*. It was a puny contrivance, so imperfect that only one page could be printed at a pull. Plainly the printer would have to work at top speed to turn off seven hundred copies in a ten-hour day.

No precise figures exist for the amount of circulation that the *Gazette* had during its early years. At first the subscribers lived chiefly to the east and southeast of Pittsburgh along the road to Greensburg or by the wooded shores of the Monongahela, the Youghiogheny, and their tributaries.

From the outset this newspaper venture encountered a number of obstacles. The problem of transmitting the paper to subscribers inevitably retarded its circulation. In Pittsburgh the printers could deliver their paper in person, but how was the rural subscriber to be reached? The Pittsburgh of 1786 lay beyond the pale of the United States government mail facilities. Now and then a friend might be counted upon to carry a letter or deliver a newspaper to a rural resident, but the more frequent story was one of long waits, of disappointments on account of the tardy appearance of the weekly intelligence or its failure to appear at all. In 1786 James Brison made his way to New York and obtained from the federal postal authorities permission to establish two posts, one from Philadelphia to Pittsburgh, the other, a branch of the first, from Bedford to Alexandria, Virginia. Early in 1787 weekly mail service between Alexandria and Pittsburgh by way of Bedford was assured. A regular post was established between Philadelphia and Pittsburgh in the course of the next year. In 1793 Morgantown, across the Virginia line, became the terminus of a post route established under the management of the *Gazette* to provide a medium for distributing the paper in that region.[1] Before the century was over the installation of regular mail boat service along the Ohio River, and the establishment of a post office at Chillicothe, one of the principal towns of the Northwest Territory, brought the *Gazette* into communication with many new points to the westward. Not all of Scull's interest in the extension of mail facilities was prompted by concern for his journal's welfare, for not long after he arrived in Pittsburgh he became the town postmaster and remained so until 1794.

Until the extension of local mail facilities, sundry individuals offered their services for distributing the newspaper beyond the town limits. John Blair, for example, advertised in the *Gazette* that "all persons on or near said river [Monongahela] who have subscribed for the *Pittsburgh Gazette* .... can have their papers brought to them every week at a more reasonable rate than any other conveyance and without disappointment." Similarly John M'Donald of Bellmont reminded his friends that his boat service was "the most speedy and sure way of transporting the *Pittsburgh Gazette* to the subscribers on Youghiogany, Peter's creek, Mingo creek and Pigeon creek."[2]

Further embarrassment was occasioned by the fluctuating supply of newsprint, to which the frequent issues of reduced size were a silent testimonial. Of course Scull was profuse with apologies. His supply of paper and printing materials had to be brought over the mountains on pack horses, this at a time when freight rates were six dollars per hundred weight. Roads were bad, the carriers irregular. Sometimes writing paper was resorted to; on several occasions cartridge paper of inferior quality had to be borrowed from Fort Pitt. On July 1, 1792, Scull petitioned Major Isaac Craig, the commandant:

Dear Sir:
John Wright's pack-horses, by whom I receive my paper from Chambersburgh, has returned without bringing me any—owing to none being finished. As I am entirely out, and do not know what to do, I take the liberty of applying to you for some you have in the public stores, (and of which I have had some), as a loan, or an exchange, for the kind herein enclosed—and as this kind is smaller, I will make an adequate allowance—or if you could wait two or three weeks, I will return you paper of a superior quality....as I have sent to Philadelphia, by Mr. Brackenridge, for a large quantity, and John Wright's pack-horses return immediately for Chambersburgh, and will bring me up some—as I conceive you will not want the paper as soon as I can replace it, I flatter myself you will let me have three reams, and as soon as I receive mine it shall be returned, or if you choose to take the inclosed in exchange, it shall be immediately sent you—if you can oblige me with the paper it will do any time this day, and I shall consider myself as under a very particular obligation.
     I am, dear sir, your most obedient servant,
                                         JOHN SCULL.[3]

Then in 1797 two Quaker mechanics, Samuel Jackson and Jonathan Sharpless, erected a new paper mill at Redstone Old Fort in Fayette County. Scull was delighted. By saving old rags and sending them to the mill, the people of the western country might assure its success and along with it the success of their *Gazette.* To celebrate the event the subscription price of the paper was cut to less than half its former figure.

Often Scull's patience was worn thin because of the inability or unwillingness of the canny Scots of the hinterland to pay their annual dues promptly. He did not mince words. Although he was quite willing to receive payments in kind (pelts, wheat, corn, whisky, barley, and wood were listed on one occasion), prompt payments were demanded in no uncertain terms. There was no sale of single issues. The yearly rate was 17s 6d ($4.37½), a large sum at best in a frontier region where ready money was remarkably scarce. By 1808 the debits outstanding were estimated to be several thousand dollars, and a number of subscribers were in arrears six, eight, and ten years. The printer might snatch what crumbs of comfort he could from the lists of sheriff's sales which periodically came his way; but he could not rely upon revenue from advertising to make up the deficit—it is probable that the average value of the advertising space in a single issue during these years did not exceed twelve dollars.

One bane of modern civilization, chronic unemployment, was blissfully unknown in eighteenth-century Pittsburgh. Scull was frequently at a loss for help in getting out the paper. In November, 1786, Hall died, and Scull, who was left as sole business-manager, reporter, type-setter, and delivery boy, turned in his perplexity to Brackenridge, then in Philadelphia on legislative business. Within a few weeks John Boyd was sent out to Pittsburgh to coöperate with Scull in the paper's management. Boyd does not seem to have had much influence in the direction of the paper. For a time his name was identified with a circulating library project for which subscriptions were to be taken at the *Gazette* office. Then one day late in the summer of 1788 he walked out of the Water Street office, climbed a hill (since called Boyd's Hill) just back of the present court house, and hanged himself, without disclosing his reasons. Scull, omitting all comment, simply dropped Boyd's name from the statement of management and stoically went on alone. In lieu of a partner, he had to depend upon the assistance of an apprentice for inking the type. This task, now performed by machine, was accomplished by means of an ink ball, which looked for all the world like a football with a handle attached.

Like most of his frontier neighbors, Scull had a number of irons in the fire. Postmaster, printer of the first newspaper in the West, he had a job-printing business too. The clamor of the country folk for almanacs to place beside the Bible on the family table meant further revenue. One stock of them was quoted at three shillings per dozen for storekeepers, who added a modest sum to the cost for the retail trade. A respectable number of books issued from Scull's press: songbooks, spelling books, and cate-chisms, for which the way was prepared by the publication in 1793 of the third volume of Brackenridge's *Modern Chivalry*, the first book to be printed west of the Alleghenies.

The *Gazette* news, like that of most eighteenth-century and early nineteenth-century newspapers in the West, was a com-pound in considerable degree of the proceedings of the European countries and Congress together with a small amount of general advertising and some political controversies. The European news varied from four to seven months in age. American intelligence, somewhat less stale, appeared in the form of letters to the editor from Boston, New York, Baltimore, and Philadelphia. There might be "an extract of a letter from a gentleman in Philadelphia to his friend in this town," a very common type of news heading at the time. While the *Gazette* had a political purpose, it was at first without editorials in the modern sense of the term. In fact Scull, always modest and unassuming, was very chary about applying the title of editor to himself. Not until political con-troversy waxed hot around 1800 was the evolution of the editorial perceptible. Instead, opinion was directed by long, anonymous letters from "Vindex," "Observer," "Farmer," and others; al-though there is reason to believe that Scull sometimes masqueraded his sentiments in this form. These savants gave vent to sage com-ments on political questions, religion, morals, popular education, and the like. Sometimes for filler, especially when the eastern mail was held up, more abstract subjects might be chosen: "Laugh-ing," "Gallantry," "Drunkenness," or "Women." Doubtless such contributions were thoroughly discussed around the hearthstones of lonely cabins or in the taverns, where there was usually someone like the schoolmaster in *Rip Van Winkle* to read the news to the gathering of loafers. Market prices, manufacturing enterprises, and the deaths or marriages of prominent citizens were the chief subjects of local interest. The brilliant marriage of an officer at Fort Pitt to a member of the Wilkins family in 1788 was viewed complacently by the *Gazette* as "a union that promises as much happiness as any that has ever taken place in this western country." The writer of an obituary announcement the same year for the "much and justly lamented" Samuel Mackay observed with all the formality of the age:

> An elaborate essay on the deceased would be but an affront to his merit,—as memory will ever represent him the truest friend, a dutiful son...and strictly moral in his principles. These traits united, render him a real loss to society, as such we drop a tear to his memory, and heave a sigh to departed merit.[4]

In common with most western journals, the *Gazette* also endeavored to improve its readers' tastes by including matter of purely literary interest. The frontier newspaper was expected to exercise many of the functions of the modern magazine; indeed, people had little else to read. It was customary to reserve a corner for nondescript verse; sometimes a few stanzas from some famous poet like Burns or Freneau, however, found their way into the literary column. The predominance of sentiment in these literary effusions is well illustrated by the tale of "Sidney, or the Parental Beggar," an orphan who befriended a pair of beggars, fugitives from an Algerine dungeon, only to recognize them at last as his long-lost parents. Did the author attempt to shield this intimate moment from prying public eyes? Not for a moment. The right touch of emotional crescendo was given, and then the moral came in on the highest note:

> "Cease, O my father, the mournful tale! behold, my parents! behold your son, your Frederic Sidney!"—He would have said more; but his excessive joy stopped his utterance; the tears poured down his face, and mingled with those of his parents. In vain do I attempt to sketch the scene; let those who possess humanity, think what they must feel, on beholding a son, a father, and a mother, after thirty years of tedious absence, meet again! Suffice me for to say, that happiness, content, and plenty crowned the remaining days of the venerable pair, and blessed the youthful, the filial Sidney.[5]

If humor was what the reader desired, he might now and then be
regaled by a ludicrous anecdote usually built around a pun, such
as the following typical example:

> Milton was asked by a friend whether he would in-
> struct his daughter in the different languages? To which
> he replied, "No, sir, *one tongue* is sufficient for a woman."[6]

From a modern point of view it is the advertisements, though
of slim proportions, which do most to relieve the otherwise dull
tone of the early numbers of the *Gazette*.

> Advertisements not exceeding a Square are Inserted
> Three Weeks for a Dollar and every continuance after
> one-fourth of a Dollar; those exceeding a square are in-
> serted in proportion.

Such were the terms offered to advertisers from the beginning.
News was not sacrificed for advertising revenue, however; often
the printer felt called upon to apologize for omitting advertising
matter on account of lack of space! Prominent among the advertisers was the general-store merchant, often listing his merchandise in a manner that invited a barter of commodities. Cor-
duroys, velvets and velverets, best beaver fustian, "sattins,"
shalloons, duroys, moreens, calimancoes, taboreens, and camblets
—the names are strange; there is even something musty about
them, as if they had been sealed up for a century and a half behind
the counters that they once brightly graced. Other advertisements
spoke briefly of "vendues" or auctions of stock and household
goods, runaway slaves, absconding apprentices, straying livestock,
and a host of other things interesting to a restless people.

Of course the outward appearance of the newspaper was radically different from that of the present day, both in size and
typographical arrangement. The sheet size of the first issue of the
Gazette, a publication three columns wide and carrying margins of
approximately one-half inch, measured fifteen inches by nine and
three-quarters inches. The front page was given over to a solid
mass of advertising, and its appearance was not unlike that of the

cover of the present-day *London Times*. A few uninspired cuts supplied practically the only bit of variety in the generally monotonous format of the paper. They were almost exclusively advertising heads, small figures of blooded stallions, perhaps, or large plumed beaver hats. Possibly the printer was groping for some means of appeal to the eye when he dictated successive enlargements of his paper—in 1799, when the *Gazette* was increased to royal size, gothic head and all, superior to that of any other paper in the western country; and again in 1811, when a super-royal sheet was adopted and the paper could rank itself with the Philadelphia journals.[7] At the beginning of the year 1813 the *Gazette* came out with entirely new type—"A new coat," Scull called it, "not a turn-coat trimmed at the treasury—not a fancy coat finished with French lining—but an honest American coat, warp and woof, durable in its texture, and creditable to the owner."[8]

All through the period the *Gazette* appeared regularly once a week. In 1800 the day of issue was changed frequently to accord with revisions of mail schedule. The paper began to publish supplements to the regular four-page issue in order to care for surplus advertising about the same time. Extras, however, were first printed during the War of 1812. There is to be found in the *Life and Reminiscences* of William G. Johnston, a Pittsburgh business man of the last century, an interesting anecdote about this:

> The first news of Perry's victory on Lake Erie, Sept. 10, 1813, came to Pittsburgh in a letter addressed to Mr. Johnston (postmaster of the town and father of the writer); and immediately on receipt of it he carried it to Mr. Scull, who issued a diminutive extra of the *Gazette* announcing the glad tidings to the inhabitants of the town; and this, in all probability, was the first extra ever issued by the Pittsburgh press.[9]

As to the historical importance of this particular issue, Johnston is somewhat in error. The first war extra appears to have been dated November 4, 1812. It contained a message to Congress from President Madison and was of regular size. In this respect it was unlike the extra of May 8, 1813, a small handbill about eight by twelve inches, relating the news of the American capture of York in upper Canada.

By the end of the century, the circulation territory of the paper had expanded liberally over western Pennsylvania and the Virginia Panhandle, including subscribers in Somerset, Bedford, Erie, Meadville, Wheeling, and other principal towns.

Through the medium of the printed word the *Gazette* afforded its backwoods constituency many points of contact with the more polished outside world. Sometimes it offended its subscribers by what it printed. While remarkably free from libel suits all through the early period, the paper did not always escape the threat of court action. Within a year after its founding it published a letter from "A Farmer" reviling Brackenridge for voting in the Pennsylvania General Assembly against a land bill and accusing him of having "sold the good will of his country for a dinner of some stockholder's fat beef." Brackenridge chose to feel greatly injured. At length, he wrote to the editors stating that this was a libel and, in law, indictable and actionable. By publishing the article the printers had made themselves fully as culpable as the author, said Brackenridge. Still, as printers were given to a great deal of license in such matters, he would excuse them if they would provide him with the identity of the writer. Scull and Boyd answered rather independently that the names of contributors were kept in the strictest confidence, especially if the protected one would underwrite any losses sustained by the printers in his behalf; but in view of the circumstances, they agreed to furnish Brackenridge the name if he would call at the office. With this the matter was dropped.

JOHN SCULL, FOUNDER AND FIRST EDITOR

THE GAZETTE PRINTING OFFICE IN 1790

CHAPTER II

NEWSPAPER GLIMPSES OF EARLY PITTSBURGH

In the Carnegie Library of Pittsburgh there is a group of paintings representing Pittsburgh in its early years—a mute contrast to what a bird's-eye view would show today. Doubtless the passage of years has lent a romantic touch to the scene. Arthur Lee of Virginia, who visited Pittsburgh in 1784, evidently thought very little of the place, for in his journal he stated that the town

> is inhabited almost entirely by Scots and Irish, who live in paltry log-houses, and are as dirty as in the north of Ireland, or even Scotland.... There are in the town four attorneys, two doctors, and not a priest of any persuasion, nor church, nor chapel; so that they are likely to be damned, without *the benefit of clergy*.... The place, *I believe*, will never be very considerable.[1]

One of Pittsburgh's adopted sons, Hugh Henry Brackenridge, was of a totally different opinion. Seizing upon the early issues of the *Gazette* as a vehicle for his "boosting," he exclaimed in exaggerated vein: "This town must in future time be a place of great manufacturing: indeed the greatest on the continent and perhaps in the world." One of his contributions, styled "on the Situation of the Town of Pittsburgh and the State of Society at that Place," presents the best contemporary account of Pittsburgh in 1786 and enjoys the distinction of being the most frequently reprinted article ever to appear in the *Gazette*. In spite of its inflated style of writing, it is, in its way, a classic, and so an excerpt from it may well preface what is to follow:

> The town consists at present of about an hundred dwelling houses, with buildings appurtenant. More are daily added, and for some time past it has improved with an equal but continual pace. The inhabitants, children, men and women are about fifteen hundred; this number doubling almost every year from the accession of people

11

from abroad, and from those born in the town. As I pass
along, I may remark that this new country is in general
highly prolific; whether it is that the vegetable air, if I
may so express it, constantly perfumed with aromatic
flavor, and impregnated with salts drawn from the fresh
soil, is more favorable to the production of men and other
animals than decayed grounds.

There is not a more delightful spot under heaven to
spend any of the summer months than at this place. I am
astonished that there should be such repair to the Warm
Springs in Virginia, a place pent up between the hills
where the sun pours its beams concentred as in a burning
glass, and not a breath of air stirs; where the eye can
wander scarcely half a furlong; while here we have the
breezes of the river, coming from the Mississippi and the
ocean; the gales that fan the woods, and are sent from the
refreshing lakes to the northward.... Here we have the
town and country together. How pleasant is it in a summer evening, to walk out upon these grounds; the smooth
green surface of the earth, and the woodland shade soften-
ing the late fervid beams of the sun; how pleasant by a
chrystal fountain in a tea party under one of those hills,
with the rivers and the plains beneath.[2]

There is a quality about such descriptions that lives and
lingers in the memory. Yet its writer was far from being simply
an imaginative dreamer. Thirty-six log houses, one stone house,
and one frame house, and five small stores extending along Chan-
cery Lane and Market Street—this was the Pittsburgh of Brackenridge's hopes. Much of its community life centered around the
tavern, where hospitality was extended to friend and stranger
alike; where well-known hosts like Josiah Tannehill or Barnabas
McShane were on hand to prove their good intentions to all who
stopped at their doors. *"Here the weary may rest—the hungry feed
and those who thirst may quaff of the best"* was the advertisement of
one enterprising tavern-keeper. Another, who opened Beaumont's
Hotel and Ohio Coffee House in 1789, promised to use his utmost
endeavors to procure punctually newspapers from Philadelphia
and other distant points for the use and amusement of his cus-

tomers. Furthermore, by an undertaking "hitherto unattempted in this western country," he proposed to cater to travelers and those "select parties" that desired "apartments without being intruded upon by others."[3]

Contributing their feathered finery to the general mixture of costume that prevailed in the post town, bands of Indians were wont to drift into the settlement to haggle with the merchants or practice petty thievery. Long after the danger of Indian warfare around Pittsburgh had been removed a surprising public notice in the *Gazette* implied that the sight of Indians in town was far from being unusual. Addressed to the merchants of Pittsburgh, it read:

> Brothers,
> Your friends of the Seneca Nation, belonging to Allegheny River, speak to you.—We hope you will be attentive, and listen to our talk. We understand that some of you are in the practice of trusting our Indians for goods &c. Brothers—We have taken this matter into consideration, and, in order that the chain of friendship may be kept bright between you and us, we now earnestly entreat you not to trust our Indians any more, as we are determined to pay no debts contracted by individuals....
> We request our talk may be put on the great paper, that you may not be deceived.
> Agreed on at a Council held at the Cold Spring 2d mo. 9th, 1807.[4]

White servants and negro slaves might be seen hobnobbing with their social betters. Scull's Quaker background did not incline him to favor negro slavery; on numerous occasions he made his attitude plain. Still he followed the custom of the times and printed many a notice calling for the return of runaway servants. A few examples will suffice to indicate the nature of these alarms. One of 1787 held out the promise of

ONE HUNDRED DOLLARS REWARD

> Ranaway from the subscriber, on the 11th of October last, an indented Irish servant Man, named JOHN BUCHANAN, about 28 years of age, 5 feet 5 or 6 inches

high, black complexion, of a very effeminate appearance, short black hair, speaks with the brogue, is very pregnant with little artifice, and a notorious liar; had on a blue broadcloth coat, with yellow buttons, moleskin jacket, black breeches, and a large cocked castor hat; took with him two horses, one black, 15 and an half hands high, with a small star, his left hind foot white, marked on the right buttock U S, almost worn out; the other a bay; he carried a case of holster pistols and a fusil; endeavoured to change the horses in the Alleghany Mountain, on his way down the old Virginia road; he had then in company with him a young woman, whom he passed for his wife; he was bought of Jeremiah Warder, Parker & Co. in Philadelphia, on the 27th of May, 1784: says he was born in Cork, and is a glove maker. As he had access to a large store in Pittsburgh, it appears that he has carried off a considerable sum of money and other valuable property; it is therefore expected that he may escape to Ireland; should this be the case, the above reward shall be paid to any person that will have him apprehended, so that he may be brought to justice, and a reward of Forty Dollars shall be paid to any person that will have him taken and secured in any workhouse or prison in the United States, so that his master may get him again, or that will deliver him to General Febiger, in Philadelphia; Walter Roe, in Baltimore; Michael M'Kewan, in Martinsburgh, Virginia, or the subscriber in Pittsburgh, and all reasonable charges.

JAMES O'HARA.[5]

Another instance, involving a slave, dates from the year 1793.

STOP THE VILLAIN!

Thirty Dollars Reward

Ranaway from the subscriber living in Washington County, Maryland, 8 miles from Hagerstown, on the 15th inst. a light coloured Negro Man, named Jack, 35 years of age, about 5 feet 7 inches high, straight and square made, has lost a fore tooth, bow legged, thick flat feet, is a shoemaker and carpenter to trade; had on striped

cotton overalls, fine shirt, old fulled linsey waistcoat, old
gray coating coat, no hat, but is an active thief and perhaps will soon get a hat and change all his cloaths if he
can steal better ones, also took a half worn Indian
blanket. Whoever takes up said negro and secures him so
that his master may get him again, shall have 5 dollars if
taken within 10 miles from home, 10 dollars if 20 miles
from home, 20 dollars if 50 miles, and if upwards, the
above reward, and reasonable charges if brought home
paid by

JOSIAH PRICE.[6]

Still another notice of 1807 suggests that all was not rosy in
the relationship of master and servant:

TAKE NOTICE

RANAWAY again, Mary Baltise, a mustee,[7] who I advertised in this paper on the 3d inst. The said girl ab-
sconded twice yesterday, the 18th inst. I warn any body
from trusting her on my account, and whoever dares to
harbour her, shall be prosecuted, as the law directs. She
is, as I solemnly before said, a *thief;* a *liar,* and unexcep-
tionably speaking, *one of the greatest monsters in nature.*
She has about 9 months to stay with me, but I offer her
for sale, to any body wishing to have a *plague* in his
family.

ST. LEGER D'HAPPART.[8]

The number of such public notices was legion. Many of them
seemed to have been dictated by an explosion of temper rather
than by any expectation of procuring the culprit's return. In one
case a reward of one cent was assured for "a promising youth for
the penitentiary addicted to lying, stealing, and drinking." Whoever returned the apprentice was promised thirty lashes in addition to the reward! From this there can be little doubt that
vagrant apprentices and persons of color constituted a floating
population that gave the authorities much concern. Some of the
regulations proclaimed by the town clerk seem petty in the light

of the present day. Five shillings' fine was ordained for the heinous
offense of firing off a gun or galloping a horse within the streets,
lanes, or alleys of the borough. The tendency of the porcine
population of the community to run riot over the town gave rise
to further regulation. There was a letter to Scull in the *Gazette*,
March 23, 1793, signed "Many," bewailing this grievous nuisance:

> It is impossible to save a garden where such an animal
> runs at large, and will insinuate itself by undermining, or
> opening a way with the snout through the paleings, or
> entering the moment the gate is opened by a neighbour,
> for the purpose of obtaining water from your pump.

To this indictment were added the opinions of Brackenridge and
William Blackstone to the effect that keeping swine in the town
was an indictable offense, and shooting the offensive invaders
justifiable. The burgesses of the town agreed that this was a
weighty matter and the next year issued an order that hogs were
henceforth not to be allowed to run at large.

What frontier lawlessness there was around Pittsburgh hardly
reached the proportions of a crime wave. Crimes there were; yet
very little crime news as we know it today appeared in the *Gazette*
at the time.

Money, watches, and other trinkets are always fair game for
thieves, but the light-fingered gentry of the Pennsylvania frontier
seem to have had a special preference for horses. Indeed the
Gazette files of those years are a veritable museum of advertisements for straying livestock. One of the most newsworthy horse
thieves of the time was James Bonine, the leader of a gang, whose
rendezvous was near the sign of the Black Horse at the forks of the
Youghiogheny. His capture and confinement in the Greensburg
jail was duly noted, but Bonine had little inclination to remain
behind bars. Soon he was out and away. In order to give the
escape full publicity, the jailer inserted a rhyming advertisement
in the *Gazette:*

Take *Care of* Your Horses!
Thirty Dollars Reward.

No doubt at all but what you'll know,
Why with our money we part so;
The following lines be pleas'd to read,
And they will shew the cause indeed.
'Twas Sunday night, on the tenth day,
From Greensburgh jail did break away,
A lusty fellow there confin'd,
And stealing Horses was his crime;
Where he is gone I can not say,
But he's a rogue both night and day.
To tell his marks I am inclin'd,
His age may be full twenty nine;
His hair is dark, if I am right,
He wears it ty'd both day and night;
His height perhaps is five feet nine,
His proper name is James Bonine—
Tho' other names no doubt he'll find,
And change as often as the wind....
To tell his cloathing I shan't lack,
His overall's is velvet black,
Drab colour was the coat he wore,
His jacket was of cassimer—
A greater coat with him he bore,
Which over all he mostly wore,
It was gray coating if I mind,
His hat was of the rorum kind...
And now this caution I do make,
To any one that may him take,
Whate'er he says, or may reply,
Believe him not, for he will lie,
Unless he tells you he broke jail,
And is determin'd for to steal,
Has practic'd evil from his youth,
Believe him then, 'tis honest truth.
And when you have him strongly bound,
Come on my boy to Greensburgh town,
And then to me without delay,
Deliver him and get your pay.
　　　　　　　　　NATHAN WILLIAMS, jailor.[9]

Two other *Gazette* crime stories offer examples of the forms that local crime might take. On August 23, 1799, a certain Samuel Johnston was caught in the act of robbing the house of Thomas Bracken and was hauled before Justice John Wilkins. Something in the bearing of the prisoner convinced the court that he was not what he seemed; a careful examination revealed that "he was of the female sex." The self-disclosed Amazon admitted that she was the mother of five children, that she had passed for a man for five years, and that she was ostensibly employed in the weavers' trade at the forks of the Youghiogheny. The astonished court directed that she be lodged in the Allegheny County Jail. Meanwhile it set to work to trace rumors of her complicity with a ring of horse thieves. On the evening of October 3 she broke jail. Her jailer, Samuel McCord, proclaimed the fact in the *Gazette* and described her as "about 40 years of age, 4 feet 10 inches high, has a scar on her left eye-lid, had on a blue petticoat and striped short gown, a small round black hat, without any shoes on...." But there is no record that the escaped prisoner was ever returned.

The second story presented features no less unusual. Early in 1813 a certain Dr. John McDowell of Kentucky sent one of his servants to Montreal to bring the daughter of the family, Esther, to his frontier home, which she had never seen. The two traveled on horseback across northern Pennsylvania. While journeying after nightfall through Lycoming County, the faithless servant robbed the girl of eleven hundred guineas, stripped off her clothing, and tied her to a tree. After her rescue she had an advertisement forwarded to the *Gazette* offering two hundred dollars' reward for the capture of her betrayer and appealing to her father, whose exact address she did not know, to come to her relief. Whether Esther McDowell ever found her family, whether or not the money was recovered—this remained a mystery, for Scull appears to have lost interest in the case very suddenly.

The *Gazette* had room for religious news as well. The population of the town in 1786 was predominantly Presbyterian, so much so that when Brackenridge the next year obtained a charter of incorporation for the first Pittsburgh church, the name Presbyterian was written into the charter in spite of Brackenridge's wish that it should be simply styled "Christian." Other sects contested the local field with the Presbyterians. In a *Gazette* issue of 1793 is an interesting letter from the Reverend Mr. Samuel Porter, a Presbyterian clergyman of Beaver Run, Westmoreland County, complaining of how "these meek, candid, persecuted, sweet, loving lambs [*the Methodists*], came into our congregations in great love to us, and mercy to our people, and...raged against us for preaching for money, challenged us to public disputation, boasted of their conquests, assassinated our doctrines, and after all, hypocritically said they loved us, as ministers and Christians."[10]

Scull believed in supernaturalism as firmly as did the most superstitious negro. He saw no improbability in the story, which had come to him in a round-about way, of an Indian who was struck to the earth mortally wounded by divine vengeance, after defying "the Great Man above" to afflict him with smallpox as so many of his fellow Indians were being afflicted.

Scull was a religious man, yet not narrowly so. At times he was accused of "infidelity" and deism. He did not refuse to advertise the writings of Swedenborg, scarcely the most orthodox advocate of religion. The irreligious phase of the French Revolution troubled him greatly, however, and made him, it is likely, more conservative than he might otherwise have been.

About the turn of the century God and the circuit rider were abroad in the land. Another series of great religious revivals were in store for the West. Sensing a new seriousness on the part of his readers, Scull came out in the *Gazette*, October 24, 1800, with a number of questions for his Presbyterian congregation: Could they hope for good morals without religion or the fear of God? Could religion be maintained without public support? Were they not able to erect a respectable and commodious church building? Would not money so employed be more beneficial to the town than horse racing, billiard playing? The implied rebuke was understood. On April 2, 1802, the *Gazette* announced that the contract for a "Brick Meeting House" for the Presbyterian congregation of Pittsburgh had been let.

What religious life in Pittsburgh was like at the time was suggested by a letter to Scull from a traveler who paid the town a brief visit in 1803:

> Mr. Scull,
>   I am lately from over the mountains and now in this place; before I left my former place of abode, the current report there was that Pittsburgh was a young hell, a second Sodom, inhabited by a set of people who paid no respect to the Supreme Being or the Christian religion. On enquiry, after my arrival, I understood there were four established churches in this place—a Dutch, a Lutheran, a Presbyterian, and a Covenanter or Ceceder. Curiosity led me to visit these churches in rotation, expecting to see a disorderly croud of people, something like play acting, in derision of the church of Christ; but to my great surprise, I found each church filled with well dressed decent people, paying the greatest attention to divine service. Being myself a Presbyterian, I have, since my arrival, generally attended that church, and am much pleased with the decent and strict order of that congregation.[11]

According to the code of the times it was the will of God that the female should be subject to the male. The *Gazette* paid very little heed to the interests of feminine readers. Now and then an article offered suggestions to the young lady for winning and holding lovers. More often she was advised that chastity was the glory of a lady or was warned against being misled by a certain edition of the Bible that had by mistake omitted the word "not" from the seventh commandment.

Marriage took place early in this rural society, and woe betide those who took liberties with the institution: old maids were felt to be a monstrosity, and widows were fair game. Ann Boyd, the widow of Scull's partner, remarried within eight months. The frontier dread of single blessedness is well shown by some stanzas called "The Old Maid's Soliloquy," which the *Gazette* printed:

> I really wish I had a man,
> As big a plague as e'er they be;
> And yet I dare not tell it them
> For fear that they will laugh at me....
>
> I sometimes wish the bucks of town
> Were in the stocks or pillory;
> For if I dance and ogle round,
> They only smile and laugh at me.

The next stanzas describe her plan to use cosmetics and dress herself youthfully in order to catch a man. She concludes:

> Then I shall ne'er when boreas blows
> In winter dread my bed to see;
> No more the sheets shall freeze my toes,
> While warm'd by him who laughs with me.[12]

Pitiful spectacle that the old maid was, she might count herself more fortunate than the wife who fled from the shelter of her husband's roof. The latter's plight was depicted in the many runaway wife advertisements of the day. Perhaps the most interesting of all such notices was one of the year 1787 written in rhyme:

> July the twenty-seventh day,
> My wife Betsey ran away,
> From bed and board did flee and say,
> She would no longer with me stay.
> Since she has left me without cause,
> I'll give her time enough to pause,
> That she may see her error,
> When I live happy with a fairer.
> Therefore I forwarn both great and small,
> To trust her any thing at all,
> For her contracts from this day
> Not one farthing will I pay.
>   DENNIS O'BRYAN.[13]

Toward the end of the period, the *Gazette* gave signs that women were becoming more self-assertive. One can well imagine

the consternation that sped around the town when a feminine
correspondent of the *Gazette* took the opportunity to say in 1816:

> On the subject of the comparative abilities, and excel-
> lencies of the two sexes, I trust a more enlightened age is,
> introducing just and liberal views, and I have every reason
> to believe, that females, dispised as they heretofore have
> been, are gradually ascending in the scale of importance,
> to their proper and natural elevation. We already see
> them begin to think, speak, and write for themselves; we
> see them successfully engaging in literary pursuits and
> labors; we see them giving birth to productions, scarcely
> excelled in merit and brilliancy; by the works of the most
> distinguished authors of the present or any past age.[14]

Almost from the very first the *Gazette* sensed the preoccupation
of its readers with the ills of the body. Scattered through the
early issues were articles written by Dr. Benjamin Rush, the most
famous physician of his day. His experiments to relieve cancer
with an arsenic powder and his conviction of the harmful effects
of alcoholic beverages were noted with especial care. The freak
remedies of the day had their showing too. For the ague, scourge
of the Ohio Valley, the sufferer was advised to take as much flour
of brimstone as would cover a half-dollar piece, moisten it to a
paste with lemon juice, mix it with a glass of rum or port wine,
and swallow it when the fit came on. For dropsy the following
simple prescription sufficed: "two ounces of bark, two ounces of
gun powder, and one ounce of coarse mustard seed, steeped in a
quart of wine, and well shaken together. Let three wine glasses
full be taken every day."[15]

The wondrous effect that sanitation was to have in lessening
the havoc wrought by disease was hardly realized as yet. Now
and then a voice was raised in behalf of reasonable precautions.
There was a letter in the *Gazette*, March 21, 1789, calling attention
to the ponds in Pittsburgh and "the noxious vapors ... exhaled
from these stagnant waters in the summer." The writer felt that
it would be wise to enlarge the sewers leading into the Monon-

gahela, the expense of which would not exceed half the annual sum spent locally for medicines.

Already the ravages of yellow fever, one of the great destroyers of modern times, were a matter of record in the *Gazette*. An account of the great epidemic of 1793 in Philadelphia, which Philip Freneau described faithfully, could hardly be kept out of the western newspapers. Pittsburgh merchants transferred their business accounts from Philadelphia to Baltimore, and all intercourse between Philadelphia and Pittsburgh was temporarily cut off. Again in 1798 the details of another yellow fever epidemic in Philadelphia were gloomily recounted by the *Gazette*. So deep an impression was made by this picture of misery that the sum of four hundred dollars was subscribed for relief by the townsmen.

With regard to pulmonary consumption, long the scourge of the Pittsburgh region, a curious hypothesis, quoted from a medical report in New York City, was propounded in a *Gazette* of 1815:

> We are authorized by one of the most intelligent Physicians in this city to state, that in very many of the cases of female consumption, that have come under his observation, the disease has been induced by the wearing of *Corsets*. Such an intimation from a respectable source should not be lost upon parents.[16]

The spirits of the community rebounded quickly, however, from tales of disease and death. Its amusements were of a simple kind. There was just enough Virginia influence in western Pennsylvania to make horses and horse racing popular. During the breeding season, columns devoted to advertising famous stud horses occupied more space proportionately than automobile advertising in the present age. Scull left no uncertainty about his views on the subject. Horse racing was in his opinion a "fruitful seminary of all vice." For some years the *Gazette* refused to accept any advertising for the jockeys and their mounts.

The races gave pleasure to some, but the animal shows had an irresistible appeal for all. The first menagerie advertisement published in the *Gazette* appeared in 1808:

A LIVING ELEPHANT May be seen in the Borough of Pittsburgh from Wednesday the 12th to Saturday the 15th instant. Those who wish to gratify their curiosity by viewing the wonderful works of nature, will do well to call, for perhaps the present generation may never have the opportunity of seeing an Elephant again, as this is the only one in the United States, and is perhaps the only visit to this Borough.[17]

Not until 1814 was Pittsburgh privileged to view a full menagerie.

To the spread of education locally the *Gazette* lent encouragement. The first school announcement printed in the paper told of a boarding and day school for young ladies to be opened by a Mrs. Pride. Needlework, knitting, reading, and English comprised the curriculum. Mrs. Pride also contracted to take the strictest care of the morals and good breeding of the young ladies placed under her care and so to merit the confidence of "inhabitants of this side of the Alleghany Mountain."

To speed the good work, Scull and Boyd published several articles on the value of education in the *Gazette* during March, 1787. Their plan called for a state university at the capital and four colleges, one at Philadelphia, one at Carlisle, another at Lancaster, and a fourth at Pittsburgh. In each county there was to be a college preparatory academy, and in every township or district of one hundred families there were to be free schools where children could learn to read and write the English and German languages. The colleges were to be supported by land grants, the lower schools by land grants and taxes. The ideas expressed were far ahead of the times, but the future was to see them nearly all realized.

The founding of the Pittsburgh Academy, Pittsburgh's first important school, was appropriately noticed, and from time to time complimentary allusions to the high grade of work performed there were made. French schools, evening schools, academies far and near, the Universities of Pennsylvania and Maryland in the East, Transylvania University in the heart of the Kentucky bluegrass country—all were extolled according to their merits in the columns of the *Gazette* from year to year.

Education provided as much opportunity for newspaper controversy as politics. During the summer of 1810 a dispute over educational methods arose among some of the *Gazette's* readers. One of the writers, "Florian," was sharply critical of the western school system, with its travesty on a classical education. He was for broadening the curriculum, introducing mathematics, natural philosophy, geography, astronomy, history, and the like. He would even devote a different day of the week to each subject instead of taking the whole group daily all in a rush. This brought one "Junius" into the lists to expose the absurdity of such views and to defend the *status quo*. A third writer praised the idea of a liberalized education, already introduced, in effect, as he said, into the best American seminaries. Thus the controversy went merrily on behind the masks of anonymity. Probably no one was deceived by the mysterious *noms de plumes*, for Pittsburgh was still a small town.

To judge from the *Gazette*, affection for the fine arts was not deeply rooted in early Pittsburgh. In the spring of 1804, the paper advised its readers of the arrival of two artists from Philadelphia, one a landscape, the other a miniature painter. At best the reception accorded them was a bleak one. Portraits were the only form of painting that signified much to the average layman of the time.

Save for announcements of balls and concerts, the *Gazette* contained very few references to musical events in the community. In the summer of 1798 the arrival of B. Holdich, a dancing master, gave rise to some musical enthusiasm. Soon a generation of young Pittsburghers were hard at work threading their feet painfully through a maze of complicated minuets, cotillions, and fashionable country dances. During the War of 1812, Dennis Loughby, "the blind poet of Pittsburgh," composed several martial airs, which the *Gazette* saw fit to reprint.

One of the first tokens of local interest in the drama was

evinced in a letter to the *Gazette* in 1790 describing a production of *Tancred and Sigsmunda* by some amateurs in the nearby town of Washington. The writer concluded his account with an ironic touch: "How the Almighty is pleased with an exhibition of this nature, as it savors of the stage, I do not know; but it is certain his creatures were much amused on the occasion; the young ladies especially."[18]

The first public theatrical production in Pittsburgh took place on the evening of January 26, 1803, when Messrs. Bromley and Arnold presented a tragedy entitled *The Gamester*. It must have been well received (the *Gazette* contained no reviews), for within a month's time John O Keefe's popular comic opera, *The Poor Soldier*, and a farce, *The Apprentice*, were played at the courthouse by the young gentlemen of the town. Tickets were to be had at Scull's printing office. That Pittsburgh still preserved the character of a country town was shown by the fact that the curtain rose precisely at half-past six o'clock.

Thus the *Gazette* reflected the varied activities of its readers and disclosed a definite influence in many fields. Pittsburgh was still very young. Shut off from the East by high mountain walls, it was forced to consult its own devices for amusement and recreation. Sophistication was markedly lacking in the community, but that deficiency was likely to be removed as the city continued to grow and justify the confident hopes entertained by its well-wishers.

CHAPTER III

LAYING THE FOUNDATIONS OF THE NEW WEST

The dawning years of the new century brought great changes to the West. Countless emigrants were advancing into Transappalachia and transforming it from a wilderness into a region of farms, clearings, and small towns. In Pittsburgh men were hurrying to the river wharves to watch the launching of one of the new ships of Tarascon Brothers, James Berthoud & Company. John Scull pondered the scene from his office window. Perhaps there was promise of future greatness for Pittsburgh after all. Nerves! Simply nerves! Ailing wives don't improve a fellow's disposition.[1] Scull sighed. Alas for the "good old days" when men turned to the *Gazette* as to the Bible. No longer did Scull have the whole field to himself. Newspapers were springing up in manifold places noising strange doctrines about.

The year of the Constitutional Convention, 1787, John Bradford, a Virginian who had shouldered his firelock in the days of '76, migrated to the bluegrass country and established the *Kentucky Gazette* at Lexington. The press for the undertaking was from Pittsburgh, perhaps purchased from Scull himself. The *Kentucky Gazette* was the second newspaper west of the Alleghenies. Not until 1795 was a second paper started in western Pennsylvania, the *Western Telegraphe and Washington Advertiser*, sponsored by Colerick, Hunter, and Beaumont and printed in Washington, Pennsylvania. In Pittsburgh the number of journals multiplied after the turn of the century. The *Tree of Liberty* (1800) was the *Gazette's* first competitor. In 1805 the radical *Commonwealth* came along; in 1811 James Gilleland established another Democratic paper, the *Mercury*. Taking the place of the defunct *Tree of Liberty*, they maintained a joint front against Scull's Federalist *Gazette*.

During these years, the *Gazette* was packed with tidings of a populace on the march; with rumors of new routes and methods

27

of transportation either contemplated or in process of construction; with data to show the inrush of trade and business in the wake of the irresistible westward trend. If the paper was to be believed, the craze for land was almost incredible. One might pick up the *Gazette* and chance upon the supposedly imperative reasons for taking up land in southern Ohio, at the mouth of the Scioto, perhaps, where natural rice plantations inspired dreams of sudden wealth, where the capital of the first state carved out of the Northwest Territory must surely be. In the columns of the newspaper every budding western metropolis had its hearing. If the number of town lots advertised for sale was any criterion, all rural America must have been struggling to secure a location on Main Street.

Now and again voices were heard in protest against the almost universal disposition to be on the move. "A Farmer," who stated that he was a resident of Pitt Township, Allegheny County, wrote during the War of 1812:

> *Hills are green a great way off*, is an old saying, yes, and a true saying.—I have from circumstances of residence been obliged for many years to observe the hordes of emigrants who have travelled through the western parts of Pennsylvania, to settle in the "state of Ohio"—or "on Congress lands"—or on lands "down the river," to use their language....
>
> I have at such times asked the head of the emigrant family, "why not buy land in this country when you can procure it on as easy terms as you can down the river?" The answer uniformly was, "We hear such a great name of the new state—we can raise so much corn there with so little labour...."
>
> It is, however, latterly observable, that this mania is now working its own cure, and will soon cease. Persons accustomed to the oak, chestnut and hickory timbered land of the eastern parts of Pennsylvania, and the advantages of the Philadelphia market, begin to discover, that if they remove to the westward, they ought to settle as near as possible to *Pittsburgh*, because it is the *next best market in America*...and can acquire land of superior fertility to that they before owned *at as low or a less price*

than lands in Ohio cost.... emigrants now reflect before
they decide on the place of their permanent residence.[2]

Each new improvement in transportation acted as a stimulus
for further westward migration. The *Gazette* allotted abundant
space to news of the preparation of new routes and means of conveyance for the immigrants. Pathfinders like Timothy Flint may
have sighed for the magic carpet of the *Arabian Nights*, but the
turnpikes and the river steamboats probably seemed scarcely less
wonderful at first glance.

Communications with Philadelphia were all important to early
Pittsburgh. An ingenious fellow, fairly bursting with a plan to
convey mail from Philadelphia to Pittsburgh in three days and a
half, about half the time then necessary, wrote to the *Gazette* in
the fall of 1804. After all his disclaimers of romantic dreaming, it
turned out that he had in mind a double-tracked wooden railroad
over the mountains. In the Pennsylvania General Assembly
Brackenridge had addressed his constituents on the subject of a
state road over the mountains through the columns of the *Gazette*.
The expense might well be met, he thought, by putting an annual
head tax of fifteen pence on the horses of the state, ninety-six
thousand in all. Indeed the saving of oats would serve to remove
all objections. His plan was not followed out completely, but in
1791 a state thoroughfare was constructed from Bedford to Pittsburgh. This helped pave the way for the opening of a line of mail
stages between Philadelphia and Pittsburgh in 1804, much to the
delight of the *Gazette* and its patrons.

Scull was interested in turnpikes. In the summer of 1806 he
gave two columns to a reprinted article from the *Caledonian
Mercury* of Edinburgh, Scotland, descanting on the utility of
"turn pike roads." An italicized statement directly under the
article indicates his partiality for the subject: "We would earnestly solicit the serious attention of the people of this country to
the foregoing publication."[3] At another time he avowed:

> The refusal of the Legislature to grant a charter to the
> trustees of the late Bank of the United States, has de-
> prived this state of the vast sum of 500,000 dollars, which
> was to be appropriated towards the making turnpike
> roads, and building bridges.—Public indignation will, no
> doubt, be the reward of such nefarious conduct.[4]

The fruit of this interest was agitation for turnpikes between
Pittsburgh, Washington, Greensburg, and other neighboring
towns. Plans for building a Pittsburgh-Harrisburg turnpike were
aired repeatedly in the *Gazette*, until finally in 1817 it was opened
for traffic. Simultaneously, mail service became more ramified
and frequent.

But turnpikes were expensive to build and maintain. Why
not utilize the water thoroughfares that nature had abundantly
provided? Only gradually did the community and the newspaper
come to realize the potentialities that lay in the town's position.
One of the first indications was a lottery advertisement in the
Gazette of July 21, 1798, submitted by a group of citizens, who
hoped by that means to raise "$12,000 for the erection of municipal
piers along the Allegheny and Monongahela rivers." One sentence
was of particular significance: "Situated as it is, on a point of land
at the confluence of two majestic rivers which, joining, flow through
an immense territory to the ocean, it must of necessity be in a
considerable degree the emporium of that territory."

The part that local boat building played in making the Ohio
River an avenue of transportation may be reconstructed from the
contemporary *Gazette*. In one of the first issues, Joseph Chester
had solicited custom for his boat-building establishment on the
Monongahela River opposite the mouth of Little Redstone Creek
at the price 20s–22s 6d per foot, "he finding everything." After
1793, when a schooner built at Elizabeth Town on the Monongahela descended the Ohio and Mississippi Rivers and continued
safely on to Philadelphia, a broad market for locally built boats
was opened. During the Adams administration, when for a time
war with France seemed no remote possibility, the local mechanics

worked long hours in their shops hammering away at the hulls of two galleys, the "President Adams" and the "Senator Ross," destined to do battle for Columbia on the high seas. The details of the launching—the crowd of spectators, the salutes, the acclamations—were proudly noticed in the attentive *Gazette*.

If, however, shipbuilding had its difficulties, river navigation presented its dangers. The river adventurer might escape the numerous sawyers, planters, and snags of which Zadok Cramer's *Navigator* warned him and then run smack into a band of marauding Indians or river pirates. In all likelihood the public was impressed by the precautions adopted by the first packet-boat line between Pittsburgh and Cincinnati. Prospective patrons read in the *Gazette:*

> No danger need be apprehended from the enemy, as every person on board will be under cover, made proof against rifle or musket balls, and convenient port holes for firing out of.—Each of the Boats are armed with six pieces carrying a pound ball; also a number of good muskets, and amply supplied with necessary ammunition, strongly manned with choice hands, and the masters of approved knowledge.[5]

The introduction of steam power wrought a gradual transformation in the navigation of the western waters. Only a few years after Fulton had frightened the superstitious and routed the skeptics with his "Clermont," a young engineer came to Pittsburgh fairly agog with an idea. A flatboat trip down the river convinced him of its merit. In the spring of 1810 he went to work in the shadow of John Boyd's hill to lay the keel of a steamboat—but let installments from the *Gazette* tell the story:

> [*October 18, 1811*] With pleasure we announce, that the Steam Boat lately built at this place by Mr. Rosevelt, (from an experiment made on Tuesday last) fully answers the most sanguine expectations that were formed of her sailing.

She is 150 feet keel, 450 tons burthen, and built with
the best materials and in the most substantial manner.—
Her cabin is elegant, and the accommodations for passengers not surpassed.

We are told that she is intended as a regular packet
between Natchez and New Orleans.

[*October 25, 1811*] The Steam Boat sailed from this
place, on Sunday last, for the Natchez.

[*January 3, 1812*] The Steam Boat, "New-Orleans,"
lately built at this place by Mr. Rosevelt, passed the Red
Banks, about 950 miles from here, on the 17th ult. all
well.

[*February 14, 1812*] The Louisiana Gazette of the 13th
of January, says, "The Steam Boat *New-Orleans*, from
Pittsburgh, arrived here on Friday evening last. The captain reports that she has been *under way* not more than
259 hours from Pittsburgh to this place, which gives
about eight miles each hour."

Scull did not know that the age of steam had reached the West.
Very likely he would not have let himself become excited if he had
known. At all events, it was to be some time before the steamboat
became the smoky monarch of the inland waters. The *Gazette*
was wont to refer to it only when some catastrophe resulted or
when a new speed record was established.

It was much less romantic for the paper to treat of trade and
of articles of commerce than to dwell upon the boatmen and their
craft. There is a more melodious sound about the swish of the
paddle or the rhythmic motion of the sweep than there is about the
jostling of casks or the shuffling about of cotton bales. Without
those steady staples of commerce, however, there would have been
few boatmen in the picture; while manufactures were still in the
rudimentary stage Pittsburgh's very existence was dependent
upon the merchant and his kind. This explains the prominence of
mercantile pursuits in the news of the day. When the *Gazette* first
came into existence, the folk of the western country were dependent

upon the slow-going pack horse, the distant ancestor of the "Iron Horse," for the delivery of goods from east of the mountains. Before the curious eyes of the townsmen quantities of groceries, liquor, salt, and iron were unstrapped and replaced by equivalent loads of furs, skins, and ginseng destined for an eastern market. After 1790 the increasing use of the Conestoga wagon relegated the pack horse to the limbo of the past. In the opposite direction the New Orleans market beckoned to the western farmers to float the fruit of their labors down the bosom of the broad Mississippi to New Orleans and the outside world.

As a western journalist, Scull was concerned by aught that affected the security of that New Orleans market. Early in 1801 he predicted the transfer of Louisiana to France, and with elaborate sarcasm saluted the prospect of protection offered to the "friends of democracy and lovers of confusion in this country" by the French legions at the mouth of the Mississippi. It was the news of the closing of the port of New Orleans against American vessels, nevertheless, which really lashed the West into a fury of excitement. The information reached the *Gazette* in December, 1802, through the medium of a letter from a gentleman in New Orleans "to his friend in this place," and was soon followed by rumors from Kentucky that General Claude Victor was coming to New Orleans with ten thousand French troops. With a hint of a belief in the "Manifest Destiny" that hypnotized a later generation, the *Gazette* spoke out forcefully in the cause of its friends and neighbors:

> Were we to take immediate possession of Louisiana, we should not be destitute of justifying reasons for our conduct....Why should we wait for the slow process of doubtful negotiation? Spain is only the ostensible proprietor, while France, the real owner of Louisiana, keeps behind the scene, and prompts her neighbor to acts of aggression....Let us, therefore, assume the sovereignty of an unfriendly precinct, contiguous to our settlements, which nature intended for our inheritance, but which mere blind casualty ravished from us.[6]

A genuine thrill shot through the West at these words, and a
ground-swell of discontent followed in the wake of such speeches
as that delivered in the Senate chamber by Senator James Ross
on the text "On the Shutting of the Port of New Orleans." The
Gazette published the speech in its entirety, declaring that it so
well reflected the sentiment of the western country that every
printer in that region should be at pains to republish it.

The information that the Louisiana purchase had been con-
summated was happy news for the *Gazette* and its readers. Scull
thought that

> no event so important to the western country has ever
> happened since the British treaty which surrendered the
> western posts, as the cession of New Orleans to the United
> States. By this every man who owns a farm may reckon
> it one half more valuable than before, and every man on
> the western waters may reckon himself one half richer.[7]

Unwilling to see glory reflected on the Jefferson administration
by this fortunate stroke, Scull attributed what had happened to
the brave resistance of the British ministry, which forced the
French to sell what they could not keep.

Scarcely had the Louisiana purchase become a matter of record
than quotations from the New Orleans market began to nudge
their way into the mass of *Gazette* advertisements. Soon enterprising importers were advertising their New Orleans wares locally.
Typical was a notice submitted in 1814 by Robinson and Barber,
offering New Orleans sugar, cotton, and indigo for sale contingent
upon the arrival of six keel boats from "down river" some time
during the month. An interesting commercial enterprise, which
the *Gazette* helped to promote was the Ohio Company of 1802.
Its foremost sponsor in the locality was John Wilkins, Jr., of
Pittsburgh, who in a letter to the newspaper recalled the many
disadvantages under which the Mississippi trade labored, chiefly
for want of suitable arrangements for adjusting the trade to
market demand and facilities of ocean transit. In order to stabilize
the risks within relatively narrow limits, Wilkins called for a

meeting in Pittsburgh to arrange for the formation of a corporation capitalized at approximately a hundred thousand dollars. Scull heartily concurred in the idea, probably the more so because the *Tree of Liberty* damned it as a partisan enterprise designed to aggrandize the influence of Wilkins, its author. The Ohio Company, it would seem, never attained the stature that was desired for it. Yet it was a signal foreshadowing of the daring ventures that were to bring fame to many a future Pittsburgh *entrepreneur.* Soon after the start of the new century, Pittsburgh market reports began to appear in the *Gazette* as an occasional feature. Beef, three to five cents per pound; butter, ten to thirteen cents; eggs, seven to twelve cents per dozen; flour, a dollar and a quarter to a dollar and a half per hundredweight—these were sample commodity prices in the Pittsburgh of 1801. There were no serious interruptions of these levels until the stress of the War of 1812 was felt. Then, under the influence of war-time inflation, commodity prices shot upward: beef, nine to ten cents per pound; bacon, fifteen to eighteen cents; flour, four dollars per hundredweight; potatoes, similarly, seventy cents to a dollar; butter, thirty-seven to fifty cents per pound; eggs, twenty-five cents per dozen.

The farmers of the vicinity were delighted as the price of wheat soared to unbelievable levels. In 1809 the two Evanses built the first steam flour mill in Pittsburgh, an establishment that Scull warmly praised as superior to any of the water mills in the West. At first the farmers adopted the policy of holding their wheat back in hopes of higher prices, for which Scull upbraided them, reminding them that the proprietors must turn to other manufactures rather than let an investment of fifteen thousand dollars lie idle. At the time, 1809, wheat was seventy-five cents per bushel, the same price as at the outbreak of the war. In October, 1812, one dollar in cash per bushel for quick delivery was offered at the Pittsburgh Steam Mill. The price remained uniformly at that point until the year 1814, when it rose steadily to a peak of a dollar and a half. A parallel tendency in the price of bread was perceptible, with the natural effect of distressing the working classes. "A Mechanick of Pittsburgh" complained to the *Gazette* of having to pay twelve and a half cents for a forty-two ounce loaf of bread and threatened to appear before the town council to obtain redress from the grasping baker!

Well before the War of 1812 the *Gazette* was giving attention to industrial stirrings in the community. As early as 1789, Scull broadcast an appeal for mechanics:

> We want people, we want sober and diligent trades-men; hatters, button makers, rope walkers, weavers, &c, will be more welcome, and will essentially promote our prosperity....I wish this state would give a bounty of forty shillings to every mechanic or labourer who arrives in it from Europe. Population and industry are the true causes of national greatness.[8]

In 1792, there were already thirty-six mechanics in the town: blacksmiths, whitesmiths, wheelwrights, rope-makers, cabinet-makers, and the like. The opening of the famous glassworks of James O'Hara and Isaac Craig in 1800 was noticed by the *Gazette*. In 1809 Scull observed with pleasure that "Pittsburgh window glass' was advertised for sale by merchants in Philadelphia. From time to time reference was made to the setting up of iron furnaces and "nail manufactories" in the vicinity of Pittsburgh, such as Anthony Beelen's Pittsburgh Eagle Foundry and George Milten-burger's Copper and Tin Ware Manufactory. Pittsburgh *entre-peneurs* were entering the field of textile manufactures too. Letters were received by the paper advising the farmers to go into sheep raising as a way of encouraging woolen cloth manufacturing. Advertisements for both woolen and cotton mills were displayed in the *Gazette* several years before the end of the War of 1812.

Early in 1812, George Evans put a card in the paper to warn the public that he possessed an exclusive right to supply steam engines on the Oliver Evans principle and to use such engines for iron manufactures in the Pittsburgh district. Like Whitney, Fulton, and countless other inventors, Evans found that he had to fight repeated battles to preserve his rights. One of the most furious of them, that with Thomas Copeland, made colorful reading for the *Gazette's* subscribers. Probably the subscribers were not very sympathetic toward Evans; monopolies and exclusive rights were not the darlings of western hearts.

Whether or not Evans was to blame, the coal-smoke haze, which hovers over Pittsburgh's hills and valleys today, was already being talked about. The first reference the *Gazette* made to the phenomenon was in a letter from "One of the People" to "The Inhabitants of Pittsburgh" in the issue of June 10, 1814:

> Although much of the prosperity of Pittsburgh is owing to its *"Fires,"* it is not to be concealed, that the effects of those immense fires, have become subjects of complaint. That the evil (if it be an evil to be enveloped in smoke) is daily increasing, and that relief is now universally called for.

Not yet, it appears, had troublesome doubts as to its morality injured another very profitable business at that time, the liquor business. "Still for Sale" was a common advertising head in the *Gazette.* "An Old Farmer," writing to the paper in 1803, saw the situation somewhat as follows:

> This liquor [*whisky*] is now become the common drink of the western people in every country house, and it is generally used in such a state of dangerous impurity... that its fatal effects are but too well and too generally known.... The use of whiskey is now become so universal, that it is considered as an indispensable necessary in all families. In short, we can neither work or play without it.[9]

These business beginnings furnished a foundation for the development of the New West. Pittsburgh could not follow the frontier, but it could draw upon the resources of the western region to furnish a workshop. To advance the business interests of the community an active newspaper was essential. The *Gazette* stood prepared to extend coöperation to this end. In its columns there was to be found abundant encouragement for the pioneer business man.

CHAPTER IV

A LONE OUTPOST OF FEDERALISM

The generation of John Scull and Hugh Henry Brackenridge was a politically minded generation. The authority of kings and magistrates and the natural rights of the individual were favorite topics of the day. The American Revolution and the chain of consequences that flowed from it had turned men's minds in that direction. Scull was perfectly honest and correct when he stated that politics was "the roast beef of the times...a dish equally sumptuous to the king and the cobler."

Scull's antecedents and early life prepared him to sympathize earnestly with the purposes of the group that drew up the Federal Constitution and supplied the leadership of the Federalist party. Yet his intention had been to set up a newspaper that should be free from party influences. As a printer he felt that he could and should do this; as a private citizen he subscribed to Federalist principles, because, as he explained, they "do but promote the interests of the Country."

Although the *Gazette* was not quite a yearling when the Constitutional Convention forgathered, it had already presented evidence of conditions that called for strong government. To the East it pled for a West that suffered from burdensome taxes and lack of cash, and feared, too, the loss of the Mississippi trade. All through the summer of 1787 the *Gazette* kept its readers closely informed of what leaked out from behind the closed doors at the Philadelphia Constitutional Convention. When the work of the Fathers was done, the *Gazette* promptly proceeded to print in full the document to which they had affixed their signatures. The loyal friends of the Constitution in the locality immediately held a meeting at Tannehill's Tavern to endorse the action taken at Philadelphia. Both the call for this meeting and the resolutions that it prepared were printed in the *Gazette*. During the contest

38

over the ratification of the Constitution in Pennsylvania, the paper printed many contributions favoring ratification along with some specimens of lampooning verse more remarkable for crude and controversial expressions than for rhythmical quality. When at length the news of the ratification by Virginia, the tenth state (supposedly the ninth), reached Pittsburgh on Friday, June 29, 1788, the *Gazette* joyfully spread the tidings and extended congratulations to the entire country.

On Saturday evening about fifteen hundred people gathered on Grant's Hill, east of the town, to celebrate the event. At the given time, Brackenridge, the orator on the occasion, rose and saluted his hearers as citizens of a new empire. Then he launched into a spirited address that dipped freely into the classical lore of which the audiences of the age were inordinately fond. At the conclusion the men of Pittsburgh rushed forward with a will to carry out a prearranged ceremony. As the *Gazette* described it:

> Three cheers were now given, and the hats thrown into the air. Nine piles of wood were then alighted, representing the nine states which had adopted the constitution. At intermediate distances, four piles were left uninflamed, representing those which had not adopted it. Fire was kindled in them, but oppressed by green leaves and heavy boughes; in spite of all that could be done the pile of New Hampshire burst out, and gave a luminous splendor; that of Rhode Island not having sent delegates to the general convention, or called a convention of their own, had brimstone, tar and feathers thrown into it; yet, still some boughs of wood that were at the bottom, catched the flame, purged off the noxious vapour and materials. That of New York and North Carolina at length took fire, and exceeded even the other piles. The whole thirteen now in one united blaze began to burn. The youths of the village danced round them on the green; and the Indians who were present, the chiefs of several nations, on their way to the treaty at Muskingum, stood in amazement at the scene; concluded this to be a great council, seeing the thirteen fires kindled on the hill.[1]

It now remained to be seen what form the organization of the new government would take and how it would exercise the broad powers conferred upon it. An early test was provided by the Whisky Insurrection of 1794, a spontaneous uprising of the four southwestern counties of Pennsylvania against the authority of the central government. The imposition of a federal excise tax on whisky was the ostensible cause for the trouble, but in truth the reasons for the conflict were less simplified. The farmers of the region felt themselves at every turn to be checked and harassed by the actions of a government whose very nature was strange to them and whose actions portended the further extension of its control over them at the expense of the independent mode of life to which they had become accustomed.

There were those, nevertheless, who cried down a resort to arms. As the only newspaper in the area immediately affected, the *Gazette* was embarrassed by the divergent views of its subscribers. Under the circumstances it felt obliged to steer a neutral course between two extremes, however unpleasant such a course might be. Scull's tolerance for the conduct of David Bradford and the other malcontents, adopted as a matter of policy at first, became at last a matter of necessity. At one time the printing office was surrounded by a mob, and Scull was held under arrest for a short period, but no violence was done either to him or his property.

Equally unpleasant was the influence of "Tom the Tinker," who was abroad in the land in the summer of 1794. "Tom" was the pseudonym signed to the otherwise anonymous notices that the whisky chiefs circulated to intimidate those who would not join the insurrectionists. Their method was to leave the missive tacked to the premises of some luckless individual, who was required to have the notice inserted in the *Gazette*. To insure his own personal safety, Scull thought it prudent to comply with the requests when he was singled out as the recipient of the notices. They usually took some such form as this:

> Poor Tom takes this opportunity to inform his friends throughout all the country, that he is obliged to take up

his commission once more tho' disagreeable to his inclination.... This is fair warning, traitors take care, for my
hammer is up and my ladel is hot, I cannot travel the
country for nothing.

From your old friend

TOM the TINKER.[2]

There was just a sufficient tinge of mystery about this to alarm
those who, courageous enough when it came to repelling savages,
were given to brooding over the dangers to be expected from an
enemy whose identity was unknown.

Scull waited long to express his real feelings; and when at
length he did so, his voice simply harmonized with a swelling
chorus. On August 30, 1794, his first direct attack against the
insurrectionists appeared in the *Gazette*. The language was plain:

> If every man would now speak out his real sentiments,
> there would be very few found to approve the late opposi-
> tion to the laws. It cannot be supported without a sepa-
> ration from the United States—a thing that could not be
> effected, and if it could, it would enfeeble and ruin the
> Western Country.

At the critical moment the courage of the rebel chieftains failed
them, and so, comforted by the information that the national
militia was on its way westward, the *Gazette* continued to pour oil
on troubled waters. Doubtless the activity on its part facilitated
the clement policy which the federal government assumed toward
the rioters.

In the midst of such disordered days the *Gazette* and the folk of
the locality were dimly aware of tremendous changes going on in
Europe, which were to stress more sharply the lines separating
the various shades of American political opinion. Scull's readers
were on the periphery of the conflict. They read of the coming of
Citizen Edmond Charles Edouard Gênet, envoy of the French
Republic; viewed with some difference of opinion the fall of the
monarchy and the proclamation of the republic; argued freely
about the rights of man and various revolutionary dogmas; and

doubtless drank many a toast in their potent western brew to honor the characters and events that best pleased their fancy. One can well imagine numbers of them listening intently to the defense of the revolutionists or rushing off to organize another of the Democratic societies—"demonical societies," as the Federalists derisively termed them.

The friends of France made capital of course out of the resentment that the English aroused by their agency in promoting Indian raids. During the year 1794, war spirit against the English ran high; to the *Gazette* came repeated letters sounding monotonously the same chord: Gênet was arrogant, but he was young and would be our friend. Great Britain, Spain, the Algerine states were our natural enemies; France was bound to us by sentimental ties that no change of government could sunder. United with her we might seize Canada, Florida, open the Mississippi River to free navigation, and finally end the Indian menace. Nor was the appointment of John Jay as envoy extraordinary to negotiate a settlement of all points of difference with Great Britain likely to allay the face of western discontent. Was this not the same Jay who had proposed to barter away the precious right to navigate the Mississippi? These doubts were caught up by a wave of disappointment when the terms of the Jay Treaty became known. Here and there a voice was raised to defend the hapless Jay, but the community as a whole joined in the hue and cry against the treaty. Scull remembered that the public sentiment as expressed in town meetings from one end of the country to the other was a unit; the treaty, in his opinion, had agitated the public mind more than any event since the Declaration of Independence. The Pinckney treaty, on the other hand, with its promise of trade opportunity in the Southwest, did a great deal to reconcile the *Gazette* and its following to the earlier disappointment. By 1796 a measure of calm had returned.

As a Federalist Scull could hardly repress the desire to applaud whenever a well directed shot from the Federalist camp made the friends of France wince. The irreligious character of men like

Thomas Paine was an especially vulnerable point. With particular relish, the *Gazette* pounced upon Paine for some ill-natured remarks directed against Washington. "America will decide between their respectable fellow-citizen, George Washington, and that degenerate moral and political monster, Thomas Paine," concluded Scull with a flourish.[3]

When the chance of war with France loomed up in 1798, Scull, though opposed to war on principle, was caught up by the excitement. While the militia of the four southwest counties prepared to march at the first call, Scull freely maintained that no nation that expressed great unwillingness to encounter war could maintain its rights in "this corrupt world." Yet the best defense was on the ocean, he thought, for ten good seamen were better protection than a hundred soldiers. Scull thought he saw in the French preparations for war "the cloven foot of Citizen Talleyrand," whose general untrustworthiness was a favorite theme. A sudden shift of French policy swept the war clouds aside, however, and permitted the *Gazette* to turn away from the spectacle of marching troops and the sound of drum beats.

Scull had matters nearer home to attend to, in any case. The development of antagonistic political parties, hastened to a large degree in consequence of the French upheaval, was transforming the *Gazette* from the neutral mirror of local opinion, which Scull desired it to be, into an out and out party organ. Scull's reluctance to see his journal undergo this change appears in a statement of policy for the year 1797:

> The Pittsburgh *Gazette* has never deserved or obtained the epithet of a party paper; because the Editor is of no party, not being greatly versed in the abstract science of politics, and not having the ambition or the skill to be any thing but a printer....[4]

But the controversies to which the French Revolution gave rise eventually forced him to take sides. As loyal opposition to the administration crystallized, Scull felt himself drawn by temperament more and more into the councils of the "monocrats," as the Federalists were sometimes called.

In the year 1798 he came to a parting of the ways. Ever since the Whisky Insurrection the Federalists of western Pennsylvania had more than held their own with the Republicans, but in that year the Jeffersonians were regaining courage. In the contest for the local seat in Congress the *Gazette* warmly championed John Woods, the Federalist candidate, but Albert Gallatin, his opponent, was too popular in the district to be overcome. Even Brackenridge was known to be favorable to Gallatin's candidacy. The next year, however, Scull entered with a will into the campaign for governor. James Ross, Federalist United States Senator from Pennsylvania, was the choice of the *Gazette*. On the opposite side was Thomas McKean, chief justice of the Pennsylvania supreme court for more than a score of years, a former president of the Continental Congress, and a signer of the Declaration of Independence. The fact that the *Herald of Liberty*, a newspaper recently started in Washington, Pennsylvania, was supporting McKean put the *Gazette* on its mettle. Absurd stories were not slow to appear. The *Gazette* told its readers that McKean was the man who had suffered his daughter to renounce her religion in order to form a connection with a Spanish nobleman. Moreover, if McKean were elected governor then Tench Coxe, "the pilot of Lord Howe and his army into Philadelphia," would most likely become secretary of state.

Neither party was squeamish about the feelings of the other. The *Gazette* never quite forgot certain self-imposed standards of good taste. Yet it was not averse to remarking that in parts of New England a Democrat was becoming as rare a sight as a bear or a wolf; that Jacobinism was on the wane there and, like the yellow fever, would probably vanish soon. A stranger from Maryland, who came west in 1800 to look for land, left with impressions of a political babel in which the Irish shouted loudest, usually against the corruption and oppression of the federal government. In a letter addressed to Scull he declared with feeling: "I was in this country in the spring of 1794, just before the whiskey insurrection, and the violence and confusion of the people then was not so bad as it is now."[5]

The outcome of the election of 1799 spelled an ill fate for the Federalists in the ensuing national election. The local Anti-Federalists were so well pleased over their triumph that they planned a dinner at Captain Smur's tavern in Pittsburgh on the evening of October 26th. Some forty or fifty were there, Hugh Henry Brackenridge among them to preside over the toasts. In the midst of the conviviality, the information was given that an armed party was parading in front of the tavern in protest against a rumored McKean parade. As a consequence the banquet broke up in disorder, and new scores were added to old.

The antagonism to which the election had given rise now brought the break between Scull and Brackenridge, which had been presaged for some time. The *Gazette* had been retreating of late from its earlier policy of allowing Anti-Federalist leaders the freedom of its columns. Brackenridge, ambitious politician that he was, was particularly perturbed. As early as 1797 he had suggested to Andrew Richardson and some others the advisability of starting an opposition paper in Pittsburgh. The present seemed the moment to strike.

On November 30, 1799, Scull funereally detailed the prospectus for a new paper sponsored by Brackenridge. The ostensible reason given for the step was a scurrilous article that had appeared in the *Gazette*, but Scull had furnished the name of the author to Brackenridge and considered himself thereby acquitted of responsibility. Brackenridge countered with a statement that Scull should have disapproved or rejected the communication for publication. The gifted lawyer admitted, however, that he had desired a private press for his own use as a literary man for some time, since Scull's press was neither well adapted to the publication of pamphlets nor given to low charges.

Scull was quite beside himself at the depreciating tone of this explanation. With an air of pathos he queried:

> What Printer prints cheaper than I do? What sheet is better filled than mine? He may indeed get a Printer to publish what may be more agreeable to himself—but I

submit to my readers, whether any can fill the sheet with
more useful intelligence.[6]

It was all in vain. Scull's monopoly in the field of local journalism
was at last to be broken. A certain John Israel, who had been
publishing the *Herald of Liberty* mentioned above, quietly went
ahead, installed a press in Pittsburgh, and began printing a small
four-column opposition sheet, the *Tree of Liberty*, on August 16,
1800.

The rivalry between the two papers flauntingly colored the
national campaign of the next year. The new venture did not
escape the favorite Federalist charge of irreligion, and Scull was
sufficiently scandalized to remark:

> I reverence the Bible, and do not like...to see the
> word of God profaned. Messrs. Brackenridge and Israel
> have taken a motto to their paper from Revelations 22,
> 2. where the Holy Spirit speaking of the Tree of Life says,
> "And the leaves of the Tree were for the healing of the
> nations." These sacred words they have profanely ap-
> plied to their newspaper.[7]

Scull also quizzed Brackenridge as to the identity of the persons
whose heads had been cut off and laid like turnips under the *Tree
of Liberty*. "We suggest the propriety of adding a Guillotine to the
Tree, and a headless trunk or two in the back ground, together
with Judge Marat smiling and enjoying the carnage.—French
things should be completely French ! ! !"[8] To all these accusations, Brackenridge returned the same bland answer. While personally friendly to Mr. Israel, he himself had no connection with
the *Tree of Liberty*. Very little credit was given this disclaimer,
nevertheless, for Brackenridge's part in fostering the *Gazette* was
not forgotten.

Whether or not he might be financially interested in Israel's
press, Brackenridge certainly did not hesitate to use it for public
expression of his views. Although he had been a member of the
state supreme court since December 18, 1799, he allowed himself

to become involved in an angry controversy with his fellow judge, Alexander Addison, and so far forgot his legal training as to write

> It ... is a strong proof of the love of order, and re-
> spect for the laws among the people, that under a sense
> of the groundless and degrading LIBEL, they were not
> fired with sudden indignation, and did not drag you from
> your seat, and tread you under foot.[9]

This bombastic sentence coming from a judge of the supreme court convinced Scull that a revolution was planned. The *Gazette* of November 28, 1800, appeared with great flaring headlines, a unique feature at the time. The word "Insurrection" was emblazoned across the head, and the public was advised that if tumult, violence, and insurrection did not take place, the failure could not be ascribed to Hugh Henry Brackenridge. In short, Scull seems to have convinced himself that Brackenridge had lost his sanity, and well he might, for he had a letter on hand from a citizen of Washington County to the effect that on Brackenridge's "late Mad circuit" through Washington County, the judge had become "terribly drunk" in Canonsburg, had stridden around the tavern naked, and had induced the local boys to throw buckets of water over him. Scull must have shaken his head dismally, as he wrote with many a lift of his goose-quill pen:

> The foregoing narrative would seem almost incredible
> to any person unacquainted with Mr. Brackenridge, yet
> it can be proved by the oaths of many witnesses. His
> cursing and swearing were shocking beyond anything ever
> heard before: A person at Noblesburgh is willing to make
> oath that the Judge damned the Landlord fifteen times
> while he was getting whiskey to make the eggnogg
> stronger. When these things are done by a magistrate
> high in office, we can not expect reformation or punish-
> ment of the profane and dissolute among us.[10]

In taking part in such controversies, Scull, always the gentleman, seems to have felt a sense of shame that impelled him to apologize for letting personalities enter into his paper. He confessed no pleasure in them; in fact, he sought to avoid them, but self-defense left no choice.

Stolidly he received the Federalist setback in 1800 and the inauguration of Jefferson. True he noted half favorably the conciliatory tone of the great Virginian's inaugural address, but this was soon forgotten in the clamor that arose over appointments and the president's friendliness toward Thomas Paine. The favor accorded Gallatin by the president offended Scull too. Statesman of the West though he was, Gallatin was not overly popular with the Pittsburgh Federalists. The five-thousand-dollar salary that he drew, they claimed, was hardly consistent with "Democratic Economy," and his first report on the treasury, with its reflections on the financial management of the preceding administration, produced only frowns and grimaces on their part.

Scull's temper was not likely to be improved anyway by the insults hurled at him by the "Laboratory of Slander," as he chose to call the local organ of the Anti-Federalists, which frequently lampooned him in the following manner:

> Poor Johnny in his last Gazette
> Begins again to bray and fret
> Swearing that Israel is not known—
> A stranger, lad, not yet half grown.
> But, of all the charges that are laid
> To Scull, it surely can't be said,
> That He's a stranger.—For he's well known,
> By his *spindle shanks & hard skull bone.*
> Aye faith By Them, he's known as well
> As Polecat is by fragrant smell,
> Or muskrat, or the bearded goat,
> Or man that's under pettycoat.[11]

Some of the accusations of Scull's writers were little better. As mentioned before, one was so very extreme that Brackenridge called on Scull, pointed out the objectionable matter, and threatened suit unless Scull revealed the name of the author. Another such blast was blamed for an attempt to assassinate John B. C. Lucas, elected to Congress by the Republicans in 1802. After the latter incident visions of a new reign of terror instigated by the Federalist editor came to Israel's eyes. He saw the streets filled with "bludgeoned Federalists exhibiting a riotous appearance" and whimpered that Scull in his paper had called upon the "faction" to attack Israel's printing office and lay it prostrate. In a disdainful way, Scull demonstrated this last complaint to be a garbled version of a remark dropped by one of the *Gazette's* correspondents. Finally the articles in the *Tree* became so violent that in 1803, Scull brought suit against Israel for libel and won the verdict.

Regardless of such episodes, the increasing power of the Anti-Federalists in the region could not be gainsaid. In 1803, the borough of Pittsburgh was carried by them for the first time. In the general ebb of Pennsylvania Federalism that year, only six Federalists were to be discovered in the newly elected general assembly of the state. Nor was it possible to attribute continued Federalist reverses in the locality to the machinations of Brackenridge and Israel alone. The former moved from Pittsburgh to Carlisle in August, 1801; Israel died of blood poisoning at nearby Washington on October 7, 1806. The *Tree of Liberty* had been succeeded by the Pittsburgh *Commonwealth* as the party organ in Pittsburgh. The crux of the matter was that the elements from which the Federalist belief drew its strength had been left out of the texture of western soil. Federalism was in the West, not of it. Whether they realized it or not, John Scull and his friends represented a system of government and politics that was destined to undergo a temporary eclipse.

When the War of 1812 came along, Scull preferred to line up with his party rather than with his section. He could not align with both. Probably the depths to which the *Gazette* was stirred by the Embargo was more a matter of political opposition to the Jefferson administration than of actual discomfort induced by economic privation. Scarcely had the War of 1812 begun when the irrational conduct of General Isaac Hull, the United States commanding officer at Detroit, placed the whole Northwest at the mercy of an invasion from Canada. With more coolness than most

of his fellow citizens could muster, Scull expressed the opinion
that this was a most unfortunate event but that little else could
have been expected from the poorly equipped and illy disciplined
army under Hull's command. The citizenry of Pittsburgh, on the
other hand, could not view the matter with such detachment.
Although immediate danger was not expected, a committee of
safety with seven members was appointed, while efforts to fill
volunteer companies and to induce the governor to equip the
militia were elicited.

Scull had little stomach for war activities. Certainly the
burlesque performance of "our heroes both in and out of Congress"
would, he thought, draw forth only fresh effusions of Napoleon
Bonaparte's contempt for American valor. The logical remedy
was a political one. A word from the people at large could in-
stantly annihilate the existence of all unworthy rulers. As if in
answer to this advice, a circle of war-weary Pittsburghers trooped
into the home of William Monroe and appointed delegates to a
county convention for the purpose of choosing candidates for the
fall election. The Peace ticket, as their slate was called, was
backed so energetically by the *Gazette* that it carried Allegheny
County by a majority of nearly two hundred votes; but Butler
County, then joined with Allegheny County to constitute the
congressional district, amassed enough votes on the other side to
return Adamson Tannehill to Congress. After some loud mutter-
ings organized opposition to the war in the region subsided.

Perry's victory at Lake Erie was the *Gazette's* best news story
during the war. So moving was it that "The Recluse," a local
rimester, celebrated it with a doggerel poem, which the paper
printed. When Scull happened on the fact that Perry was a Federalist, his joy knew no bounds. "We state this with the greater
pleasure," he said, "as all the disgrace and defeats which our
armies have met with, were solely owing to the treachery, coward-
ice, or incapacity of their Democratic commanders." [12] From time
to time the exploits of the Pittsburgh Blues, the local contingent,
came in for their share of reporting. When the local sons came

home, a year after their departure, their eager reception may be imagined. A discharge of artillery from the fort broke the silence as they crossed to the Pittsburgh side of the Allegheny River, where they were met by the garrison and escorted to the public square. Crowds of citizens were out in the streets to welcome them, and of course there was a bountiful public dinner for them, with that rising young political light Henry Baldwin presiding.

Scull was plainly irked by the repeated calls for militia levies to plug the holes in the regimental ranks. The *Gazette* went so far as to predict that in the face of public discontent with the war "Mr. Madison" might be compelled "to adopt the favorite plan of his friend Bonaparte, and send the *conscripts* chain'd and handcuff'd to their places of rendezvous." [18] Newspaper advertisements spoke eloquently for the prevalence of desertions and bounty jumping in the vicinity. In the *Gazette* itself there was a standing offer of fifty dollars posted by Captain James Reed at Fort Fayette for any deserter brought in. With the offer went the promise that as soon as a desertion was reported a charge would be fired from a twenty-five pounder on Grant's Hill so that the citizens might be placed on the alert.

Jackson's victory at New Orleans was a long-delayed compensation for the many humiliations of the war. The *Gazette* hastened the news to its readers in an extra. For several weeks it had grumbled that neither the western mails nor the *National Intelligencer* (Washington, D.C.) brought tidings from New Orleans. At last on February 6, 1815, nearly a month after the battle, an extra brought the news to the Pittsburgh public. On February 26 the *Gazette* made known the full terms of the treaty of peace. Both events were celebrated in the town on February 28 with a public illumination and general hilarity.

The feeling of joy was not materially diminished by repeated indications that Napoleon's imperial days were numbered. His sweeping campaigns had been generously though not sympathetically reported in the *Gazette*. On August 12, 1815, the paper published the news of the Battle of Waterloo, but cautiously waited a week's time before celebrating the unexpected victory. It was glad to see him banished to St. Helena. Scull started at the rumored possibility of Napoleon coming to America. This must never be. "We most fervently pray that our soil may never be polluted by the landing on it of this demon of discord, this fiend in human shape." [14]

Notwithstanding the fact that this great bogey-man of the Federalists had made his last bow before the footlights, the old Federalist party itself was about to breathe its last. There was a momentary interruption of the sinking spell in 1814 when Woods, the local Federalist candidate of Congress, slipped under the wire by a slender majority. After that a strange coma settled down upon the Pittsburgh Federalists, which all Scull's scoldings and warnings could not dispel. It was unquestionably time for the emergence of new factors to revitalize the party system, if a party system there was to be. The Federalists had stood by helplessly while the Jeffersonians took over, one by one, the separate features of Federalist policy—a course of action that might be soothing to the vanity of the Federalists, but that was ruinous to their party organization.

Scull, about to leave his old desk, regarded the political pot with a wry face. The Virginia dynasty kept marching on without halt. "To what a pitiable pass has democracy come!" mourned Scull. "James Monroe, the *profound statesman* and *intrepid soldier*, the *only* man of the party, who unites *all* the requisites for the office!—O Tempora!" [15] It was a fitting elegy.

PART II—1816–1841

THE CRUSADER

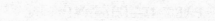

CHAPTER V

NEW PILOTS AND CHANGING WINDS

Thirty years had come and gone since Scull first entered the little office on Water Street. He was not old, as the world counts years, but he was perhaps a whit discouraged at his poor success in keeping the Federalist lamp trimmed and burning in western Pennsylvania. Brackenridge was dead; the news had just come from Carlisle. Old faces were passing from the scene. Then, too, son John yearned (or was it perhaps the old man's desire?) to step into his father's shoes and continue the paper as a family venture. Whatever the reason, on the thirtieth anniversary of the founding of the *Gazette*, John Scull the elder stepped down, and young John Irwin Scull entered enthusiastically upon his career as editor.

The elder Scull clung to his printing business for more than a year. After its discontinuance he left his home on Sixth Street near Smithfield and moved to a spot in Westmoreland County not far from Irwin. Adjoining it was Brush Hill, the residence of his son John, to whom it had been deeded by his maternal grandfather, Colonel John Irwin, "in consideration of the great love he bore him, and the sum of one dollar." Yet John Scull, Sr., was not quite resigned to the quiet existence of a country gentleman. Late in life he experienced a desire for political honor, which was satisfied by successful candidacies for the offices of justice of the peace and county commissioner. Other posts of honor and trust were conferred upon him. Not only was he one of the incorporators of the Western University of Pennsylvania; he also held for a time the position of president of the Farmers' and Mechanics' Bank, one of the first institutions of the sort in Pittsburgh. When death came to him on February 8, 1828, he might well have looked back with pride on a full and useful life. His last will and testament was an interesting commentary on his careful and prudent mode of life. Prefaced with a full acknowledgment to God for his "infinite mercy" in prolonging his servant's existence to that time,

55

it bequeathed all his property, $13,600 worth, carefully itemized, to his wife, Mary Scull, and appointed her sole executrix. In comparison with the princely fortunes of some present day newspaper owners, the amount is small. It was, however, a tidy sum for that day, and, one may suppose, it enabled his widow to spend her remaining days comfortably.

Like a subsequent editor of the *Gazette*, John Irwin Scull, the second son, was sent to Princeton University. On November 7, 1804, his grandfather Irwin had booked passage for himself, for little John, and for another grandson, James Irwin, on the new stage line to Philadelphia. It must have been an exciting trip for the lads just in their teens. Philadelphia was a grand place! There grandfather bought a box of paints for "Jimmy," as well as other fascinating things and, of course, necessaries for the year. The individual cost of board, room rent, tuition, wood, servants' wages, etc., for the winter session was estimated at $92.17. The boys were each provided with twenty dollars for pocket money and for miscellaneous needed articles. Nine days after the coach left the two rivers, the cousins were at Princeton, ready to open a new chapter in their lives.

John I. Scull came back from Princeton gripping his sheepskin proudly and began at once the practice of law in his home town. Then the War of 1812 came and shunted his brother Edward into its maelstrom. James Irwin, too, marched merrily off to the sound of fifes and drums, but John Scull's second son remained at home with his law books. It may be that the father's prejudice against the war was an initial factor in keeping him there; certainly a disinclination to enter the fray was not; and letters filled with military ardor from cousin James away at the front were scant comfort to John. He itched to grasp a commission and go off to join his comrades; such as Holmes, for example, who wrote back from Sackett's Harbor expressing the desire that they might fight together "as we have been accustomed to do everything from our infancy." One of the letters implies, however, that young Scull was not entirely disconsolate:

How do your *love* affairs come on & who are you in love with? for you are so *fickle* & *inconstant* that it is impossible for one to *even* guess. I think the fair one that can catch and hold you as her Captive for any length of time must not only possess Beauty but some share of address & must not make the least *faux-pas* or you'll *be off....*

Do you frequent Kerrs as much as you used to do for the purpose of playing *Cards?* What would I not give to be among you for a day or two, that we might saunter about the streets, visit the Girls, & at nine o'clock adjourn to the tavern, meet with the *Old Crew* & have a genteel game of—but alas those times are over! & now instead of sauntering through the streets, [I] am *drilling the men* & in place of visiting the Girls & playing Cards, drinking &c am obliged to be Officer of the Guards, set up all night & drink *cold water*.—I must request that you visit the Girls directly on the receipt of this & tell the dear *Creatures* that *a time may come* when I shall again *live and fatten* on their *smiles*.[1]

Another of young John's soldier friends wrote home in the summer of 1815 to reprove him for his silence and to bid him "awake from your dream of bliss and devote half an hour to creatures of this sublunary sphere." Meanwhile his hopes of military service had failed to materialize. At the very end of the year 1814 Ephraim Pentland wrote from Washington to the father advising him that young John's name was on the list of nominations to a lieutenancy and would be presented to the Senate for confirmation in a few days. The ink was already dry on the parchment of Ghent![2]

So it was that on August 9, 1816, John Irwin Scull, now happily married and anxious to distinguish himself as he had not in the soldier's profession or the law, took over active control of the *Gazette*, moved the establishment to a point opposite the post office on Front Street, and changed the weekly *Gazette* into a semi-weekly. It was now to be published on Tuesdays and Fridays, at three dollars per year in advance or three and a half dollars "on time." The width of the sheet reverted to four columns, but the paper was still a four-page publication.

Doubtless the young editor entered on his task with great confidence. He had come from Princeton with the best classical training that the times could afford; his literary taste was admittedly superior. His appearance was handsome; his manners fascinating; his disposition at all times genial. In making his bow to the public, the new editor gave an expression of his views none the less interesting for its lofty style:

> The prospectus of village journals, has heretofore been as little attractive, as a "tale thrice told," or as the periodical ebullitions of the fourth of July. A country Editor, when sitting down to announce his intention, and to explain his principles, commonly does it more for the sake of form, and of complying with established custom, than from the anticipation of being generally read, or from the still more delusive hope of increasing, by these means, the list of patrons. Provincial gazettes have been destined to be viewed as village appendages, too much in the light of an alehouse, or blacksmith's shop; as these are necessary for the temporary accommodation of individuals, so are *those* considered merely as convenient vehicles, for announcing to the world, the important intelligence of stray cattle, runaway apprentices, and cheap stores. But the present Editor feels happy, that at the moment he enters on his duties, a new era is commencing in the western country; his predecessor began his publication before science had even dawned, o'er the "wild," and before politics were thought of as a system; he, on the contrary, commences his career, at the instant Pittsburgh takes her place among the Cities of the Union.[3]

It was clear that young John had a facility of expression and a light and airy manner that his father never possessed, but unfortunately he did not live up to his promising beginning. The newspaper business in 1816 was far from booming. There were at the time nearly five hundred newspapers being printed in the United States, and fully half were facing a hard struggle to pay expenses. Poverty and disappointment were often the reward of years of active exertion.

From his father Scull had inherited a newspaper staff of indeterminate size, contributing to a high overhead of expense. As a result, the most notable change in the appearance of the paper was the increasing prominence of the revenue-providing advertising material. The front page had become a solid bank of advertisements, with somewhat larger lettering than before. Scull was conscious of this change: "Our advertising custom, though necessary for our support," he declared, "is already too great for our limits; and is daily encroaching upon that portion of our paper which we would wish to devote to useful and interesting matter." [4]

The circulation of the paper had its routine worries. Complaints of irregular subscription service arose. Early in November, 1817, Scull was called to account on this score several times, and a kindly admonition came even from old Colonel Irwin:

> Dear John
> I hope you are not very strong with foreign news you can the better share a column for a letter of the Domestick kind. I take great pleasure in reading your Paper, but do not receive much over the half of them. I Recommend, that all the Papers for our neighbourhood may be put up in one Packet & directed to Mr. Fullerton, as he will Pay attention to the Stage Passing so close to his door. Single Papers given to the Drivers are Generally treated with neglect, by being trodden under foot in the Stage or Picked up by the passengers. A Sealed packet will be treated with more Respect.
> It would give me pleasure to find your Paper abound with Such Native or Domestick Productions, as may be Supposed to flow from the Penn of the Editor. The Proceedings of the General & State Governments, will always afford a large field for Critickism.
>
> Most affectionately,
> JOHN IRWIN.[5]

All that Scull could say in reply was that he was satisfied the fault lay not in the Pittsburgh post office but in some of the offices east of the city, and that the *Gazette* was regularly and strongly packed and deposited in the post office on each day of publication.

The paper had not been in Scull's possession for two years

when he announced the sale of a half interest in it to Morgan Neville, a grandson of General John Neville, who was a central figure in the Whisky Insurrection, and the son of the accomplished Colonel Presley Neville. It soon became obvious that the heavier share of the editorial duties had fallen on the newcomer, an attractive figure and, in some respects, the ablest editor the paper ever had. Henry M. Brackenridge, his classmate at the Pittsburgh Academy, spoke in the highest terms of the ability and the gentlemanly qualities that quite set Neville apart from his schoolfellows. Admitted to the bar in 1808, he became the associate of such distinguished attorneys as Walter Forward, Alexander Johnston, and Charles Shaler. Three years later he was married to Jeremiah Barker's Nancy and settled down. It was high time. In the days when Aaron Burr was sowing intrigues up and down the western country, Neville had been one of a party of fourteen youths who were detained on Blennerhassett's Island for several days under suspicion of complicity in the conspiracy. At the investigation that followed it was set forth that they had simply started down the Ohio River on a trip to New Orleans without any idea of hostile designs against the United States government. This point established, they were set at liberty and permitted to return to their homes. This incident indicates Neville's adventurous character.

From the beginning Neville's editorials were brilliantly written, sometimes to the point of being strained and sophomoric. The verbiage and the frequent quotations were the fruit of a capacious mind; the liberal point of view expressed in them was partly a matter of Neville's convictions, partly a result of the political calm that for the nonce the country enjoyed. The newspaper guild at large admired the product of Neville's craftsmanship. Even the newspapers at the national capital occasionally reprinted editorials from the *Gazette*.

Unquestionably Neville had a high opinion of his calling. In many a Pittsburgh household, as he put it, "The columns of a *Gazette* are frequently folded beneath the cover of the sacred book, and the implicit credence that is given to the one, is very generally transferred to the other." [6] This, he admitted, gave him considerable pride, and so it was with regret that he saw the style of many country editors descend from the high plane upon which gentlemen should be addressed. The prating familiarity of the Jacksonian period and the nicknames it affected were likewise distasteful to him.

Neville barely made a living from his newspaper work. Partly for this reason, partly on account of his restless nature, he also engaged in other pursuits. When the Thespian Society was organized in 1817 he daubed himself with grease and took part in amateur theatrical productions. In 1819 he waged a triumphant campaign for the office of sheriff of Allegheny County, which threw a goodly share of legal advertising in the direction of the *Gazette*. From 1819 to 1824 he was the captain of the Pittsburgh Blues, the local militia contingent.

Early in 1820 the community was surprised by another change in the *Gazette's* management. Old citizens rubbed their eyes in amazement. Could the *Gazette* continue without one of the Sculls in control? It seemed incredible. Some were heard to say gloomily that the paper was tottering to an early grave. The burden of debts was indeed very heavy. During the period of twenty-one months since Neville had joined the staff, a period of stringently hard times, the amount of debts owing to the paper had reached four thousand dollars. It was evident that the *Gazette* editors could no longer afford to issue the paper twice a week. Under the circumstances, the firm of John I. Scull and Morgan Neville was dissolved. Scull explained in his valedictory editorial that a new residence far from the city prevented him from carrying on his editorial duties satisfactorily—hardly the whole story.

Into the breach came the printing firm of Eichbaum and Johnston, to purchase the paper and retain Neville as editor. The *Gazette* emerged with an elongated name that must have inspired some consternation in the community. The *Pittsburgh Gazette and Manufacturing and Mercantile Advertiser* was the appellation with

which it was to be saddled for several years. Neville remained
with it until the autumn of 1821, when he stepped out with seeming
reluctance. He was obliged "for the present" to relinquish the
editorial duties of the *Gazette*, but he hoped at no distant day to
resume an employment, "to which, I confess, I am much attached."
This aspiration was never fulfilled. In 1824 he removed to Cincinnati, where in the course of his activities he founded the short-
lived Cincinnati *Commercial Register*, the first daily newspaper
west of Philadelphia.

The story is told that when Lafayette reached Cincinnati on
his famous tour of the United States in 1825, he inquired at once
for Morgan Neville, whose father he had known well in Revolutionary days. Tosso, one of the general's aides, nudged him and
whispered that Neville was lying ill with ague at his home. "I will
go to him at once," the general said. He was shown the way, and
after a little talk he asked, "Well, Neville, what are your circumstances?" "Not good, general," was the reply. "I spent every
thing I had to pay my father's debts." The general then rang for
pen and ink and wrote an order on the United States Bank for
stock to the amount of four thousand dollars in favor of Morgan
Neville and slipped it under the pillow. Neville was too proud,
however, to use a penny of it. It remained untouched in his possession and was transferred along with the rest of his estate to his
family at the time of his death.[7]

For a short time Eichbaum and Johnston coöperated in the
editorial direction of the paper as well as in the publishing of it,
but in the summer of 1822 they turned over a portion of the editorial duties to Benjamin Evans, a lawyer of the town. Either he
tired of the task or they of him, for his name was withdrawn from
the paper in October of the same year. Nothing, it seemed, could
prevent the *Gazette and Manufacturing and Mercantile Advertiser*
from lurching into the grave that has swallowed up hundreds of
Pittsburgh newspapers. The new publishers bemoaned the fact
that during the two years since they had acquired it, the paper
had brought in scarcely enough to pay the bare cost of labor and

materials. Nearly all of its subscribers were back two years on their payments. Indeed, if it had not been for "other resources," the publication of the *Gazette and Manufacturing and Mercantile Advertiser* must have stopped ere this. By other resources, the publishers meant, in all likelihood, the proceeds from their book-printing business.

Near the close of the year 1822 the paper changed hands once more. David Maclean, the new owner, was no novice in the newspaper business. In 1805 he had wandered into John Scull's office, a Scotch-Irish lad from Westmoreland County who desired to become a printer's apprentice. At the end of the prescribed period he had returned to Greensburg, taken employment with the *Greensburg Gazette*, a Federalist organ, and had at length become its owner. There he had remained until his arrangement with Eichbaum and Johnston had been effected. Very soon he associated his brother Matthew with him in the management of the *Gazette and Manufacturing and Mercantile Advertiser*. Neither was inclined toward spectacular journalism. As long as twenty columns of news and advertisements were regularly dished up for the subscribers, they considered their task well done. Acrid Anne Royall, who visited Pittsburgh in 1828, set the elder brother down as a "blue stocking" and dismissed him curtly with the words "his countenance bespeaks him what he is, though he is not devoid of talent." [8]

Times were picking up, however, and newspaper patronage with them. In the fall of 1825 the brothers planned to expand the paper to what they styled the imperial size—a width of six columns. They were moved to take this optimistic step by increased advertising patronage and a larger subscription list—a greater percentage of paid-up subscriptions. About this same time, the paper reverted to its original title; it remained a weekly at two dollars per year until September, 1828, when a semi-weekly edition, at four dollars per year, was put out to supplement the weekly.

The greatest exploit of the Maclean *régime* came in March, 1829, when what may be called the *Gazette's* first big news scoop was printed. Jackson had just entered the presidency, and his first words after his induction into office were awaited anxiously by everyone. At 12:35 P. M. on March 8 express riders left Washington with the message; they reached Pittsburgh with it just twenty-four hours later. Within a few hours Old Hickory's words were in type at the *Gazette* office, ready for the edition. This was accounted a great achievement at the time.

As yet the *Gazette* still derived most of its national and foreign news from exchanges. High lights in the panorama of foreign news during those years were the reports of the passing of Napoleon, George Canning, and King George III. Of the latter the *Gazette* spoke with surprising moderation, concluding that his character was not properly appreciated and that it must be left to the future historian to do him justice. One of the most sensational stories from abroad was the divorce trial in which King George IV appeared against his unhappy consort, Queen Caroline. The *Gazette* printed a great deal about it, although with some reluctance about entering into the details of the "disgusting proceeding." To the plaints of revolutionists abroad the *Gazette* inclined a sympathetic ear. It displayed a continuous and friendly interest in the struggles of Bolivar and San Martin for the cause of independence in South America and stirred up local excitement by reports of the hard fight the Greek patriots were making to throw off the yoke of their Turkish overlords; during the year 1827 nearly two thousand dollars were raised by local agencies to succor the suffering Hellenes.

Such benevolence was well rooted in the sentimentality of the times, a quality with which the issues of the *Gazette*, along with those of contemporary newspapers, were likely to be saturated. Filial love, frustrated affection, wanton seduction might be the excuse for a heart-wringing essay of column length or more. An effective antidote for such artificial writing might be found, however, in the rough and ready humor that the *Gazette* retailed along with other western journals. Even at that time the Irish joke was a stand-by:

A Pat, an odd joker—and a Yankee more sly,
Once riding together, a gallows pass'd by:
Said the Yankee to Pat, "if I don't make too free,
Give that gallows its due, and pray where would you be?"
"Why, honey," said Pat, "faith that's easily known;
I'd be riding to town by myself all alone."[9]

In this way the *Gazette's* new pilots carried on their task of providing their friends with the news of the day. The paper had passed through a dangerous transitional crisis; the next decade was to see it safely back in its course under new and expert guidance.

CHAPTER VI

A FIGHTING EDITOR

Changes of ownership and control recurred at such frequent intervals in the years following the departure of John Irwin Scull from the *Gazette* that there could have been little surprise when the Macleans sold the paper in the fall of 1829. The newspaper business was none too profitable at the time. The elder Scull had died the year before, muttering mysteriously that he had all his life neglected "the one thing needful" and now must perish. His brain child, it seemed probable, would not outlive him long. Certainly its transfer to a young man who knew nothing of the printing and publishing side of the business boded ill for the paper's future. Yet this same young man, a first cousin of Morgan Neville, was to extend the *Gazette's* influence farther than had any of his predecessors; and he was to become one of the most distinguished persons connected with the early journalism of Pittsburgh.

Neville B. Craig came from a family that had from the beginning turned a useful hand toward building the city. The major, his father, has already appeared as Scull's benefactor when a paper shortage threatened. Soon after the surrender of Yorktown Isaac Craig, a veteran of the American Revolution, was ordered with his detachment to Fort Pitt. There he settled down as deputy quarter-master, married into the influential Neville family, and bestirred himself to take advantage of the tempting business opportunities that he saw in the region.

Such was the environment in which young Neville Craig grew up: watching soldiers come and go, skating on the broad moat near the redoubt, playing ball with the young Butlers, Nevilles, and O'Haras, or listening to the tales that his father and uncles told about Colonel Boquet, General Forbes, and other heroes of the French and Indian War days. He was just seven years old when David Bradford's whisky rebels marched from Braddock's Field into Pittsburgh. Mrs. Craig, fearing that in her husband's absence young Neville might get into mischief, locked him in the front room that served both as a parlor and ordinance office. As platoon after platoon of the marchers filed by the house on their way to Kirkpatricks, the young prisoner took up a cannon ball, which he had found in the room, hoisted the window, and let the missile fall amongst the insurgents. Surprised and provoked, one of them whirled around and leveled his gun at the youngster. Fortunately an officer was on hand to strike up the rifle with his sword and preserve the Craig child's life.

After some preliminary instruction at the Pittsburgh Academy, young Craig, with letters addressed to his father's old military friend, Major Ercurius Beatty, was sent in his seventeenth year to Princeton. Before he had finished his course there his collegiate career was abruptly terminated by an affray in which he took sides with the students against the police and unluckily wounded one of the constables with a sword cane. He was arrested and held for bail; Major Beatty was his surety. In the trial, at which his father was present, the testimony was clearly against him, but the memory of his father's gallantry at the battle of Princeton influenced the court and saved the day. Expelled from college, sobered by his experience with the law, Craig started home. He stopped at Philadelphia and fought a duel with an old schoolmate just back from a sea voyage. Neither was harmed; they parted the best of friends; and Craig resumed his westward journey.

After spending some time in the law office of the great jurist, Alexander Addison, Craig was admitted to the bar in 1810. The next year he spent in the law firm of Walter Forward and Henry M. Watt. About that time he married Jane Fulton, daughter of Henry Fulton, a merchant of the town. Hard put to it to support a family on his meager income, Craig moved to New Lisbon in Columbiana County, Ohio, and became a village storekeeper for a time. In the course of his stay there he made three trading voyages with flour to New Orleans, financed in part by his father and his father-in-law. When the War of 1812 broke out he quickened to the sound of fife and drum and yearned to rush away to the battle field. In fact, he went so far as to return to Pittsburgh and accept a commission in the "Pittsburgh Blues," but the entreaties of his aging father kept him from marching away with them.

The war passed. Back at his law practice Craig turned an eye now and then to politics. In 1822 he was appointed deputy attorney-general for Allegheny County by the attorney-general of the commonwealth. While holding that office he became involved in a scrape that threatened serious consequences. The occasion was a legal tilt with another practicing attorney, John Henry Hopkins, which led to heated words, lie calling, and finally a scuffle under the eyes of the court. This imprudent conduct brought about his arrest and a heavy fine. Craig's slender resources were quite inadequate to raise the sum required, but a spectator, an old Yankee sea captain named Richard Bowen, generously came to the rescue. Many years later Craig had the opportunity to return the favor by giving his endorsement to a stay of execution of Bowen's note.

Craig's decision to turn from the law to journalism is not readily explained. He was for a while employed as an attorney by the brothers Maclean while contributing at the same time some material to their paper. Perhaps the connection of his cousin Morgan Neville was a factor. Probably he paid no great price for the paper and all its effects. To pay for it he had, in addition to any savings of his own, a decent competence from his father's estate and his wife's considerable legacy.

It is commonly agreed that the new editor was in 1829 a man of striking appearance, tall and of commanding presence, the more remarkable for the large green-colored glasses made necessary by his weak vision. His friends agreed that he was a great worker. He employed all the hands, selected the material for the paper, wrote all the editorials, and kept the books. So meticulously careful was he to have the paper delivered on time that he would trust no one but himself to see to the mailing. Every morning regularly at seven o'clock he entered the office and headed for his editorial sanctum on the second floor. Once there, he donned overall sleeves and an eye shade and plunged into his work. Scissors, pencils, and paste he scorned. Instead he took a quill pen and marked the articles he wanted to publish. Between times he read proof and saw to all the other details. For callers he had a congenital dislike. Only one chair was kept in the editorial room—that was Craig's. Intruders were likely to find him utterly oblivious of them.

The story is told that one day the English traveler and lecturer, James Silk Buckingham, called on him. When he entered Craig was sitting with his back to the door, hard at work. "Hoch!" went Mr. Buckingham, with the intention of attracting his attention. "Spit out," shouted Mr. Craig, who had a perfect horror of the habit of clearing the throat. The Englishman's face crimsoned, and he stood completely nonplussed. His conductor indicated to Mr. Craig that there was present a gentleman who wished to speak with him. Craig turned and said, "Be seated, sir," and then went on with getting out copy. Buckingham's embarrassment was only increased when he realized that there was no chair in the office save the one Mr. Craig was occupying. After a little while, however, the editor arose and gave him a cordial greeting and his chair and sent upstairs for another to be brought down. The two had an animated conversation that ended in Craig's writing a half-column leader about Mr. Buckingham's proposed lecture. [1]

After 1833 the *Gazette* employed a considerable number of hands. The foreman of the office was for a time Matthew Maclean Grant, a nephew of Craig's predecessors. In 1835 Grant was admitted to the firm, but Craig retained editorial control, with some assistance from B. F. Nevins. The old Ramage press, which had printed the first numbers of the *Gazette*, was still being used in 1829, but its career was nearly over. Its successor, a new imperial-size, one-pull press, is said to have created a great sensation among the populace when it arrived from Philadelphia.

Craig followed the custom set by his predecessors in putting out separate weekly and semi-weekly editions. Before long he began to turn over in his mind the advisability of issuing the

Gazette daily. The experiment had already worked in Cincinnati and Louisville. Why not in Pittsburgh? After several delays, which consumed nearly two years' time, the momentous step was taken. At that time (Tuesday, July 30, 1833) Craig made it clear that the *Daily Pittsburgh Gazette* was to have more of a commercial character than before, that it was to be an afternoon paper, and that it would cost six dollars per year, strictly in advance. Viewed retrospectively, the delivery of the first number of the *Daily Gazette* was an historic occasion. The paper then had only one carrier in the city. To him was given a list of the widely scattered group of subscribers in Pittsburgh and Allegheny, most of whom were already taking the weekly. In no sense was he a newsboy, for he collected no money; instead, he had instructions to distribute papers only to those whose names were on his list. The route was an extended one; the carrier admitted that on account of this he was often tempted to skip subscribers in outlying parts.

A daily edition would not have been undertaken had Craig not felt sure of a steady patronage. As the volume of advertising increased the policy of the paper grew less lenient. At a meeting of Pittsburgh newspaper publishers in May, 1836, it was decided that thereafter charges would be made for all notices except obituaries and political notices. No longer would the editor continue to publish at his own expense unlimited amounts of material having to do with railroads, canals, societies, fire companies, or weddings.

Among the new features that found their way into the *Gazette* in the thirties were the steamboat columns containing lists of arrivals and departures of boats and the names of new guests at the city hotels. An evidence of increasing interest in the conduct of the government at Washington, D. C., was the employment in 1837 of a Washington correspondent, "Junius," to retail political gossip from the capitol in the form of random letters. Perhaps the most novel feature was the carrier's address, which appeared in the paper on or about New Year's Day. Each subscriber served by the carrier was expected to respond to the address with some

NEVILLE B. CRAIG, EDITOR 1829–1841

THE FIRST NUMBER OF THE DAILY GAZETTE

small sum. One of the best addresses was that for the year 1838, from which extracts follow:

> A Carrier must support his station,
> Must keep in funds his corporation;
> The universal custom claim,
> To borrow—in the muses' name,
> In paper speculations dip,
> And issue his poetic scrip.
> But as it seems his friends to pinch
> To find the silver change for Lynch,
> That nothing but hard money passes.
> Now, with your Kendalls and DeHasses—
> Your faithful, humble poetaster
> Will thank you for a good shinplaster.
> Another year of Van's reverses,
> And ye will ope your silken purses
> To better auspices and—verses! . . .
>
> The Southern States would fain annex us
> With that new negro market, Texas;
> And Vicksburgh mobs and Alton murders
> Gleam ominously o'er our borders. . . .
>
> As Van himself did once support
> Our dignity at England's court,
> By making himself mean and little,
> He sends to London his lickspittle;
> And Rush and Stevenson have been
> On gracious terms with Briton's Queen. . . .
>
> In Prussia, we have Mr. Wheaton
> In Madrid, we have Mrs. Eaton;
> Ex-secretary Lewis Cass
> Has sailed to the Levant at last. . . .
>
> Van Buren hired the Dutch and Poles
> To crush the half starved Seminoles;
> He hired the Indian, and imbrued
> His red hand in his brother's blood:
> But all in vain, till Jesup stole a

Trick upon poor Osceola,
And proved what Indians won't deny,
That now we beat them at a lie.
Van Buren's press, his party organ,
Brands Lovejoy as it branded Morgan;
This press condemns the brave and good,
Who sought its freedom with life's blood.[2]

The editor was still wont to depend upon his exchanges for news political and otherwise, for there was as yet no systematic attempt on the part of the paper to gather local news. Its contents were very largely selected from such eastern journals as Poulson's *Daily Advertiser* and the *United States Gazette* both of Philadelphia; the *Boston Atlas*, and the widely quoted *National Intelligencer*, from the national capital. A particularly delectable bit of news was the president's message. Long before it arrived, the proprietors of the various city newspapers were at work lining up journeyman printers and apprentices to help hurry it to press in advance of competitors. As many as three or four sizes of type might be used in one column, a practice that was generally interpreted to be very enterprising, as it signified the disposition of the paper to put all its resources at the command of its readers. President Jackson's message of December, 1836, for example, was hurried into print by the *Gazette* with amazing speed. It was received at eight A. M. on the morning of December 9 and issued before noon. The *Gazette* proudly boasted that this was the most expeditious printing of the message that had ever taken place in the city.

More and more in this period did it become plain that the editor was the newspaper, and that the editorial was the most original matter in the paper. On several occasions Neville Craig affixed his signature to editorials; beginning March 31, 1838, they were printed in larger type than the rest of the paper in order to draw attention to them. One can hardly picture Scull composing a breezy paragraph like the one Craig indited on the morning of August 6, 1839: "We do not feel much disposed to write editorial this morning, and having nothing to say, we have deliberately concluded to say nothing."

The extent to which editors of the thirties went out of their way to vilify and insult each other can hardly be indicated by mere statements to that effect. One of the greatest offenders was Craig, who at one time or another ran the gauntlet of practically everyone of his Pittsburgh fellow editors. It is a great wonder that sooner or later he did not become a victim of personal assault, for he wrote as if his pen were dipped in gall. According to one authority he had a faculty for making the warmest friends and the most bitter enemies of any Pittsburgh newspaper man of his times.[3] His favorite adversaries were such local Democratic papers as the *Allegheny Democrat*, the *American Manufacturer*, the *Mercury*, and the *Pittsburgher*.

At first the tone of the controversies was mild, but as time went on epithets like "vile and speckled reptile" and "scalded hound" were freely passed back and forth. Present-day public opinion would not tolerate the gutter language with which these rival editors abused each other. In the first example quoted here the *Gazette* takes the *Mercury* to task for its sudden attachment to William Wilkins after his desertion of the cause of the United States Bank:

> Our remarks upon Judge Wilkins' toast have drawn out a paragraph, in reply, from (the vile spaniel of the Mercury, as we would call him, if we were not unwilling to do that animal injustice, by the comparison,) the editor of the Mercury.
>
> In the various chameleon like changes of that unprincipled paper, none seems to us more striking than its present zeal in the cause of Judge Wilkins. In the campaign which preceded the election of our Senator to Congress, that paper was the selected sewer through which all kinds of filth was poured upon the devoted head of "our present distinguished Senator." Low, and disgusting, and vile, and abominable, as that paper has been, during the last four or five years, its conduct in relation to our "present distinguished Senator" was *then* supereminently base and infamous. Every charge that could be raked up from the filthiest kennels, were freely, nay cheer-

fully, belched forth from the office of the Pittsburgh
Mercury.... Now Mr. Stevenson is in his grave, and
William Wilkins is "our distinguished Senator," and is
shortly to have a hand in the public funds, which are so
conveniently scattered to the four winds, and so lavishly
wasted, upon printers.[4]

In the second example the *Mercury* is seen to strike a wicked
blow at the redoubtable editor of the *Gazette*:

Again has old *"Vinegar Cruet"* of the Gazette dis-
charged himself upon us. His pent up wrath—the "swel-
tering venom sleeping got," vented itself on Saturday
last:—the moral tumour of his black heart burst, for the
nonce, and, we presume, is again accumulating its usual
secretions.... The snakey editor of the Gazette is, un-
consciously we presume, much like the rattlesnake—he
gives warning of attack. He has a lately been gracious
enough to nod to us in the street—to smile and be courte-
ous. Upon this, so well do we know the man, we immediately told our friends that the editor had singled us out
for a spring....
If the abuse of the ruffianly editor of the Gazette was
any disgrace, who would have a character left? He attacks every one who crosses his path.... He has a malignant ferocity, a sanguinary appetite, such as "Boz" has
delineated in Bill Sikes's dog,—a Pythagorean would say
that his soul had served an apprenticeship in the body of
a wolf or a West India bloodhound.[5]

The third example shows Craig's partner, Grant, being vic-
timized by a gross attack in the *Pittsburgher*:

There is a cowardly, and withal malignant puppy, who
publishes a daily paper in this city, but whose insignifi-
cance has heretofore protected him from reproof and
chastisement—I of course mean that lying whelp Matthew Grant, editor of the Gazette. When his brutal master, Craig, has been "cornered," or "dumfounded," ...
so that he cannot put pen to paper on any political topic,
it is then that this sneaking cur, Grant, puts forth his
dolorous whine for "copy," and suggests to the brute, his

master, that if he cannot argue on politics, he can at least *assail private character*. Craig forthwith sets to work, and the big brute then gives the little brute a full charge of brutality and scandal, which is soon sent round by the hands of the carrier to all the old maids in pants who subscribe for the Gazette.

For the information of that "vile," "*white-livered*," "miscreant," MATTHEW GRANT, I have to inform him that at the rate he has been going on for some time, he will be apt soon to get his head among hot coals. I warn him once for all. He understands me. I have heretofore let him pass unscathed, and this time I let him off *pretty easy*.—But the next time that his blackguardism induces me to notice him, I will give him his *full deserts*.[6]

Craig welcomed such warfare, and it was almost inevitable that he should give a good account of himself. His impeccable logic, that of a trained lawyer, was hard to meet. It was easier to attack him than find flaws in what he said. Something of his ironic touch is illustrated by a fling that he took at the *Advocate* and its gradual withdrawal from the war on Jackson:

What has befallen that war? Is it carried on so quietly that no person can hear it? Are the combatants of that party cheered to battle with drums so muffled that no person can hear them? Or have our neighbors—those modern Hannibals, who have sworn an interminable war against the old *Roman*, concluded an inglorious peace with their enemy? Most persons would suppose that the recent interference of Van Buren in our State concerns would have excited our neighbors into still more ardent exertions against him. Have the incursions of the modern Roman, into our own Africa, been as injurious to our modern Carthaginians, as the invasion of Scipio was to the old practisers of the *punica fides?*

We will call again—in the meantime we leave our card.[7]

No action for libel seems to have been instituted against the *Gazette* while Craig was the editor. On the other hand, it is known that he initiated at least two libel suits of his own. The first, in

1834, compelled the editors of the *Advocate* to retract their charges
of a treasonable connection with the Burr conspiracy on the part
of Craig. The other was directed against Zantzinger McDonald
and Thomas Phillips of the *Manufacturer* in 1839. They had published in their columns a letter written by James Callan, impeach-
ing Craig's character as a parent. The suit was discontinued after
a letter of apology and the payment of costs had been received
from the defendants.

At the very end of the decade Craig began to tire of the heavy
responsibilities that the joint duties of editor and publisher placed
upon him. On June 25, 1840, the transfer of ownership to Alexander
Ingram, Jr., a member of the firm of Ingram and McCandless,
Booksellers, was announced. Craig remained as editor. The new
ownership proved temporary: on New Year's Day, 1841, Ingram
made known that he had disposed of the *Gazette* to D. N. White &
Company, Printers. White changed the time of issue from afternoon to morning, but he too kept Craig in the editor's chair. But
Craig was ready to say farewell to his journalistic career. He had
a desire to enter politics again, and he also wanted to do some
literary writing of his own. On July 29, 1841, the fifty-fifth anniversary of the founding of the *Gazette*, he at length made public
his decision to resign from the editorship. The resolution, interpreted by his enemies as quitting under fire, released a stream of
comment. William H. Smith, the editor of the newly combined
Mercury and Democrat raised a paean of delight, observing maliciously that Craig "retreats snarling and snapping, more like a
half-starved wolf when scared and driven from his prey than a
vanquished combatant retiring from an honorable and well-fought
field."[8] Fortunately this was not the general opinion. From far
and wide came tributes to his honesty and ability.

Craig had rescued the *Gazette* from sinking into a state of
respectable mediocrity. Under his immediate predecessors it had
become quite indistinguishable from the mass of country newspapers; but Craig had endowed it with a cause and made it at

once distinctive and widely appealing. During the thirties the paper's circulation boomed. In 1829 it claimed something over a thousand subscribers. About a hundred householders signed for the daily edition when it was first issued in 1833. In 1839 the entire subscription list of the *Pittsburgh Times* came into the possession of the *Gazette*. When Craig's stewardship came to an end in 1841, the *Gazette* was in the lead. In his hands the *Gazette* had become something more than a tradition—his dynamic leadership had made it a strong force to be reckoned with, whether as friend or foe.

CHAPTER VII

THE ANTIMASONIC HERESY

In 1816 the Federalist party of the nation was tottering to its grave, and the country beheld the spectacle of a democracy all but bereft of a party system. The next year the new president, James Monroe, made a triumphal tour of the land. At Pittsburgh, as elsewhere, everyone was out to greet him and to share in the general good feeling of which he seemed the harbinger. Basking in the atmosphere of good will, the *Gazette* rejoiced at this "brilliantly conciliatory" act and called for a party truce to select the best qualified men for county offices and the legislature. In 1820, Neville, the editor, was of the opinion that the "fever of party feeling" had well subsided and that the term Federalist had completely lost its terrors.

During the twenties, the *Gazette* was politically apathetic. In 1824, it claimed to be the only Federalist paper left in the district; yet even it could not escape the charm of the new idol of the West Andrew Jackson. For that matter there were few in western Pennsylvania who could. Pittsburgh, once a Federalist stronghold, gave a smashing popular verdict for Jackson in the presidential election of 1824, 1385 votes against the 18 counted for his victorious rival John Quincy Adams! The Macleans were rather easily reconciled to the result, however. They liked the qualifications of "Old Man Eloquent;" they liked his policies too, and so in 1828 they made some effort to check the popular tide that swept Jackson irresistibly along the road to the White House.

From that time on the *Gazette's* political principles were of cardinal importance, for in the Jacksonian period, Pittsburgh became once again the scene of tightly drawn political contests. Long afterwards Horace Greeley, recalling the days when he was employed for fifteen dollars a week on an Erie, Pennsylvania, newspaper, remarked: "The quality for which its people were most remarkable in 1831 was an intense addiction to partisan strife.

An ardent politician from childhood, I was fairly appalled by the assiduity and vehemence wherewith political controversy was prosecuted by nearly every man and boy I met in Erie." [1] What was true for Erie seemed to be true for western Pennsylvania at large.

Before Craig took over the *Gazette* in 1829 a movement directed against secret societies had crept into western Pennyslvania.[2] It was the product of a jealous feeling toward secret orders that had been quietly fostered in America for nearly a half century. A strange tale concerning the supposed abduction and murder in 1826 of William Morgan, a critic of the Masons, was enough to cause Antimasonic agitation to spread like wildfire over the rural districts of New York and Pennsylvania. Seeing an opportunity to employ this agitation as a political vehicle, a number of enterprising politicians hastened to organize an Antimasonic party, in opposition to Jackson.

Craig was at first undetermined as to which way to turn. For one thing, he had placed himself upon record as a Jackson man as early as 1824 Then again, his cousin Morgan Neville had been a participating Mason and a good friend of the order. Craig looked at his circulation list. It was almost evenly divided between adherents of the Masons and the Antimasons. Only one person who had subscribed to the paper from the day of its founding was still living, and he was a Mason. In view of all this, the editor determined after much deliberation that the *Gazette* should not become the advocate of either party in the coming contest. As time went on, his leanings became more evident, however. His old attachment to Jackson had by degrees turned into something akin to active animosity. Probably the preference shown by Jackson's politica managers for rival editors in Pittsburgh touched the quick-tempered *Gazette* editor in a vital spot. "Who," asked Craig, "is simple enough to expect independence from a man who, like Mr. Johns lives in double dependence upon Jacksonism; being both a *printer by authority*, and an *office-holder?*" [3] By 1831, the *Gazette* was definitely within the Antimasonic camp, sharing quarters with the *Pittsburgh Times*, a sheet established for the express purpose of spreading the principles of Antimasonry.

The Masons for their part bowed momentarily before the storm. Many of their lodges were forced to disband; panic spread among the rest. The leading Masonic paper in Pittsburgh at the time was the *Statesman*, whose editor, John B. Butler, was an active opponent of Craig's. One night the Butler household was aroused by heavy knocking at the postern. The latch was carefully drawn back to disclose the bespectacled countenance of Craig. He had come to warn his antagonist that he had overheard some ill-favored individuals making plans to burn the Butler home that very night. The warning was gratefully received, and speedy precautions were taken to disappoint the plotters. In time, after their first fright, the Masons collected their forces and fought back fiercely at their foes. In August, 1834, they held repeated meetings to denounce Craig for his efforts against them. Years later Craig wryly recalled the episode:

> This was the grand effort of Masonry to overawe me . . . .
> Immediately after these meetings and their resolutions against the *Gazette* and its editor, the masons began to discontinue the paper—Judge Riddle, Thomas Scott and Samuel Fahnestock taking the lead. That was the time I would have cowered before the wrath and the influence of Masonry, if I had been willing to abandon my principles. I shrank not, however, but met their machinations in such a manner as convinced them that masonic trickery and menaces were wasted upon me.[4]

As a political party, the Antimasonic organization was committed to battle for preference with the adherents of Jackson and with the National Republicans of Adams and Henry Clay. In the election of 1832 the enemies of Jackson, Craig among them, made capital out of Jackson's veto of the bill for the recharter of the United States Bank. The fact that the opposition to Jackson was divided was a handicap none the less, to say nothing of the fact that William Wirt, the presidential standard bearer of the Antimasons, was himself a Mason! At the last moment, the local National Republican ticket was withdrawn; as a result many Antimasons who had been Jacksonites feared that Wirt was to become merely a stalking horse for Clay. They decided either to vote for Jackson or to abstain from voting at all, and so Allegheny County contributed to the Democratic landslide, which swept all before it.

The removal of the government deposits from the United States Bank by the executive made Craig more wrathful than ever. As a director of the Bank of Pittsburgh, he was especially disturbed. Still this "high handed measure" might be a blessing in disguise if by it the opponents of Jackson were brought into a tightly knit organization. A great public demonstration was prepared by Craig and his friends to arouse opinion against the action. Resolutions of protest were prepared under Craig's supervision, and copies were carefully forwarded to Congress. A delegation was even sent to Washington to petition for the return of the deposits. The Pittsburghers did not know Jackson, however; after a promising beginning, the president lost his patience and broke out into a tirade against the bank. "I will not bow down to the Golden Calf; the Spanish Inquisition could never make me bow down to the monster," he thundered. The delegates threw up their hands in despair and came back to Pittsburgh to report their ill success. There they found the *Gazette* and the other anti-Jackson papers bewailing the "pressure" that had followed hard upon the president's ill-advised action.

The fruit of the agitation against this strong-handed executive was the Whig party, whose nucleus was the remnants of the National Republican organization. In May, 1834, the newly fledged Whigs of Pittsburgh held a jubilee celebration of some recent victories in New York State to arouse enthusiasm for their cause. Troubled by doubts as to the wisdom of his course, Craig consented to serve as one of the vice presidents of the gathering. A few days later he journeyed to the first state convention of the Whigs at Harrisburg and allowed himself to be named its secretary.

Withal, Craig was only passively favorable to this "harmony" movement. He saw no reason why his own Antimasonic group should not be the center around which opposition to Jackson might crystallize. He was disagreeably affected, too, by a stratagem employed by the Whigs at the jubilee to foist a ticket upon the large number of Antimasons present. Beneath the veneer of friendliness affected by the *Gazette* and the *Times* on one hand and the *Advocate* and *Statesman* on the other were suspicions that would not down.

The year 1835 brought new developments. Internal dissensions crept into the party organization of the Democrats that year and led to the nomination of two candidates for governor, George Wolf representing the Jackson men and Henry Muhlenberg the Van Burenites. With hopeful enthusiasm the Whigs and Antimasons forgot their differences momentarily and carried the day for their candidate, Joseph Ritner. The *Gazette* and its friends now felt that their long awaited opportunity to smoke the Masonic enemy out of his lair had come. Early in January, 1836, a legislative committee appointed for the express purpose of investigating the evils of Freemasonry began its hearings. The *Gazette* gave full space to the investigation. When the Masonic papers condemned Thaddeus Stevens's Star Chamber proceedings, Craig replied: "We trust that he will persevere in the investigation, until its charity and excellence are universally known, or till its rottenness stinks in the nostrils of the whole people."[5]

At first the investigation proceeded smoothly. The initial witnesses were present by choice, and they answered readily questions put to them concerning their membership in the order and the authenticity of the various exposés of Masonry. When it came time for the other witnesses to be subpoenaed, however, there was another story. From former Governor George Wolf down, a score all told, they refused to be sworn to give testimony. Try as he might, Stevens could not whip the legislature into compelling the refractory witnesses to answer his questions. Craig was greatly disappointed. The collapse of the investigation he viewed as a deadly blow struck at the very heart of Antimasonry.

In the national election of 1836, a few months later, both William Henry Harrison and Daniel Webster were mentioned as likely possibilities to oppose the candidate of the Jackson men. Craig much preferred Webster and hoped that he might be the candidate of the Antimasons. The hope was not realized. Dissensions arose among the Pennsylvania Antimasons. They met at Philadelphia in national convention but turned homewards without naming a candidate. This left Harrison, who had been nominated by an irregular convention in December, 1835, the only alternative to Van Buren in Pennsylvania. Craig had no choice except to set his course and ignore the patent fact that Harrison was no Antimason. The local Antimasons were grievously perplexed. They saw the *Times*, Pittsburgh's other Antimasonic paper, throwing its support to Van Buren. When the ill feeling between the two papers came to the surface, the local Democrats were gratified. The *Mercury* observed cheerfully: "The Times and Gazette are fighting like Kilkenny cats; and the fur begins to fly from the thin shirt of Antimasonry in which the latter has been masquerading." [6] Craig for his part took keen pleasure in going into the back files of the *Times* for material to answer its attacks. One quotation in particular he used with effect: "The Boston Advocate lately observed that the Pittsburgh Gazette was the most ably conducted Antimasonic paper in Pennsylvania; and we think it no disparagement to any other one to say that we 'endorse' that opinion."

Such quarreling did the cause of the Antimasons no good. At length the *Gazette* injected a new note into the campaign by publishing the text of "Mr. Van Buren's Popish Letter" [7] to arouse the latent anti-Catholic prejudice that was to be evident in subsequent campaign years. The bank question was also well hammered about, but all in vain. Jackson's influence was too strong. The *Gazette* vainly promised its friends in the West a ten thousand majority in Pennsylvania for Harrison. Actually the state went for Van Buren by a majority exceeding four thousand. Swallowing his disappointment, Craig comforted himself by reflecting that at least the country was well rid of Andrew Jackson!

In the course of the election of 1837, the editor of the *Gazette* figured in an affray that was typical of the times. Just before the election certain Democratic leaders in Pittsburgh decided upon a bold stratagem to sow discord between the Whigs and Antimasons. This took the form of a handbill, supposedly of Antimasonic origin, designed to be very offensive to the Whigs. Copies of it were freely distributed. Craig promptly pronounced it an "infamous forgery" and expressed his suspicion that it had been printed, to judge from the type, by either the *Mercury* or the *Manufacturer*. The proprietors of the *Gazette*, the *Times*, the *Advocate*, and the *Democrat* formally denied all complicity. The editors of the *Mercury*, however, when called upon by Craig, refused pointblank to certify to the same. On the following morning Craig, in no pleasant mood, walked briskly to the polls to cast his vote early. On the way he passed a knot of loafers reading and discussing one of the forged handbills. According to Craig:

> The remark was then made that it looked like the Gazette type. We were confident that it was the infamous production of one of the Loco-Foco presses, and being, we admit, of a very excitable temperament, we offered to bet Dawson Wadsworth fifty dollars that it was printed in the Manufacturer office. He declined betting, and we were moving off, when a fellow, whom we never saw before, stepped after us, and said he would bet fifty dollars; and as we turned toward him he added—*in gold*. We were provoked at the impudent equivocation, and very foolishly gave him a slap in the face with the back of our hand.[8]

In spite of the explanation, Craig looked rather ridiculous. The *Mercury* contented itself with a sardonic sentence: "Mr. Craig does wisely in betaking himself to his *fists*—his practice in that line will soon enable him to throw down the gauntlet to Deaf Burke or O'Rourke." [9]

It is probable that Craig lost caste with few for his willingness to "mix it up" with his political enemies. Political dementia was quite inescapable in the atmosphere of hard fought political contests. The strength of the Whigs, the Antimasons, and the Democrats was so evenly balanced in Allegheny County during the thirties that any untoward incident, a handfull of fraudulent ballots for example, might decide an outcome. In the fall of 1838 a friend of Craig wrote a letter to the *Gazette* expressing his disgust at the extremes to which party conflict was carried:

> Our city has been scandalized, for some days past, by street fights. The excitement of politics seems to have deprived men of their senses, and persons, from whom we could have expected other things, have conducted themselves in such a way as to merit the most decided reprobation of every good citizen. Ridiculous disputes at the street corners, and in bar-rooms have ended in calling liar and in fisty cuffs.[10]

Before the year 1840 was rung in, the direction that the presidential campaign that year would take was predictable. Personalities, as usual, clouded the issues. Craig was inclined to support Harrison, for Clay's connections with the Whigs and with Masonry were beyond the editor's endurance; and as early as 1838 Craig exerted himself to resist the blandishments of the Clay Whigs and to advance the cause of Harrison. On December 20, 1839, the *Gazette* reprinted from an eastern newspaper an article showing that the campaign tactics of 1828 had not been lost upon Harrison's lieutenants. In an editorial the *Gazette* decried the tendency of the "nabob Martin Van Buren" to make the poverty of his opponent a matter of jest and reproach, and gloried in the honesty of the brave old soldier, Harrison, who preferred "a pure and undefiled name, with a 'cottage' and 'hard cider,' to infamy. a palace, and the most costly wines." From then on the country witnessed the astonishing spectacle of a political campaign fought with all the fervor of a religious revival. The followers of Van Buren, the levellers of the last decade, were on the defensive because of their presumed aristocratic tastes. Tippecanoe textbooks, Tippecanoe almanacs, and Tippecanoe clubs advertised everywhere the military prowess of the new idol. Campaign

ballads, some of which the *Gazette* printed, were on the lips of
everyone. One can well imagine those rough partisans roaring
out with vast enthusiasm and faint traces of melody the lines of
"Reynard's Transformation":

> The lion's the king of the beasts, like thunder he roars,
> But I sing of the fox who steals while he snoars,
> With his long bushy tale and whiskers so red.[11]

Or following the cadences of

> The *People* are coming—Van Buren is down,
> Let a loud shout of triumph be heard in our town;
> Tom Benton is beaten and Amos is loo'd,
> The "pip" and "blind staggers" have reach'd the whole
>   brood;
> Huzza, then, huzza! mid the cannon's loud roar
> Let's resolve to be rul'd by Van Buren no more.[12]

Early in August Pittsburgh participated in a log cabin raising.
The Harrison House, as it was called, drew many to labor and
many to watch. A "noisy Loco" had to be driven away, and a
rain fell in the midst of the occasion, but many former Van Buren
men were on hand to take part. If such meetings smoothed the
path to victory, the Harrison leaders stood ready to provide them.
A great jamboree was planned for October 5–6 to commemorate
Harrison's victory at the Thames. Craig took a strong personal
interest in the convention. In the *Gazette* of September 24, 1840,
appeared the announcement:

> The editor of the Pittsburgh Gazette takes this mode
> of inviting all his brethren of the corps editorial, who may
> attend the Convention ... to make their homes with him,
> while they remain here.
> His residence is at the corner of Penn and Marbury
> streets, where he assures them "the latch string will not be
> pulled in," and all who come will find a cordial welcome,
> and an anxious desire to make their stay comfortable.

The Tippecanoe Convention, as it was called, surpassed all expectations—Craig declared that the lowest estimate of the numbers was twenty-seven thousand. By all odds this was quadruple the number of any previous political assembly in Allegheny County. Even the *Pittsburgher*, an unfriendly journal, was quoted as saying: "Yesterday afternoon, the cities of Pittsburgh and Allegheny looked like a couple of spacious harbors, in which the hulls of ten thousand ships lay almost invisible amidst a forest of masts, adorned with cider barrels, streamers, and flags." [13]

In spite of themselves, the Democrats caught the excitement. A Loco-Foco mob, according to Craig, paraded the streets on the evening of October 6 and insulted many of the Harrison men:

> They passed by our house, but behaved much better than we expected. We were standing in front of the house, with some of our family, and some persons who were staying with us. They offered no violence, threw no stones, and said nothing indecent to the females of our family, as they had done, we are told, at other places.
>
> The whole amount of their offence to us, if it could be called offence by Loco-Focos, was crying out, "Hiss Neville B Craig;" "Hiss the British Lighthouse;" "Hiss the Green Eyed Monster, &c."
>
> It happens to be our misfortune to be both short-sighted and weak-eyed, which compels us to wear green spectacles; this circumstance originated the very witty and generous epithet of "Green Eyed Monster." [14]

Only the merest tyro could have doubted that a political landslide would ensue. The election proved that Craig and his friends had done their work well. Harrison carried the county by 7,620 votes to 4,572 for Van Buren. As the state went for Harrison by not more than three hundred votes, it is apparent that the *Gazette* had been a vitally important factor in effecting the result. Try as he might, however, Craig could not ignore the fact that this was a Whig victory, and that the Antimasons as a group had lost their separate identity. The fault had not been his. One of the *Gazette's* readers declared that the Antimasons considered the *Gazette* to be "one of the best conducted Antimasonic presses in the state or in the United States." The *United States Gazette*, itself an outstanding paper of the time, was authority for the statement that the *Pittsburgh Gazette* was "the leading Antimasonic paper of the Commonwealth." Yet Antimasonry was already on its way to the junk heap of lost causes. The *Gazette* came to realize this in the course of time, but not until after Neville Craig had retired from the field of party journalism.

CHAPTER VIII

THE GAZETTE ADOPTS THE AMERICAN SYSTEM

Our shores exhibit one of the most animated scenes of bustling emigration, we have ever witnessed. The beach of the Monongahela has been for several days completely lined with flat boats, destined for the Illinois and other districts below the Falls of Ohio. The great body of emigrants now are of a different kind from those which we have been accustomed to see in this place; it is composed of English, who appear to come *full handed*, as we term it. The rage for emigration from the land of our forefathers, appears to pervade the whole kingdom. We have lately conversed with families, speaking all the dialects from Liverpool to London, from the Tweed to the Land's End. We anticipate the most beneficial effects from this kind of population. The comforts and conveniences which they carry with them, bespeak them of a class who have been useful at home, and their ruddy, healthy complexions, prove the total disuse of ardent spirits, that bane of all our new settlements.... May all their anticipations be realized! May the deep forests of the west possess no gloom for them! and may a few years of intrepid industry enable them to enjoy what was formerly the boast of the English yeomanry, roast beef and plumb pudding, undisturbed either by the frequent tax gatherer, or the brawling orators of reform.[1]

It was Morgan Neville writing in the year 1818, writing with peculiar enthusiasm as if he might be conjuring up in his minds-eye a place for himself among those restless marchers. In his hands the *Gazette* tingled with the heady nationalism for which the West was famous in the years after 1815.

The West is no longer inhabited by a set of Bedouin Arabs, or hunters who are not sufficiently important in the scale of society, and only intended by nature to purchase from the eastern merchant with what little money they can scrape together by laborious enterprize. We

89

must also be attended to. We have the population, and
we possess the will to demand consideration.[2]

Neville and his friends had a proper sense of the fact that the
country was swiftly growing, that Pittsburgh was no longer in
the backwoods. The *Gazette* recorded the blandishments of land
agents and bubble promoters, each one hopefully assuring the
world that the road to fortune wound through the woods to his
front door.

In 1840 the situation was rather different. Pittsburgh was no
longer West. The West had leaped over an imaginary barrier into
the distance. Preemption rights, the darling of the frontiersman's
heart, were being debated in the halls of Congress, and Neville B.
Craig, the editor of the *Gazette*, was asking his readers:

> Will our citizens, who are so deeply involved in debt
> for improvements which benefit the whole west, consent
> to give up her [*Pennsylvania's*] share of lands won by the
> toils and perils of the "Old Thirteen." Will they, at the
> very moment when they are oppressed with low prices,
> and threatened with taxes, consent to make a gift of pub-
> lic lands to the new States? We trust not." [3]

Craig blamed the westward movement for destroying the even
balance that had once existed between the producers and con-
sumers of farm products. In his opinion the low state of farm
prices around Pittsburgh in 1840 would continue until that balance
had been restored.

The *Gazette* was alive to a function that had not seemed so
important at one time. The importance of the city's geographical
location was becoming apparent to Pittsburgh's sons and daughters. Whether eastern or western, the city might well grow into a
great center of inland trade, and so it was the duty of its presses
to struggle ceaselessly for improvements that would enable it the
better to cope with its municipal rivals. The nearest competitor
was Wheeling. Warming to its task, the *Gazette* seized upon what
weapons it could to ward off the danger from the Virginia river
port.

With no easy eye, the paper viewed the steady progress of the great National Road westward from Cumberland, Maryland, in the years after the War of 1812. If Pittsburgh had been its western goal, all local objections would have been removed, but alas! it was directed to Wheeling. Pittsburgh was being shelved by an improvement, built at the expense of the national government. By the close of 1818 it was complete, and the disastrous effects that the *Gazette* had expected from it were freely evident. With a burst of energy Neville wrote:

> The present is a period which calls for every exertion on our part to avert impending danger; look at our manufactures, listen to the news from the Cumberland road! look at our rivers! a short time since we spent a day with a friend on Montour's Island; during the whole day but one sluggish flat boat passed! two years ago, fifty boats would have passed in the same time! We could not help exclaiming, "is this Pittsburgh? can such a change be possible? where is the merchandize, where the barges and keels which but two years, two short years ago, never suffered the eye to dwell on a lifeless surface of water? is it possible that a circumstance will be realized, which we have been in the habit of ridiculing as chimerical and impracticable? is it possible that even a portion of our trade can be changed to Wheeling? No, we will not believe it!"[4]

This was the signal for a skirmish between the presses of the two towns. The *Virginia North-Western Gazette* took umbrage at Neville's air of superiority. The *Pittsburgh Gazette*, on the other hand, was annoyed by the small stratagems practiced by Wheeling against Pittsburgh. Neville declared that he had affidavits to show that on a recent occasion a group of Wheeling merchants had warned the passengers of the steamboat *Velocipede* against proceeding farther upstream, as there was not enough water above Wheeling to float the boat over the riffles. Only the urgent pleas of some indignant passengers from Pittsburgh had induced the captain to continue up the river. For his part, Neville was prepared to show that freight rates from Philadelphia to Pittsburgh were cheaper than from Philadelphia to Wheeling and that it cost no more to send goods from Pittsburgh to the falls of the Ohio than from any other point within a hundred miles downstream. To berate Wheeling was more satisfactory to the feelings than conducive to permanent good. Consequently Neville and his successors took it upon themselves to make Pittsburgh's position the stronger by a well-integrated plan of improvements, which should be a part of a broader program contrived to develop the transportation facilities, instruments of finances, manufactures, and agricultural wealth of the nation at large—in the parlance of that day, "The American System."

Throughout Neville's editorship, the *Gazette* labored for a two-fold plan that included a first-class turnpike between Philadelphia and Pittsburgh and improved navigation of the Ohio River between Pittsburgh and Wheeling. The editor soon discovered an ally in a young army officer named James Hall, who was temporarily quartered in Pittsburgh. Under the pseudonym of "Orlando," Hall, later to become famous as one of a brilliant group of young Ohio Valley literateurs in Cincinnati, contributed to the *Gazette* some able articles stressing these needs. Both he and Neville sought to play upon Philadelphia's fears of being overshadowed by New York and Baltimore. The goal was not to be easily won. The Philadelphia papers did not take kindly to strictures upon Philadelphia's commercial shortsightedness. Other Pittsburgh newspapermen were not very encouraging. Pentland of the *Statesman*, when appealed to, berated Neville for indulging in abusive language against Philadelphia, and Snowden of the *Mercury* launched into a veritable tirade against "the noble captain," as he called Neville, and "Man-Friday" Hall. More comforting was a letter from a Philadelphia reader assuring the *Gazette* that "Notwithstanding the severity in which you have sometimes indulged towards us; your paper has done much good. It has had the effect of bringing the great interest of the state before the public, and the eastern people, since your commencement, have turned their attention seriously to the West."[5]

In bringing about improved navigation of the Ohio, the *Gazette* had more immediate success. In the fall of 1819 a commission drawn from the four states immediately affected was selected to survey the river, and before the season was over an artificial channel had been cut through the shoals and riffles as far as Wheeling.

Both the Macleans and Craig were strongly attached to the cause of "internal improvements," but their interest was directed toward canals. Doubtless the early completion of the Erie Canal in 1825 was a factor in this. The *Gazette* had a prominent part in issuing the call for a canal convention that year, and lent itself with enthusiasm to discovering ways and means of building a canal over the mountains from Philadelphia to Pittsburgh. When the task was completed in 1834 it was hard to refrain from an outburst of triumph:

> The *Canal* and *Rail Road* are now in full and successful operation.—Goods arrived yesterday, in eleven days from Philadelphia....
>
> We have been informed that the New Yorkers have contracted to deliver Goods at Portsmouth, on the Ohio, by the way of the New York and Ohio Canal, and Lake Erie, for $2.06 1-4 per hundred, *when their Canal is opened.* By the Pennsylvania Canal, Goods will be delivered at Cincinnati, for $2.05. By the first of May, this will probably be reduced to $1.80.
>
> In the *time of transportation,* we will possess a still more decided advantage. Merchandise will be delivered from Philadelphia at Cincinnati in 14 or 15 days. From New York to Cincinnati will require 25 days.... The *risk,* by the Lake, is very great—by the Pennsylvania Canal and Rail Road, almost nothing.
>
> The New York Canal will not be opened for more than three weeks yet—in that time, Steam Boats may proceed to St. Louis or Nashville, and return to Pittsburgh.... Our prospects in relation to these great improvements, are truly encouraging, if they are not obscured by the folly and madness of General Jackson.[6]

To satisfy his curiosity about the new improvement, Craig concluded to view the route for himself, and in the summer of 1835 he allowed himself the pleasure of his first ride on a canal boat. Both canal and railroad he regarded as "truly noble works." The accommodations on board the "Nigara" he pronounced excellent; of the inclined planes in the mountains he remarked that they were "great defects in our system of improvements" which he hoped to see dispensed with before many years.

Other inconveniences were not slow to appear. The spirit of competition between the various lines of transportation that plied the canal was keenly pitched. The excesses to which this might run were a source of steady complaint on the part of the long suffering public. The following newspaper notice, to which the names of a score of passengers were signed, is proof enough that the complaint was not without basis:

> The Corsair started from Pittsburgh a few minutes before the Niagara, a boat belonging to the Pioneer Line, on the evening of the 10th. inst. Almost immediately after starting, the Niagara was perceived in pursuit, coming with great speed; having, in addition to the horses, about thirty men and boys attached to the tow-rope, and accompanied by a large mob, whooping, yelling and using the most abusive and outrageous language. The horses of the Niagara were soon abreast of the Corsair, and subjected to the most cruel and inhuman abuse, several persons being employed in beating them with whips, sticks, &c. Matters continued in this situation for some time, when some miscreant attached to the mob, finding that the Niagara was losing ground, ran ahead and cut the tow-rope of the Corsair. The consequence was that the Corsair lost her head way, and was run into by the Niagara, amidst cries of *"run him down,"* "stave him to pieces," &c &c. The tow-rope of the Niagara drawing with great force across the after part of the Corsair's cabin was then cut by some one on board of the latter boat. The ropes were however soon mended, and the race proceeded, the Corsair still keeping the lead. Her tow-ropes was cut again, and a *third time*, and the Niagara was thus finally enable to pass.

As may readily be supposed, the whole affair was exceedingly unpleasant to the passengers on board the Corsair, among whom were several ladies; and the undersigned, while deprecating in the strongest terms the conduct of those engaged in it, cannot at the same time avoid expressing their entire satisfaction with the conduct of Captain Stroman, and his gentlemanly treatment to them while under his care.[7]

A fortnight later a group of passengers from the "Niagara" published just such a card arraigning the captain of the "Corsair" for his efforts to run them down. The gross conduct of the "Corsair's" crew was enlarged upon, and people were warned against taking passage on such a boat. Other stories were told of packet lines that were guilty of unjust charges, overcrowding of passengers, and unsanitary conditions. The only remedy seemed to be to "publish the line."

To Craig the Pennsylvania Canal was in itself a good beginning, but in order to realize on its benefits to the fullest extent, Pittsburgh needed to do all in its power to connect the Pennsylvania Canal to the Ohio Canal system by what Craig called the "Cross Cut Canal." As early as 1825 he submitted several long articles upon the subject to the *Gazette*. In one instance the article was accompanied by a diagram or rough map of the country between Pittsburgh, Erie, and Cleveland. The sketch was familiarly called "Craig's Spider"; facsimiles of it were republished in some of the Ohio papers. During the year 1830 the *Gazette* printed editorial after editorial delineating the danger lurking in the coquettish advances that New York was making to the Ohio canals and reiterating the fact that, by building a waterway not more than 140 miles long from Pittsburgh to the Ohio system, Pennsylvanians might divert to Philadelphia the trade with which New York was gorging herself.

Such activities were not popular in all quarters. Erie, now become a place of some consequence, took offense at the crosscut canal scheme. Granting that the Pennsylvania Canal ought to be extended, the *Erie Gazette* asked, why not extend it to Erie? To this Craig replied that both routes were to be wished for, but if a choice must be made, a route linking Pittsburgh to both the Ohio Canal and Lake Erie was to be preferred to a route to the lake only. Time and again Craig returned to this position. After many disappointments he saw his dream realized at last in 1840. In April of that year shipments of iron, nails, and other merchandise began to move over the new route by way of New Castle and Akron.

Craig also showed some interest in the Chesapeake and Ohio Canal project. Both Wheeling and Pittsburgh aspired to be its western terminus, and so the *Gazette* lost no opportunity to impress upon Baltimore the superior advantage of a connection with Pittsburgh. Craig even traveled to Baltimore in 1834 to be present at a canal convention for deciding the route that the improvement should take. It was of no use. The Baltimore merchants were already showing symptoms of railroad fever; soon they would conclude to abandon the canal scheme to apply all their capital to railroads.

The *Gazette* displayed some interest in railroads. In 1813 John Scull had printed an item probably little noticed at the time: "Steam Waggons. Mr. Oliver Evans, the great constructor and improver of steam machinery, states, in a late Philadelphia paper, his conviction of probability of propelling by steam, on turnpike roads, carriages with passengers or merchandize, at the rate of 150 miles per day!" [8] The good citizens of Pittsburgh must have shrugged their shoulders. Another inventor's pipe dream! Not until the thirties did the *Gazette* pay any serious attention to the locomotive. "Railroads form a more dashing mode of conveyance, and seem latterly to have obtained more éclat than the slow and sure mode of transportation by canal," concluded Craig in 1831. Gradually he became more convinced of the importance of the railroad. One day late in the summer of 1835 he walked up to the establishment of McClurg, Wade & Company in the Northern Liberties (that part of Pittsburgh lying east of the Allegheny River and back of the Pennsylvania station) to watch the construction of a new locomotive engine, "The Pittsburgh," reputed to be the first locomotive built west of the mountains. To Craig its "beautiful smoothness and regularity" were inspiring Stimulated, he returned to his office to pen editorials in anticipation of the day when such a locomotive might come puffing into Pittsburgh. Already there was talk of a railroad from Connellsville to Pittsburgh. So heartily was Craig in accord with the idea that a number of citizens wrote to the *Gazette* expressing their appreciation for his efforts to direct public attention to the subject. The editor hoped to see such a route become a unit in a railroad connecting Pittsburgh with Baltimore. But he could not blind himself to the fact that the fatal attachment of Baltimore merchants for Wheeling left very little hope of a Baltimore-Pittsburgh line.

All through the period the *Gazette* preserved the character of a river paper. Steamboat news was always welcome in a river town like Pittsburgh. In 1819 the paper noted in passing the enormous program of steamboat building in process in every respectable-sized village between Pittsburgh and Louisville. The framework of large frigates towered up like enormous skeletons in the woods stretching back from the river. During the eighteen-thirties Pittsburgh was visited as a regular port on the schedule of river palaces that offered a degree of luxury and comfort quite amazing to the jaded land traveler. While the steamer "Moravian" was in dock in April, 1836, Craig went on board and examined with pleasure the boat's substantial furnishings. Even in the space of his own lifetime the editor could see great changes in travel conditions along the river. Once, musing in a reminiscent vein, he said:

> Truly, when we look back at the facilities (if they can now be called *facilities*) for traveling twenty or twenty-five years ago, and compare them with the present temptations to travel, the contrast is really wonderful. It is now just about twenty-three years since the senior editor of the *Gazette* made his first trip to New Orleans with two flat boats. At that time there were in Pittsburgh an officer of the U. S. Army and a merchant from New Orleans, both bound to the latter city. Our boats were the

first conveyance which offered; those gentlemen waited four or five days until we were ready, and were about six weeks making the trip to New Orleans, confined all the time in a low flat boat, and living, of course, on no very dainty fare. Now real facilities, nay, even strong temptations to go to New Orleans present, themselves three or four times a day. The whole trip down can be made in less than ten days, living in the most luxurious manner, enjoying generally the best society, male and female too, and sweeping along by a highly cultivated country, only too fast for accurate observation.[9]

Traveling by stage was not so commodious. Frequently letters were addressed to the *Gazette* reciting charges that stage drivers were heedless of the lives and comfort of their passengers. One traveler grumbled that on the pretext that oats were then very dear he had been charged eight dollars to come from Erie to Pittsburgh. The coach had moved at a snail's pace—only ten miles in one period of four hours, because the horses had been fed nothing but hay for a week. "The drivers were impertinent, careless—some times drunk; and I may say, without fear of contradiction, almost uniformly profane and blasphemous." [10]

A national bank was another objective upon which the *Gazette* concentrated its efforts as the years rolled on. During the Panic of 1819, the newspaper was so disturbed by the way in which specie was being drawn out of the local banks into the government branch banks that it expressed strong opposition to the United States Bank. After the emergency was over the *Gazette* abandoned this policy, and when the spectacular war over the United States Bank broke in the thirties, the paper planted itself solidly back of the Bank and what it stood for.

Above all, the *Gazette* reposed its faith in manufactures. During the period of hard times that succeeded the panic of 1819 the paper dwelt constantly upon local manufacturing as a means of escape from "the merciless fangs of British and foreign monopolists, manufacturers, and merchants." The choice, in the editor's opinion, lay between starvation and manufactures. Societies for the purpose of introducing American-made clothing were advocated, and the citizenry was asked to keep the money ordinarily spent for imported commodities such as glass and sandpaper "on this side of the mountains." Morgan Neville was only too pleased when his doctrines were put to the test. One day a country friend came into his office with a tale of great distress. In need of iron, nails, and some cheap clothes, he had come to town with produce to apply on his purchases. To his dismay the merchants on Market Street would not sell him what he wanted without cash. At this point the editor interrupted him. "Have you been to any of the manufactories?"

> "Manufactories?" echoed my friend, "No, I went to all the stores in town; I see no use in trying any further, and except you lend me fifty dollars, I must go home as I came, my children must wear linsey, and my barn remain uncovered!" Without making any reply I took my country friend to James Aitkins; this worthy citizen immediately supplied him with an excellent piece of cassinet, took a quantity of potatoes, oats and flour in part pay and agreed to wait for the balance; I then hauled him half stupefied to the rolling mill; here William Robinson soon struck up a trade for what iron he wanted, and took a quantity of produce for his workmen; we next visited the nail factory, where Richard Bowen completed the countryman's order on the same terms and with the same liberality as the other two gentlemen. My friend was delighted but said nothing until we arrived at the office. He then took his seat by the fire and said—"Sir, I have been deceived; the last hour has completely opened my eyes. I acknowledge I had taken up the ridiculous notion that manufactures and agriculture were incompatible and that all manufacturers were monopolists. I see my error and read my recantation." [11]

Such a story was worth a score of editorials.

In the campaign to build up Pittsburgh manufactures the *Gazette* discovered a redoubtable ally in a rising young political figure of the district, Henry Baldwin. As congressman from the Pittsburgh district from 1816 to 1822, Baldwin was greatly instrumental in focusing national attention upon the subject of domestic manufactures and adequate tariff protection for them. The *Gazette's* influence was placed squarely behind Baldwin's efforts. It printed his tariff speeches in the paper and out; it defended him against newspaper critics; it persisted in its course in spite of muttered threats that subscriptions would be withdrawn. In reply Neville could only say: "We shall repel every attempt like dictation at the very threshold. The attempt to limit the liberty of the press by restricting its patronage, we shall ever treat with scorn and contempt." [12]

By the end of the eighteen-twenties, these efforts had sown a fruitful seed. As Neville Craig took over the *Gazette* in 1829, he stopped for a moment to survey the picture of mounting industrialism around Pittsburgh. He beheld thousands of tons of metal being poured annually into Pittsburgh foundries and rolling mills for conversion into steam engines, bar iron, boiler iron, anchors for the northern lakes, and sugar mills and sugar kettles for Louisiana. Pittsburgh-built steam engines were being marketed in the Mississippi Valley, on the sugar plantations of Louisiana, and in the mines of Mexico. Pittsburgh window glass sparkled in the homes of dignified Boston, and Pittsburgh flint glass graced the White House table.

Like his cousin Morgan Neville, Craig was thoroughly convinced of the vital importance of manufactures to his native city. Consequently he stood ready to challenge those who impugned the virtues of tariff protection. When President Jackson launched his thunders at the head of the South Carolina nullifiers in 1832, Craig forgot for the moment his distaste for Jacksonian measures. It was enough that the president had struck a blow for the tariff. "Have the manufacturers, the mechanics, and the farmers of Western Pennsylvania made up their minds to consent to the abandonment of the protective policy, in obedience to the mandates of the South Carolina politicians?" asked Craig. His answer was to call for a public meeting to express approval of the president's noble and patriotic conduct.

The panic of 1837 and the hard times that followed administered a sudden check to the expanding industrial economy at
whose shrine Craig knelt. The editor showed a confident face
when he perceived the first signs of the storm, but as the money
market became more stringent, he could no longer conceal his
forebodings. The author of all these calamities, the *Gazette* opined,
was Jackson. Had not the first bank to suspend specie payments
been one of the "pet banks" located at Natchez? A clever scheme
was utilized by the *Gazette* to hang the millstone of the depression
around the neck of the administration. It took the following form:

A CONTRAST—OR, THE EXPERIMENT

1829	1837
Down with the Administration	*Hurra for Jackson*

1829

Down with the Administration
A sound, healthy, and uniform
currency—money for all legitimate purposes easily obtained
at 5 and 6 per cent. Canals and
railroads rapidly progressing—
manufactories every where re-
sounding with the hum of the
spindle, the strokes of the hammer, and the cheerful laugh of
the artisan—the Star Spangled
Banner proudly waving in every
part of the world—commerce
whitening every sea with its
bellying canvass—our vessels
filling every port—mechanics
every where engaged—office-
holders at their posts—the
President treading in the footsteps of Washington, Madison
and Monroe, and prosperity
crowning the land.

1837

Hurra for Jackson
Shin plasters or hickory leaves,
as thick as flakes of an April
snow—exchange high—no
money to be had, even at 4 per
cent a month—canals and railroads suspended—manufactories stopped and silent—opera-
tives, of all ages and sexes, idle,
downcast, poor, hungry, and
naked—merchants and manu-
facturers bankrupt—commerce
driven from the ocean—ships
laid up in the docks—tide
waiters hovering about as car-
rion crows over a dead carcase—
office-holders electioneering, the
author of the Sherrod Williams
letter treading in the footsteps
of "the Greatest and Best," and
universal despondency and
gloom hanging over the country.[13]

The picture was sufficiently depressing but hardly overdrawn.
For several years the country was in the downward swing of a

business cycle. Even as late as 1840 the "forgotten man" of the period, an unemployed mechanic in this case, wrote a pathetic letter to the paper describing the exhaustion of his savings, the accumulation of debts for necessaries, and concluding: "This state of things can not last long. What am I to do?" It almost seemed as if the paper's attempts to bring prosperity to its community had been for naught. In 1841, nevertheless, the signs of business upturn were already evident. Blighted as it had been, the Pittsburgh community was struggling to regain its feet and resume its onward journey.

More or less consistently in this period the *Gazette* had contended for a program by which Pittsburgh and the country at large might realize an ideal of national greatness based upon a secure economic foundation. Internal improvements, the United States Bank, domestic manufactures, and the tariff were means by which that program might be achieved. The *Gazette* had a good word for all. Thus it earned for itself the title of champion of the "American System."

CHAPTER IX

SMOKE STACKS AND STEEPLE TOPS

On March 8, 1816, Pittsburgh graduated from knickerbockers into pantaloons: the borough was granted a charter and began to take on city ways. It could boast of a mayor and all the other appurtenances of city government. As the oldest paper in the city, ready itself to undergo a change of control soon, the *Gazette* was palpably pleased by this evidence that Pittsburgh was growing up. Certainly the enterprise of its citizens was not at fault. After the panic of 1819 had subsided, artisans and tradesmen enlivened the town with the sound of their activity. Those who visited Pittsburgh in these years were greatly moved by what they saw—a youthful giant, suddenly conscious of his powers, reaching out for mighty tasks. At times it seemed to some that the giant was a trifle impetuous. The *Gazette* on December 27, 1833, quoted a traveling correspondent of an eastern newspaper as saying: "The great defect in the town, is the total want of public squares.... The Pittsburghers ... I fear are more bent upon increasing their 'father's store,' than in beautifying the favored spot in which they dwell." Unquestionably Pittsburgh was prosperous, for another observer complained of factories set down in the midst of churches, colleges, and private dwellings, bedaubing all with clouds of black, bituminous smoke. "Dust, smoke, soot is upon everything, and is breathed, eaten, and drank. It rains dust, snows dust, blows dust." In March, 1835, Craig wrote: "Our city is now the scene of the utmost bustle.—Our wharf is literally covered with merchandise going westward, and produce going eastward." [1]

In becoming a city Pittsburgh had not disposed of the problems of which the *Gazette* had reminded her many times before. To be sure the maze of city transportation was much less complex than it is today; but in 1816, as before, the only way to cross the two rivers from the Point was by ferry. With much satisfaction the *Gazette* in 1818 welcomed the indications that this inconvenient condition was at last to be removed. While the construction of two bridges proceeded, the paper indulged in a pardonable boast:

> The beautiful Bridge over the Monongahela has nearly reached the northern shore; it will probably be crossed before Christmas. The one over the Allegheny is not so far advanced, but yet enough is done to ensure its completion. Pittsburgh will then exhibit what no American city or town has ever yet done; two splendid Bridges over two mighty streams within 400 yards of each other.[2]

The modern visitor to Pittsburgh is fascinated with a view of the city by night—a city of a million lights scattered over the tops of the hills that are uniquely Pittsburgh's. In 1816 the city was not so profusely lighted. Not until 1837 did it enjoy the luxury of street lighting by gas illumination, and for the improvement Craig was partly to be credited. There is still extant in his private papers a copy of a letter to Alexander Johnston, president of the city council, bespeaking his desire that pressure should be put on the committee to whose care the improvement had been entrusted. When the details were finally completed the *Gazette* took special pains to congratulate those responsible for a civic enterprise well worthy of the city's gratitude.

Another pressing need was a city waterworks system. The council talked about it, and the *Gazette* commended the idea, but nothing was done. In 1823 the paper printed a humorous petition from the good housewives of the city to the gentlemen of Pittsburgh that requested them "to arrest in its progress a small portion of that element nature has so bountifully permitted to flow around us, and have it conveyed into our houses." For such audacious behavior on the part of women silence was deemed an appropriate answer, and no action was taken. But the ever pressing need of fire protection emphasized the importance of tackling the water problem. A bad fire in Pittsburgh on the night of November 17, 1823, inspired one of the awakened citizens to lecture the *Gazette* and the community on the unsatisfactory state of the fire-fighting apparatus. Most shameful of all was the presence of many "females" among the firefighters, while able-bodied men stood idly by. Fire protection was so much the hobby of Neville Craig that, in recognition of his interest, he was elected an honorary member of the Vigilant Fire Company in January, 1834.

Public health problems first drew the attention of the *Gazette* upon the approach of a destroyer whose mysterious nature spread terror in its wake. The *Gazette* first referred to the danger of Asiatic Cholera in its issue of June 22, 1832. All doubt that "Indian Cholera" had come to North America was removed by dispatches from Quebec; fears that it would spread widely and rapidly were well grounded. "To Pittsburgh, particularly, it will travel with no snail's pace—the same Irish emigrants who brought it to Quebec will bring it to the head of the Ohio." No precaution against its ravages should be overlooked, warned Craig. Streets, alleys, and cellars must be cleansed and purified. Above all, intemperance should be guarded against. The *New York Spectator* warned that "the cholera is emphatically THE SCOURGE OF DRUNKARDS." In answer to the many queries it received, the *Gazette* published a long article written by the health department of Paris listing preventives and suggesting remedial treatment. For those who put their trust in no earthly power, the intercessions of the clergy and the recommended days of fasting and prayer had to suffice. The summer passed and the destroyer had not come out in the open. With September nearly over, Craig cheerily observed: "This pestilence, which walketh in darkness, and which has already, with giant stride, extended its ravages from Quebec to Norfolk, has not yet even made a sensible approach to Pittsburgh." [3] Not until November 9 would the *Gazette* concede that the disease was in the city. Fortunately winter was only a few weeks away; with its approach, the cholera withdrew for a spell, content with but six victims.

The next year it returned. By August there had been fifty-two deaths from the malady in Pittsburgh. The city might count itself lucky, however, that it had not been struck so hard as Wheeling and other river cities. In 1834 there was another epidemic, the last during the decade of the thirties. Whether the reason for this comparative immunity was the natural healthfulness of the place, the influence of the sulphur given off from stove coal (according to contemporary wiseacres), or, on the other hand, panic or race suicide in the microbe world, it is hard to say. In any case, Pittsburgh was well content with the fact and very willing not to pry too curiously into its explanation.

In spite of the alacrity with which the townsfolk consulted the doctors in such emergencies, a number of them were convinced that the medical profession put too high a value upon its services. A vindictive note appears in a notice that was printed in the *Gazette* of February 8, 1836:

WAR OR PEACE!

It appears beyond all doubt, that a large proportion of the medical gentlemen have met, and determined to add 100 per cent to the present bill of murderous prices, and it appears the unanimous desire of the inhabitants of St. Clair township, and all that I have talked with in Pittsburgh, that there be township and borough meetings for the purpose of entering into resolutions to know whether we will let the Doctors have all we have after we are dead—therefore, the last Saturday in February is thought best to hold said meetings, the township meetings to be at 3 P. M., the borough meetings at 6 P. M., at the several election districts. By request of many persons.

EZEKIEL HARKER.

The masses of the people could hardly be stirred by controversy over physicians' fees. Most of them continued to dose themselves with the specifics extolled in the advertisements—and to place upon nature the double burden of checking the illness and repairing the damage done by the remedy. Only a hardened skeptic could resist the potent spell of such an advertisement as the one for Houck's Panacea, a versatile remedy prepared solely from vegetable matter by Jacob Houck of Baltimore, to be taken "with perfect safety by all ages and in all diseases." It was guaranteed to cure the following distempers:

Dispepsia, Loss of Appetite, Indigestion, Inflamation of
the Stomach, Heart Burn, Dirathoea, Dysentery or Flux,
Piles, Fistula ... Ague and Fever, Bilious or Remittent
Fever, Typhus Fever, Scarlet Fever, Small Pox, Ery-
sipelus or St. Anthony's Fire, Asthma, Pleurisy, Measles,
Yellow Fever, Costiveness, Wind on the Stomach or
Bowels, Cholera Morbus, Consumption, Influenza, Colds,
Coughs, Inflamation of the Chest, Palsy, Gout, Rheuma-
tism, Inflammatory Sore Throat or Quinsey, Whooping
Cough, Thrush or Sore Mouth, Putrid Sore Throat,
Croup, Inflammation of the Heart, Dropsey, Rickets,
Diseases of the Liver, Jaundice ... Gleet, Hysterics,
Nervous and Scrofulous affections of the Members and
Ligements, Mercurial and Venereal Diseases, Ulcers,
Sores, Affections of the Skin, and all diseases arising from
Impure Blood, &c PRICE PER BOTTLE $1 50.[4]

Truly this must have been a witch's brew.

Another municipal problem that the editor could hardly overlook was the elimination of crime. There were frequent complaints
of the misconduct of the young hoodlums of the town running
around naked on the wharves, disturbing funeral processions, de-
facing churches and theaters, insulting "delicate females," and
making every square resound with "their yells, and their infernal
orgies." Yet crimes of violence seem to have been comparatively
few. The public execution of John Tiernan for the murder of
Patrick Campbell in 1818 was declared by the paper to be "the
first scene of the kind ever witnessed in this part of the country,
since civilized men have occupied the soil." The very uniqueness
of the spectacle drew a crowd of eight or ten thousand persons,
some of them from neighboring counties, to look upon this exhibition of vindictive justice.

The celebrated robbery of the Farmers' and Mechanics' Bank
on the night of April 6, 1818, was in all probability the most sensational crime story published in the *Gazette* during the period. It
provided all the elements for a front-page story—it was the first
bank robbery in Pittsburgh, the president of the bank was John

Scull, the cashier was Morgan Neville. The culprits were Pluymart and Emmons, two Yankee gamblers who effected an entrance by stealing the watchman's key and taking impressions of the bank vault keyhole so as to fit keys of their own fashioning into it. Making off with $104,000, the entire liquid capital of the bank, the two fled downriver. When the crime was discovered the *Gazette* published the facts, handbills were circulated, and a reward of one thousand dollars was offered for the recovery of the property and the apprehension of the thieves. William Lecky, one of the directors, organized a posse and pursued them in a skiff. Pluymart and Emmons were overtaken at Wheeling and subjected to search, but no evidence of their guilt could be found, and they were allowed to proceed. Later, when fresh evidence turned up, they were pursued anew and overtaken about thirty miles from Cincinnati, where they were lodged in jail. At first there was difficulty about extraditing them, much to the wrath of the despoiled Pittsburghers. Finally, about June 1, Emmons was brought back to Pittsburgh, where he made full confession. What is more, he revealed the location of the cache, about twenty-five miles below Pittsburgh. As a result, a number of citizens accompanied him to the spot and recovered a portion of the loot. In spite of this, Scull's bank was so much embarrassed by the loss, coming as it did in the midst of a banking crisis, that the board of directors decided to close up the bank's affairs and liquidate as soon as possible.

Such stories were exceptional. The *Gazette* was uniformly willing to open its columns to those who had been robbed or defrauded, but it had no stomach for sensational crime news. The Macleans were prone to criticize the New York papers for their unnatural interest in criminal personalities, and Craig, for all his legal background, shied away from such news. On one occasion he delivered himself of the opinion that the conception of a newspaper as a mirror that must show deformities as well as beauties was a mistaken one. Instead, he chose to consider a newspaper as a schoolmaster "bound to give publicity only to those matters which intend to inform the mind, or improve the heart." Detailed accounts of crime, said Craig, were published chiefly to satisfy a morbid public appetite.

It was next to impossible for a newspaper of the period not to be affected by the waves of social reform that beat high upon the shores of public indifference. The *Gazette* was commonly known as a religious paper, and so the causes that it championed were likely to link hands with the aims and purposes of the church. Pittsburgh's steeple tops towered high in the heavens alongside the ubiquitous smoke stacks that stained the city with an indelible hue. A traveler who stopped in 1840 counted sixty places of religious worship in the town and commented on the fact that the streets were filled with church-going people on the Sabbath. The great religious excitement prevalent just before the end of the period was freely testified to by a writer in the *Gazette:*

> Though here, as everywhere else, there is now, and always has been, much vice, yet religion has received as much attention in Pittsburgh at every period of her existence, at least for the last thirty years, as any other place of the same amount of population. Revivals have often taken place, in which many have ceased to do evil and learned to do well. They have, however, usually been isolated, confined to one part of the city, to one denomination, in one congregation. It is now very different. Almost every denomination, and nearly every congregation in Pittsburgh, Allegheny, and Birmingham, are enjoying a season of religious refreshing.[5]

Methodists; new school, old school, and Cumberland Presbyterians; Episcopalians; Baptists were all joining together to proclaim a new-found zeal in the cause of the Lord. Individual congregations were enlisting scores every week. It was small wonder that the writer piously concluded: "These are the Lord's doings, and are marvelous in our sight."

Naturally the *Gazette* welcomed this wave of religious emotionalism. Two groups alone were exempted from its favor: Roman Catholics and Atheists. There was appearing at this time a great quantity of lurid Anti-Catholic literature, which influenced newspaper editors and their readers alike. The spread of Catholicism was undoubted. Craig beheld with some misgivings the fact that Pittsburgh had already become the seat of a bishopric and that religion had not availed to exclude Roger B. Taney, a Catholic, from the office of Chief Justice of the United States Supreme Court. If the *Gazette* was on the way to becoming militantly Anti-Catholic, however, toward Atheism it was positively uncompromising. Atheists, Deists, Unitarians were lumped together with small thought as to their differences. When a certain Cohen, an unbelieving young chemist of the time, was blown to pieces in the midst of one of his experiments, the *Gazette* printed a long account of the affair and noticed it editorally:

> Cohen, the Atheist. Our readers will find in, our columns today, a full account of the awful death of this man. We trust that the editor of the Manufacturer, and all those who participated in the recent orgies, in commemoration of the birth of Tom Paine, will give this article a careful perusal.[6]

Situated as it was, only a few miles north of the Mason-Dixon line, the *Gazette* was inclined to ponder the slavery question in these years. Editor Neville for his part was troubled by the problem of the free negro. "Pittsburgh is becoming a perfect St. Domingo," he observed in 1819. The free blacks in his opinion constituted a privileged order. They enjoyed all the rights of freedom, yet were exempt from the burden of militia duty and fines. They were customarily to be seen lounging about or leaning against lamp posts, never engaged in any regular employment. Still they were always well fed and generally well clothed. The editor scratched his head reflectively and wondered how this was accomplished. Yet he was far from wishing the slavery area extended. When the Missouri Question assumed a troublesome form in 1820, Neville was impressed with its "features more appalling, than ... possessed by any other political matter ... since we have become an independent nation.... every thing that has the slightest tendency to disunion makes us tremble;" he averred, "this is

the evil which must, we fear one day fall upon our country, and ...
we wish to put off this day, beyond the limit of *our* existence in
this world." [7]

During Neville Craig's editorship, antislavery feeling in Pittsburgh grew and blossomed. In 1833 Pittsburgh became the seat
of an antislavery society. Craig was in full sympathy with it. In
1836 he pledged himself to contribute one hundred dollars a year
to help the cause of colonizing Liberia on the coast of western
Africa with manumitted slaves. The next year he took a portentous step when he refused to reprint from the *Cincinnati Whig* an
advertisement for a slave who had escaped from a Tennessee
master. The *Gazette* had finished with that sort of advertising.
Sixteen years before, old John Irwin, the father-in-law of John
Scull, had himself advertised for the return of *his* runaway slave.
Truly the tables had been turned.

Of all the social reforms advocated in those days, the temperance movement was dearest to Craig's heart. Like Scull before
him, he saw in it a "noble cause ... destined to exert a blessed
influence upon the morals and happiness of so many millions of
human beings." With pleasure he spoke a good word for Mrs.
Lusher's "Temperance Hotel," opened on Hand Street near Penn
Avenue in 1836, and his paper printed advertising for lots on sale
in a "Temperance Village" at the mouth of Saw Mill Run opposite
Pittsburgh. In 1841 a great wave of temperance sentiment (a
reaction possibly to the "Hard Cider Campaign") swept over the
Pittsburgh region. Craig attended one of the meetings at Dr.
Swift's church in Allegheny, where "Mr. Vickers, a reformed
drunkard," spoke, and came away so full of what he saw and
heard that he resolved to tell his readers all about it:

> He had sunk so low that he would send his children
> into the street to pick up a nail here and there, to sell for
> *a cent to buy rum!* while his wife and children were suffer-
> ing the pangs of hunger to such a degree, that, as he ex-
> pressed it, his sick and suffering wife was denied a suffi-
> ciency of *cold corn-bread* to appease its ragings! His

physical energies were prostrated, his body bloated, while his trembling limbs refused their office.[8]

A change for the better, Craig affirmed, had been brought about by signing the pledge of temperance.

The *Gazette* reported that the number of Pittsburghers who were doing likewise was reaching into the thousands. Craig was convinced by this that the great mass of the community was set against intemperance. He warned those who continued to manufacture and sell intoxicating liquors that in so doing they were braving public opinion and calling down upon themselves the "scorn and abhorrence" of a large majority of their fellow citizens. Before the end of the year the excitement had worn itself out. It remained to be seen how lasting the change would be.

The cause of women's rights was one reform movement that won little encouragement from Craig. Militant females like Anne Royall and Frances Wright were quite beyond his endurance. At the time of the Eaton affair during Jackson's administration, some remarks in the *Gazette* reflected so severely upon Secretary Eaton and his championship of a "bold and designing female" that a public meeting was called in the town to criticize the newspaper for its attitude.

As trade and manufactures increased in Pittsburgh, only a flickering interest in cultural concerns was reflected in the *Gazette* from day to day. The theater existed on sufferance; the limitations of its role were explained by the *Gazette* in 1817: "The stage conveys a moral in colours more vivid than the awful and elevated station of the preacher permits him to use—it is his coadjutor in good, and goes with him, hand in hand in exposing vice to ridicule and honouring virtue."[9] For a while during the season of 1817, when Mrs. Entwisle, the celebrated actress, visited Pittsburgh, the *Gazette* had a correspondent, "Dramaticus," who wrote reviews for the paper praising her extravagantly, denominating her the "Siddons of America," etc. Four years elapsed before another theatrical company of real merit came to Pittsburgh, bringing with it the youthful Edwin Forrest.

Too many felt like the puritanical citizen who wrote to the *Gazette* in 1820 stating that he was fond of plays but was satisfied with merely perusing them. Exhibiting them, he thought, had a bad effect. Pittsburgh had no respectable theater, but it did support many houses of religious worship. For this there was a reason.

> Yes, and the cause is too palpable to require a formal induction. My bosom swells with exultation when I advert to it. The citizens of Pittsburgh would rather build churches than theatres; they would rather support the ministers of the gospel, than the profligate race of the green-room; they would rather be door-keepers in the house of the Lord, than dwell in the tents of wickedness.[10]

When a showing of a panorama of the battle of Waterloo was advertised in the *Gazette* of August 22, 1834, the sponsors thought it prudent to add: "The public are most respectfully informed that the above is nothing of a theatrical exhibition, so that no religious scruples need prevent any from visiting it."

Craig himself honestly looked upon the theater as a school of vice. One of the *Gazette* force, who was in the habit of attending the old Drury Theatre, told the story many years later of how Craig called him in one morning and charged him, the next time he went out to his mother's home beyond Emsworth, to carry a letter from the editor to her. When the mission had been performed it was found that in the letter the stern old editor insisted that his employee would have to give up the theater or depart from the paper.

The fine arts in general seem to have been hardly better patronized. The only hope of a local genius like A. Bowman was to accumulate enough means to establish himself in New York, where his ability might be recognized. In the thirties, however, occasional advertisements for showings of paintings appeared; in one instance a display of Flemish and Italian masters was noted. Craig was personally more interested in George Catlin's Indian sketches, of portraits of chiefs, scenes of villages, and pictures of

animals. Catlin, who had made an extensive tour of the Northwest, came to the Exchange Hotel with his paintings and a lecture
upon Indian customs in April, 1833. The popular response was so
hearty that he remained for two more lectures and arranged return
visits in 1835 and 1836. From these and similar exhibitions,
Pittsburghers graduated to the panorama, a series of paintings
shown in rapid sequence, the germ of the idea that produced the
cinema. Samples of this it is evident from the *Gazette*, were appearing in Pittsburgh during the thirties.

The *Gazette* was on the lookout for better educational opportunities. "We have got over these colonial notions," rejoiced
Morgan Neville in 1819, when the opening of a medical school at
Lexington, Kentucky, obviated the need for medical students to
go east for their professional training. In the same year the Western University of Pennsylvania was incorporated, with both John
Scull and Morgan Neville on the board of trustees. The first
faculty, however, was not formally installed until May, 1822.
During its early years, the new school had rough sledding and
drew much criticism from busybodies. On December 7, 1830, an
irate citizen wrote to the *Gazette:*

> Mr. Craig,—Will you be good enough to inform the
> citizens of Pittsburgh how it happens that the Western
> University of Pennyslvania is used for a carpenter's shop?
> That splendid edifice, that every person is desirous to see
> completed, is now used for a shop to prepare materials for
> the erection of other buildings. Is it the intention of the
> trustees, that the mere shell should stand, a monument of
> taste and want of energy? Are funds wanted to complete
> the building?—Perhaps the trustees, in their wisdom, are
> waiting until a gust of wind shall blow down the old
> academy, and bury professors, students and all in its
> ruins. If that be the intention, it would be well enough
> to inform the public, that those no ways connected with
> the institution might be on their guard, and keep out of
> the way.

The great majority of children were affected by neither academy nor college. Governor after governor had proposed free

schools to the legislature, but not until 1834 were they guaranteed by law. Allegheny County hastened to take advantage of the new opportunity. On August 9, 1834, the *Gazette* printed a proclamation by William Lecky, the sheriff, establishing a general system of common schools and fixing an election date for choosing the necessary officers. By 1840 Pittsburgh had a hundred schools of various kinds, many of them "public schools," where, as the *Gazette* put it, "the children of all are educated at the expense of the public as they should be."

Theater, art gallery, schooling were enjoyed by a relatively small proportion of the population. Occasionally the *Gazette* provided glimpses of interests that appealed more generally to the masses of the people. Animal shows came to town frequently. Waxwork shows and exhibitions of ventriloquism were hardly less popular. In 1830 the town was privileged to gaze upon an Egyptian mummy that had been removed from the ruins of Thebes. In 1836 A Fong Moy, a Chinese lady, diverted Pittsburgh for two days with her sallies in English and Chinese and her "astonishing little feet." Around 1820 the craze for lotteries reached Pittsburgh and provided the *Gazette* with good advertising business. The leading chance firms in town were Allen's and Towne's, both of them affiliated with large eastern concerns. Who could resist such an enterprising invitation as this:

> FOR A SNUG FORTUNE OF $20000 go and pay $7 to ALLEN'S who have had the pleasure of granting in *two late lotteries* to different deserving people the following handsome fortunes, viz one of $30000, one of 25000, one of 20000, one of 15000, two of 10000 each, besides many of 5000, 2000, 1000, 700, 500, &c. The ticket which drew the above 25000 dollar prize, was, by S. & M. ALLEN sent to Pittsburgh and there repeatedly offered for sale, but as no person could be found in all this populous, wealthy, flourishing, and enlightened city possessing a disposition to purchase the 25000 for the trifling sum of 7 or 8 dols. the poor, despised and neglected ticket was compelled to undergo a retrograde transportation over the mountains

to one of the Atlantic cities from whence it came; after
which S. & M. Allen divided and sold it in shares, one
share to a poor soldier who had lost a leg in the service of
his Country.

It is presumed that the citizens of Pittsburgh and its
vicinity on reflecting how easily they might have obtained
that splendid prize, and that they can now easily obtain
20000 or 10000 dols. that they will without delay repair
to Allen's truly lucky Lottery office.[11]

Often such advertisements were accompanied by cuts showing an
old soldier carrying a sack of money on his shoulder or a wagon
piled high with lucre and drawn by dancing steeds. In time the
abuses of the lottery system became apparent to most thoughtful
people; when lotteries were finally abolished by state law in 1833,
the *Gazette* came out with an editorial warmly endorsing the step.

Surprisingly Pittsburgh was, to use a modern phrase, air-
minded in the eighteen thirties. Balloons were the aircraft of that
day. In 1837 R. Clayton, an amateur balloonist, planned an
endurance flight eastward from Pittsburgh. On the afternoon of
August 30 he floated skyward and disappeared from view. "Such
a congregation of people as were assembled in and around the
enclosure we never before saw in or near the city," declared Craig.
Nearly a week later a full account of the "aerial voyage," penned
by Clayton himself, appeared in the *Gazette*. The reader is allowed
a place in the basket as the balloon rises higher and Pittsburgh
with its striking physical features drops away. The air has the
piercing quality of autumn and seems very cold, for Clayton says
—imagine!—that the balloon is moving along at the rate of forty-
six miles per hour. Near Johnstown the canal is seen and, struggling along at the pace of horses and mules, a canal boat. The
passengers are on deck. A balloon! A general craning of necks is
observed and what appears to be some excited talking. Then
abruptly the aerial bag heads into a storm that forces it to descend
on the top of Laurel Ridge. The fall wrecks the balloon, and
Clayton is forced to spend a rainy night in the basket, suspended

fifteen feet above the ground. After daylight he escapes, finds aid, and returns to Pittsburgh in the despised canal boat.

In 1840, Pittsburgh began to buzz with gossip about the new air-mail line that was to be opened between Pittsburgh and the Atlantic seaboard. The announcement was in the *Gazette* if one cared to read it:

CLAYTON'S AERIAL MAIL PACKET,

Will, in a few days, take its departure from PITTS-BURGH, and cross the ALLEGHENY MOUNTAINS. *Letters and Newspapers carried with Despatch....*
The inflation will begin on Wednesday, April 29th, 1840, and the ascension will probably take place in the latter part of the same week, or the beginning of the next. A short notice will be given at the time of ascent.

This immense and powerful Aerostat is between forty and fifty feet in height, and is formed of the strongest materials ever used for a similar purpose. The Car, which is in the form of a boat, is watertight, and furnished with oars, &c.

The Amphitheatre in which the Aerostat will be exhibited, and from which it will ascend, is erected on Liberty street, near the Canal.

Admission to the Amphitheatre when the Aerostat is inflated 50 cents, which sum will again admit the visitor on the day of ascension. Children admitted at half price.[12]

On May 4, 1840, the balloon took off for its eastern destination. The same evening it landed—at Tarentum, about twenty miles east of Pittsburgh!

PART III—1841–1866

THE SENTINEL

CHAPTER X

A DEACON AT THE HELM

In 1827 a printer lad of Yankee extraction entered Pittsburgh for the first time. Like many another who had been brought up along the shores of Massachusetts Bay, he had decided to go west. The country was growing in that direction. Printers were almost as much in demand as rail-splitters and canal-builders, so David N. White headed hopefully towards Pittsburgh. There he found employment with the *Gazette* and later the encouragement to set up a book- and job-printing business for himself. Then in 1840 the urge to be on the move seized him anew. After closing up his business he struck out for the prairies of Illinois where he threw himself with a will into the task of editing a campaign sheet. Once the campaign was over, though, he did not find that country congenial. Turning his face eastward, he headed back for Pittsburgh and acquired an interest in the *Gazette*. For a while he submitted to a partnership arrangement. First Z. H. Costen, and later Matthew M. Grant were associated with him. In April, 1845, a young Methodist preacher named Benjamin F. Harris, formerly a missionary among the Delaware Indians, entered the firm. White and Harris remained together until April, 1847, when White surrendered his holdings to a certain Erastus Brooks and temporarily retired from the paper.

Brooks was the first figure connected with the *Gazette* to be possessed of any experience on the large eastern newspapers. In the short span of his life he had seen a good sized portion of the world. The posthumous son of a sea captain from Portland, Maine, he had worked in a Boston grocery store, served as apprentice to a compositor, worked his way through Brown University, become Washington correspondent for a large group of eastern dailies, and then had capped his experiences by touring Europe from Queenstown to Moscow to collect material for articles to be submitted to the Portland *Advertiser*. Brooks did not remain in

121

Pittsburgh for more than a few months. His temperament was unfitted for settlement in any one place. Soon he was off to the national capital to observe political trends there. He left his partner, Samuel Haight, to attend to the more mundane details of newspaper management. The arrangement was unsatisfactory. On July 1, 1848, Brooks let it be known that for reasons of a "domestic nature" he had dissolved the partnership. The stage was set for White to come back as editor and proprietor of the *Gazette*.

His health now completely restored, White continued the second phase of his editorship for nearly a decade. Finally, in the fall of 1856, he was forced to yield to his physician's advice and retire to the pleasures of rural life in Sewickley. The *Gazette* then passed into the hands of S. Riddle & Co., a firm that continued to publish it up to the days of the Civil War.

The paper came out all through the period in three separate editions, a daily, a tri-weekly, and a weekly. At first the daily was priced at six dollars a year in advance and the tri-weekly at four dollars, and the weekly was priced at two dollars in advance or three dollars at the end of the year. In 1846, the price of the daily shifted to eight dollars, but five years later it returned to the original figure. In 1844, the *Gazette* underwent a significant change. Up to that time it had been issued as an afternoon paper. In that year it became a morning journal, which it has remained ever since.

When White first took over the paper the Franklin hand press that Craig had purchased was still in use. At the time of the great fire of 1845, however, it was tasked beyond its capacity to meet the demand for news. Consequently, White proceeded to stock his new office on Third Street with a handsome one-cylinder Napier steam press built to order in New York at a cost of nearly two thousand dollars, the first steam press used in Pittsburgh to print a daily paper. The press quite set off the new office. With a sense of pride the editor permitted his eyes to survey the dimensions of his establishment; three stories high it was, some fifty-seven feet long, and nineteen feet wide. There was ample space in the building, he claimed, for a counting room, editorial room, packing room, press room, and composing room, besides accommodations for the *Christian Advocate*, a Methodist publication for which the *Gazette* had the printing contract. In the counting room customers were looked after and all financial business transacted. In the packing room, where the supply of paper was stored, all the folding and packing was done. Along the walls were six berths similar to those in a steamboat, with bedding to accommodate the night hands. In the composing room, nine men were kept busy at typesetting. Evidently the *Gazette's* force had grown; by 1858 it numbered twenty-two. But White had no thought of making use of the services of newsboys. When significant grumblings at the removal of papers from doorstoops came to his ears, he said pointedly: "We wish the public to *take notice*.—None of our papers are placed in the hands of the boys to sell. If any boy offers to sell them, he has *purloined them*, and we wish the boy detained, and notice given to us immediately." [1]

During this period the paper went through a succession of enlargements and other changes in appearance. In 1851 it put on a "new dress" of somewhat larger type "in compassion to the eyes of our readers." A tardy concession this, for the tendency of contemporary newspapers seemed to be to make use of smaller type in order to fit an increasing mass of reading material into the paper. An enlarged sheet size supplied some of the needed space, but aught than a four-page publication was unthought of. The appearance of a new dress usually meant an eastern marketing trip by the editor for a new and improved set of type.

The *Gazette* of the eighteen-forties looked much more like a modern newspaper than ever before. The arrangement was more uniform and orderly; it evinced apparently a more conscious desire on the part of the editor to make it conform to the tastes and interests of his readers. For the most part illustrations— figures of coaches, steamboats, bells, perhaps a tailor measuring a man for a suit—were confined to the advertising section.

The *Gazette* was particularly proud of its commercial department, which provided Pittsburgh market reports, often supple-
mented by reports from the Cincinnati, Louisville, and New
Orleans markets. This new service was first instituted January 30,
1844; within two weeks a prominent rival, the *Advocate*, was
sufficiently alarmed to appeal to its patrons among the Whig
merchants not to desert to the *Gazette*. At first Harris had charge
of this department of the paper. Later Russell Errett took it over
with such success that he was credited by White with having
made it "equal to any in the West, if not in the East." The possibilities it afforded were hinted at in an anecdote related by the
editor before the department had been well organized. In the
Gazette an article had appeared taking exception to the high freight
rates imposed on cheese and ashes. A Brownsville merchant,
clipping it from the paper, sent it to the president of the Baltimore
& Ohio Railroad. The outcome was the immediate reduction of
the rates on these and other similar articles.

By 1848 a column of local affairs had become a regular feature.
In the skillful hands of William E. McLaren, regarded by his
superiors as "a young man of a liberal education...thoroughly
acquainted with Pittsburgh and its vicinities," it throve and
proved highly interesting to the people of a city that had at last
become too large to make the comings, goings, and doings of all
common property.

The *Gazette* was equally well fortified with news from the
national capital. In the fall of 1842 it employed once more the
services of a Washington reporter to look in upon the proceedings
of Congress. With an eye to what was going on at Harrisburg, the
paper dispatched a reporter there too. Soon "Pencillings at
Washington" and "Pencillings at Harrisburgh" were accepted
features of the *Gazette*. It was represented at Washington first by
"Penn" and later by "Oliver Oldschool." Ultimately it re-em-
ployed the services of that able individual, Junius, who combined
an ingenuous point of view with a distinctive style of writing, light,
airy, and drily humorous. Even the *Post*, the *Gazette's* political

arch-enemy in the period, expressed the grudging opinion that Junius wrote the only "readable, original article" published in the *Gazette*. This he might well do, for he was allowed complete freedom of expression by his employer at all times.

The correspondence of the *Gazette* ranged ever more widely. Late in the period letters began to reach the paper from a wandering correspondent, who delighted his readers with descriptions of New Orleans and its sleepy Creole population, of the fur-trade capital, St. Louis, of that hustling, western lake port and railroad center to be, Chicago. In 1857 the *Gazette* essayed the experiment of retaining a traveling foreign correspondent. His articles seem to have been popular. When the Westminister *Herald* extended compliments on his good work, the *Gazette* made proper acknowledgment and declared: "The correspondent so handsomely referred to is the worthy Bishop Simpson, of the M. E. Church of our city, who is now, probably, in the Holy Land." [2] But the paper was doing more than printing foreign news dispatches. It was now for the first time taking an active *editorial* interest in what went on abroad. At the time of the great Irish potato famine it aroused itself and aroused the community to make donations for the relief of the starving Irish. With keen satisfaction it viewed in 1848 the impending collapse of absolutist governments in Europe. The proclamation of the Second Republic in France seemed to herald a new order of things. "We trust"—the *Gazette*, April 8, 1848—"that our citizens will turn out, en masse, tonight, for the purpose of expressing their congratulations to the French Republic, on the triumphant overthrow of Monarchy in France, and the adoption of a government based upon principles similar to our own." When a sympathy meeting in Philadelphia bespoke undying devotion to the cause of Hungarian independence, White thought that Pittsburgh could do no less: "If we can do them any good by sending our shout of sympathy across the waters, let us meet, and give it with a will. Hurrah for the brave Hungarians! Success to the cause of liberal principles in Hungary!" [3] Louis Kossuth, the great Hungarian leader, was popular in Pittsburgh long before he came to America. His popularity was not diminished when the distinguished refugee landed in New York. If anything, it was intensified. In apology for the fact that almost every other subject was crowded out of the paper, White could only say that Kossuth and his great mission had so completely absorbed the public mind that nothing else seemed worth publishing.

It was expected that the country's guest would visit Pittsburgh about the middle of January, 1852, but he was held up at Hollidaysburg by deep snows on the mountains. In fact the cold was so intense on January 21 (old-timers said that they had seen nothing to compare with it for twenty years past) that deliveries of the *Gazette* could not be made. Finally on January 23 the paper was able to announce that the indomitable Hungarian had been brought in from Blairsville by sleigh. An escort met him in Wilkinsburg and conveyed him to the St. Charles Hotel, where he was glad to nurse his chilblains and recover from a slight illness. After three days he was ready to make another of his winning speeches before a cheering and respectful crowd packed in at the Masonic Hall. What Kossuth said and did was news. Extra editions of the daily *Gazette* were gobbled up almost immediately; to satisfy the craving for news, more news, the editors culled the most interesting happenings from several consecutive issues and sold this "digest" over the counter.

In order to make Kossuth's visit tangibly worth while, White reminded the public that "every dollar contributed by patriotism or benevolence...strengthens the cause on both sides of the Atlantic." Even firearms would be received by the "Friends of Hungary." The appeal was royally answered. The "ladies of Pittsburgh" donated eleven hundred dollars in gold; others subscribed in proportion. On the last day of January Pittsburgh said Godspeed to Kossuth as he departed for the Northwest by the way of the Ohio & Pennsylvania Railroad. White accompanied him as far as the Ohio line and introduced him to crowds assembled at the railroad stations in New Brighton, Pennsylvania, and Palestine, Ohio.

The viewpoint of the *Gazette* toward liberal movements in Europe being what it was, it was to be expected that the editor would take the side of the patriots who were struggling for a united Italy. The Austro-Sardinian War of 1859 was covered for the *Gazette* by the *London Times'* trusty correspondent, William H. Russell. When the war was over, when Lombardy had become a part of the new Italy, and when Modena, Parma, Tuscany, and Romagna had applied for annexation, White speculated as to Italy's future with remarkable prescience:

> With the certainty that Venice will soon be added to it, may we not hope that Naples will follow, and Italy be free, not simply from the Alps to the Adriatic, but to the southern extremity of Sicily? ... That hour is fast approaching; and with it will come the full dawn of the day of Italy's redemption.[4]

Within eleven years the vision had become reality.

The new magnetic telegraph, an invention of these years, completely revolutionized the methods by which the *Gazette* acquired its news. As late as 1845 White was grumbling about periodic lapses in the southern mail and vowing that a few round fines imposed on the government mail contractor would bring a marvelous improvement. Already Morse's invention was on the way to terminating these difficulties. At the very close of the year 1846 a special telegraphic news column, containing latest dispatches from Philadelphia and Washington, D. C. and occasioned, as it proved, by the completion of a telegraph line from Washington to Pittsburgh, was introduced into the *Gazette*. At the same time work proceeded rapidly on a line from Philadelphia to Pittsburgh. The enterprise shown by the *Gazette* drew attention from the East. The *North American* of Philadelphia commented:

> The *Pittsburgh Gazette* publishes every morning the reports of the markets in Baltimore, Philadelphia, and New York up to the previous evening. This shows the great benefit of the Atlantic and Ohio Telegraph, and also a degree of liberal enterprise on the part of Messrs. White & Harris which is of the "very kidney" we like. We hope

the thousands residing in the vallies of the Ohio and
Mississippi, who will be benefitted by such energy, will
take good care to reward it.[5]

The new step was remarked upon in the West as well. In fact
White suddenly found himself burdened with more requests for
exchange from western newspapers than he could attend to. Would
it not pay western dailies, he suggested, to subscribe for the
Gazette as long as the western terminus of the telegraph line remained at Pittsburgh? In order to distribute the load, the *Gazette*
led the way by concluding an agreement among several papers to
join in paying for telegraphic news. Thus it was a pioneer once
more—in initiating telegraphic news service west of the Allegheny
Mountains.

During the Mexican War, the *Gazette* distinguished itself by
its willingness to spare no pains to satisfy the almost frantic desire
of the public for reliable information. In enterprising fashion it
established a pony express between Lock No. 3 on the Monongahela River and the city of Pittsburgh, a distance of nineteen miles,
with relays of swift horses every six miles. At regular intervals a
certain James Walker took up his station at the lock to await the
arrival of dispatches from the war front on the Monongahela mail
packet. Within one hundred minutes after their arrival, the
dispatches were rushed into Pittsburgh by the express, so that
when the selfsame packet docked at the Point, printed slips from
the *Gazette* office were already conveying the news to all parts of
the city.

The *Gazette's* need for advertising was as great as the public's
desire for news. In order to stimulate custom, the paper preached
the gospel of advertising to the unimaginative business men of the
city. White in 1844 alluded with feeling to the fact that

> The general advertising of the city is mostly confined to
> Wholesale Grocers, Produce dealers and Commission Mer-
> chants. Our Dry Goods, Hardware, Queensware and Shoe
> merchants, and our manufacturers of all descriptions
> with few exceptions, make no use of this means of ex-

tending their business or exhibiting the amount of business done here.[6]

In 1846 he remarked:

> We pick up a leading business paper from either of those cities [*Cincinnati and St. Louis*] and find such an enticing array of advertisements from all these branches as fairly throws Pittsburgh into the shade. If we could afford it we would advertise gratuitously, for no other reason than to counteract the unfavorable effects which the Cincinnati and St. Louis papers exercise on the minds of western and country merchants through their advertising columns.[7]

The indifference of Pittsburgh business men toward advertising (classified for their benefit by the *Gazette* after 1847) was hard to explain, especially in consideration of the disparity between the advertising rates charged by the Pittsburgh papers and those charged in other large cities. To drive this point home, White reprinted a table from the *Cincinnati Gazette* showing relative charges for yearly and "casual" advertising.

	Yearly	One Square Insertion	Each Continuance
Cincinnati	$30.00	50 cents	25 cents
Louisville	40.00	100 cents	25 cents
St. Louis	40.00	75 cents	37½ cents
New Orleans	——	100 cents	50 cents
New York	40.00	75 cents	50 cents
Boston	——	100 cents	50 cents

The charges in Cincinnati were very moderate, it seemed, but, said White, advertising in Pittsburgh was even cheaper—cheaper, in fact, than in any other city in the United States. One square yearly in a Cincinnati paper was thirty dollars, but in a Pittsburgh paper, only twenty.[8] How, then, explain the lack of advertising spirit in Pittsburgh?

If low advertising rates could not move the Pittsburgh merchants, increased circulation must. So White trained his eye upon spreading the territory of the *Gazette* to the farthest limits. In the summer of 1845 notice was given that the paper had agents in Philadelphia, Baltimore, Boston, and New York, fully authorized to receive advertisements and subscriptions to any edition of the paper. Soon Cincinnati was added to the list. According to White's own figures, the combined circulation of the daily and weekly *Gazette* in 1845 must have approximated fifty-five hundred. The editor appeared to be more proud, nevertheless, of the quality rather than of the extent of his subscription list. It meant more to him that the paper was placed in the hands of eighteen hundred merchants residing in every quarter of the Ohio Valley and in many portions of the upper Mississippi and Missouri valleys; that most of the subscribers were active business men in various walks of life. The quality of its subscribers, said White, was what gave the paper its value as an advertising medium. The *Gazette* was particularly popular in the Monongahela Valley, where it had circulated freely from the beginning. Many in that region had remained subscribers for nearly a half century.

White was not at all sorry, though, to see his subscription list wax fatter from year to year. By 1854 he was pleased to announce that the daily circulation had increased nearly sevenfold and the weekly nearly fivefold. A considerable share of this steady growth was traceable to the campaign clubs that the *Gazette* organized. These were initiated during the national party campaign of 1848, when preparations were made to mail the weekly *Gazette* from June 10 until election day to subscribers in packages of ten copies for five dollars, fifteen copies for seven dollars, twenty copies for nine dollars, and one hundred copies for thirty-five dollars. In 1852, and again in 1856, the *Gazette* returned to similar projects with enthusiasm. After the campaign of 1856 the weekly edition had an extensive circulation in almost every one of the free states of the Northwest. In 1858 western and central Pennsylvania, Ohio, western Virginia, Kentucky, Indiana, Illinois, and various sections of Wisconsin, Iowa, Missouri, and the Kansas, Nebraska' and Minnesota territories provided its field. The combined circulation of the daily and weekly editions exceeded twelve thousand copies. From the foothills of the Alleghenies to the far away Pacific coast the *Gazette* carried the news of the world.

Advertisers now trooped in without visible effort on the part of the paper. As a matter of fact, none of its proprietors had ever bestirred himself greatly to make a personal canvass for advertising. This attitude created something of a tradition—which the *Gazette* on one occasion saw fit to explain:

> We are sometimes asked, "why did you not come in and ask us for an advertisement?" We will answer briefly: Our business-manager may always be found at our counter, to attend to the business of his department. We have always acted upon the principle that this was the proper place to make contracts with our friends, and shall not change until convinced that they prefer being bored by us.[9]

No small credit for the steady growth of the paper's influence belonged to Editor White. Lacking many of Craig's advantages, such as family prestige and good schooling, White won respect for himself by his refusal to indulge in editorial revolver play. The nickname "Deacon," usually prefixed to his surname, suggests a man of solemn demeanor. White was wont to shy away from "personal journalism" and to refrain from alluding to editors as individuals lest such a procedure detract from the dignity of the profession, lead directly to personalities, and debase the press to a mere engine for individual encounters. Not that one should run away from a fight. In 1852 the *Gazette* gave full publicity to an affray between the editors of two Steubenville (Ohio) newspapers. The editor of the *Herald* claimed that the editor of the *Messenger* had entered his office, locked the door, drawn a dagger, and threatened to murder him upon the spot unless he signed a paper held by the editor of the *Messenger*. The victim signed, and then had his persecutor arrested afterwards. "It seems strange," said White, "that the editor of the Herald should not have been able to find a poker, or some other weapon, to defend himself with; and it seems to us that his friends would have thought more of him, if he had not signed the paper tendered him upon such compulsion." [10]

Along with his distaste for controversy, White nourished a desire to avoid the charge of blind partisanship. In 1854 he decided to remove the name of the party slate from the head of the editorial column. He felt that its retention was an insult to the intelligence of the readers and was, besides, injurious to independent journalism in the sense that it constituted a tacit endorsement of a group, some members of which might be unsatisfactory to the editor.

A press with high standards—this was his guiding ambition. He may be discovered writing in 1851:

> Of what exceeding importance is it, in view of the far reaching influence of journalism, for a community, a state, a nation, to have a sound, judicious, moral, conservative, and intelligent newspaper press. While the press exerts its immense effects upon the people, they, in turn, greatly influence the character of their journalism. If they support a venal and unprincipled press, they may expect it to re-act upon themselves, and make them partake of the spirit of their daily teacher.[11]

Essentially the *Gazette* was conservative—had always been so in fact. For this reason, it had never quite caught the popular imagination. Freely admitting this, White ascribed his paper's success to its faithful allegiance to certain principles. These may be summarized, on the one hand, as opposition to secret oath-bound societies, to the encroachments of slavery, and to the pretensions and demands of the Roman Catholic hierarchy; on the other, to the advocacy of a protective tariff and the rights of the workingman and to the encouragement of local industrial enterprises.

As the outstanding newspaper of a large community, the *Gazette* commanded high respect. A correspondent in 1846 referred to it as standing "in the front rank of the heralds of news." Even more flattering was praise from a man who was himself an outstanding influence in American public life during the middle

DAVID N. WHITE RUSSELL ERRETT

NELSON P. REED GEORGE T. OLIVER

TYPICAL ADVERTISEMENTS OF
THE EIGHTEEN-THIRTIES

of the nineteenth century. In an eloquent sermon delivered in the Plymouth Church of Brooklyn, New York, on Thanksgiving Day, 1853, Henry Ward Beecher said, in speaking of newspapers:

> They are not merely journals of *news* of the last happenings.... Such papers as the *Tribune*, the *Times*, the *Pittsburgh Gazette*, *Cincinnati Gazette*, *Indiana Journal*, *Boston Commonwealth*, and *Traveler* contain more religious matter every week than do religious papers; more scientific matter than journals of science; more literature and art than monthlies devoted to literature and art. The tone of papers is *rising* and not falling.[12]

Such a paragraph was worth a thousand subscribers.

CHAPTER XI

POLITICAL CROSS-CURRENTS

In 1841 the *Gazette* family was still inclined to support the paper for its loyalty to a particular set of political views. During the early forties the local Whigs and Antimasons were beginning to lose their separate identity, but for the time being the *Gazette* remained staunchly Antimasonic and withheld its support from the Whig party. At length the editor awoke to the fact that he was likely to be cast in the rôle of a general without an army. The *Gazette* could hardly gloss over the fact that the Democrats were profiting from the dissensions in the ranks of their opponents. The Pennsylvania Democracy had been halted by the Whig victory of 1840 for a moment, but three years later the Whigs could muster only enough strength to win twelve of Pennsylvania's twenty-four seats in Congress.

The Clay leaders of the Whigs in Pittsburgh attributed the die-hard attitude of the *Gazette* to the fact that Matthew Grant, a sworn enemy of secret societies, still owned an interest in the paper. It was an open secret that Editor White would not remain a "bitter-ender" at the cost of Whig defeat in the coming election. So it was that in January, 1844, fifteen leading Clay Whigs clubbed together and advanced two hundred dollars each to enable White to buy out his partner's interest. Leaving White in exclusive possession, Grant departed from the firm before the end of the month.

This transaction could not escape running the gauntlet of the paper's enemies. The *Post* chuckled mightily over the notion that some of the fifteen Whigs who had purchased an interest in the *Gazette* were "members of the lodge" and would almost certainly suborn White into following the lead indicated by them. With a dash of temper, White retorted that the *Post*'s statement was "false in its conception, false in its details, false in every particular." Within a short time, it became manifest, however, that something more than a routine change was involved, for scarcely more than two months later, Judge Baird disposed of the Whig organ of the city, the *Advocate*, to White, and a merger was effected. The *Gazette* assumed a new title, the *Pittsburgh Daily Gazette and Advertiser*, and fell heir to the patronage belonging to its erstwhile rival.

At first the *Gazette* endeavored to avoid the extremes of opinion that were called forth by the slavery question. Jane Swisshelm, who was brought up in an abolitionist family, tells of writing for publication in a Pittsburgh antislavery paper verse in ridicule of three local ministers of the gospel who had voted for the "Black Gag" law at a general conference of the Methodist church. To her surprise, the *Gazette* came out with an editorial full of "pious horror" and denunciation of the article. Finding that she was liable for criminal prosecution, Mrs. Swisshelm addressed a reply to the *Gazette*, which it refrained from publishing. Yet the columns of the paper were not without signs of a passive opposition to slavery. Once it presented an account of a town meeting at which Neville B. Craig offered resolutions condemning the seizure of an abolitionist press in Lexington, Kentucky, by an angry mob. Another time it ran a series of articles on emancipation in the West Indies. Sometimes an editorial betrayed the undercurrents of feeling. The precedent set by Craig of refusing notices for runaway slaves was followed. *"Am I My Brother's Keeper"* asked White on one occasion:

> The Gazette must decline the publication of an advertisement, headed $100.00 Reward. We are not aware that such a paltry sum would tempt a reader of the Gazette to catch a boy about "ten years old, rather spare and delicately made, with black eyes, hair straight, though somewhat inclined to curl...."
> It is to be hoped that no one who reads the Gazette is so poor that he can be tempted to gain his bread by money thus earned.... No man who has read the Gazette could eat bread which would be literally soaked in the bitter tears of a mother and her little ones.... We

are sure the advertisement has been sent us for one who
does not read the Gazette, for no one who does, could
thus insult its conductors and readers.[1]

The events of the early forties half revealed, half concealed the
slavery issue. In the election of 1844 the Whigs of western Pennsylvania were eager to carry the tariff issue into the battle. The
Democrats, from Polk down, would not admit that the Whigs
could be more protective than they, but the *Gazette* was not wont
to look upon Democratic promises with any great amount of
confidence. What did the "Equal Protection for All" of the
Democrats mean? White saw in it the reduction of the duties on
such important commodities as wool and iron. Let the factory
girls of the cotton mills take heed, he advised. The withdrawal
of protection from cotton fabrics would have to be paid for by
them.

The Texas question was fat poured upon the flames. Before
the campaign was over, White convinced himself that the annexation issue had become more important than even the tariff, inasmuch as, aside from its own intrinsic merits and demerits, it might
affect the tariff and every other northern interest. The *Gazette*
could not forgive President Tyler for his efforts to bring Texas into
the Union. It recommended nothing less than impeachment for
the conduct of "His Accidency."

The campaign was hotly contested. Everywhere were great
Whig poles standing like sentinels against the sky. Plans were
made for one pole that was to be two hundred and seventy feet
high. Pole raisings innumerable, crowds, mass meetings, Ashland
clubs were the order of the day. The optimism of the local Whigs
was reflected in an auctioneer's notice in the *Gazette*, which offered
for sale seventy-eight acres of good land in Darke County, Ohio,
the deed to become payable on the day of Henry Clay's election
to the presidency of the United States. Alas for Clay and alas for
the men who followed his political fortunes through thick and thin,
thirsting for the day when they might see their favorite enter the
White House! White was quite worn out with his exertions. On

the day of the election he excused himself from editorial duties for the reason that "we are too weary and fagged out with our vigils to say anything today." Allegheny County turned in a handsome majority for Clay (2,369 votes), but Pennsylvania went for Polk. With mingled hope and dread the friends of the *Gazette* waited for the returns to filter in from the outside. The atmosphere of suspense was recalled in a later issue of the paper:

> Saturday and Sunday last were days of the most intense excitement, amounting almost to agony, among the Whig citizens of this city, we have ever seen. The news from New York on Friday evening filled every Whig bosom with gloom, and the most dread forebodings. Saturday evening the intelligence was rather more cheering, but not enough so to lift the load from American hearts, while it only added to the intensity of the suspense. On Sunday evening the die was cast. New York had gone for Polk.[2]

If the tariff policy of the new administration contributed to its unpopularity with the *Gazette*, so too did its expansionist policy. In vain did public meetings sponsored and encouraged by the *Gazette* attempt to stay the hand of Congress. When the news came that the Texan Congress had accepted the terms of annexation, White's cup of bitterness quite overflowed. "This monstrous iniquity, this most stupendous fraud upon the free states of the Union is accomplished," he said with powerful emotion. Turning to the Birney men, who had drawn enough votes from the Clay standard to defeat Clay, he bade them accept the credit of the "adulterous marriage" and adjured them to drown by their shouts if they could "the wailings and groans of the fathers, mothers, husbands, wives and children, whom their accursed instrumentality has torn from fond embraces of earth's dearest ties, to sweat and groan and bleed and die, upon the burning soil of Texas!"[3]

Confronted by the prospect of an expansionist war, White was sadly troubled. With some reluctance, he composed himself for the ordeal of armed conflict with England over the Oregon question. The conquest of Montreal would at least be easier and of more value than the acquisition of Mexico and her eight million "mongrels." Then on May 12, 1846, the news of the outbreak of war with Mexico reached Pittsburgh. White was straightway indignant. What justification had Polk for sending Taylor's little army into the disputed territory? To invade the country of a foreign power was absolutely beyond the constitutional powers of the executive. Yet the war was good for news. Every edition was sold out, and extras had no difficulty finding a market.

The *Gazette* was denounced for its pro-Mexican bias and lack of patriotism. To this the paper replied that to attack Polk's policy was not to attack the government, whatever the *Post* might say, and so White continued to hammer away at the administration. He predicted accurately that the "pestilential climate" of the Mexican country would prove deadly to the army, and he argued that from a military standpoint it would have been much better to invade the country from the direction of Vera Cruz. But after Mexico had been conquered, what then? She would constitute another Ireland to the United States, too weak to make war, too weak to make peace. For his part, White thought that the Whig party would have to adopt an anti-war platform at the next election in order to win.

It was hard to repress a sense of pride in the repeated military successes of Generals Taylor and Scott, however. Finally, in April, 1847, the city officials decided on a public illumination to celebrate the recent victories. There was a vigorous note of dissent from one *Gazette* reader: "So we are to illuminate, are we? For one I shall not do it on the present occasion. So long as blood is flowing in torrents, not only of soldiers and those whose trade it is to kill, but of helpless and innocent women and children, I cannot, will not illuminate." 4 The *Gazette* received several communications of a similar character, but while sympathizing with them, it decided to support the celebration. On Saturday evening, April 24 at 11 o'clock, the celebration was held, and, like Belgium's capital by night on the eve of Waterloo, the city presented a brilliant appearance.

Hard on the heels of the great victory of Buena Vista, the Whig papers in Philadelphia began to boom General Taylor for the presidency. Brooks, the editor of the *Gazette* for the time being, was not impressed by their reasoning. He had already decided that the military spirit rampant in the land must be curbed. Let other candidates be sounded out. When the Allegheny County Whig Convention assembled in March, 1848, it instructed its delegate to the national convention to cast his vote for Clay. But in vain. The Whigs at large had set their hearts on Taylor. They had won with a military hero in 1840. Why not again? Impelled by the discipline of party regularity, the *Gazette* reconciled itself to the nomination as best it could. Soon it was proclaiming to friend and foe:

> The glorious name of Taylor
> Has spread from sea to sea,
> And Mexico (his field of fame)
> His monument shall be.
> His name's a talisman to us,
> The dread of every foe;
> The synonym for victory,
> From Maine to Mexico.[5]

The electoral contest was far from being a tame affair. The local Whigs indorsed the Wilmot Proviso and denounced the tariff of 1846. The Democrats provided color by concealing themselves in one of the town graveyards and pelting a Whig parade with rocks and occasional shots. The *Gazette* took stock of the results of this "shameful, dastardly outrage," and reported that several men had been wounded and a woman knocked down. On the eve of the October election the Whigs put on a torch-light procession that was a thing of pride to all concerned. The *Gazette* thus described it:

> As the living throng poured along the streets, amidst a blaze of light, attended on either side with a snow-storm of handkerchiefs in the hands of beautiful women and smiling children,—the song of triumph, the shouts of exultation, the loud hurrah, the deep roll of the drum,

the wild notes of the bugle, and the grand bursts of music
from the full bands,—all made up a scene which will long
be remembered by the citizens of Pittsburgh.[6]

Successful party journalism required a constant reiteration of
the issues in order to keep the party *morale* high. No let down
must be permitted. In "A Last Word to our Weekly Readers,"
White delivered himself of the opinion that Pennsylvania was the
real battle ground for the presidency:

> Under this impression, the eyes of the whole Nation
> are upon us. The friends of Whig principles and Whig
> measures, in every State of the Union, stretch out their
> hands to us, and implore us to do our duty, to save our
> country, and to recover our downtrodden and degraded
> constitution. Their prayers go up for our success, their
> anxieties are most intense—they sympathise with us, and
> implore us not to fail them now. Shall we? *No!* No! NO![7]

The largest vote cast in Pennsylvania up to this time was
rolled up on election day. Taylor carried the state by a plurality
of 13,500 votes over Cass, his Democratic opponent. His majority
in Allegheny County was 3500. Even the Democrats had to admit
that this was unprecedented. Add to this the fact that the unaccountable populace had veered around and in the act of crowning the general who won the war had returned to power the party
that had opposed the war. It was a puzzling time for editors and
all good folk, a time of political cross-currents.

The sudden death of President Taylor in the early summer of
1850 was a hard blow to a Whig editor. The shock was the greater
because it came at a time when the country was in a state of
nervous tension over the debates in Congress on the Omnibus Bill.
The community was already agog at the prospect of a fugitive
slave law with teeth. Fugitive blacks who had counted themselves
safe in Pittsburgh were departing in droves for Canada; one citizen's meeting after another was being held in protest; the *Gazette*
was full of warnings that this law was dangerous to the South,
dangerous to the Union, dangerous to the very existence of slavery

itself. Within the year, called upon to report the proceedings of a convention at Nashville whose purpose was to consider the advisability of secession, White made short shrift of its doctrines and promised that if they were acted upon, "nothing can prevent a most bloody Civil War." This was not the propagandist utterance of an antislavery stump speaker. It was the earnest expression of an editor who prided himself upon his conservatism.

Under these unpromising circumstances the campaign of 1852 began. White made it a point to be on hand for the Whig national nominating convention at Baltimore in June. His trip *via* packet and railroad was a pleasant one. He arrived in Baltimore to find the hotels crowded, the town in commotion, and the prospects of General Scott's nomination reasonably good. A deadlock in the balloting and the arrogant attitude of the southern Whigs, however, left forebodings in the editor's mind as to the future of the Whig party. The campaign proceeded with the customary features—and some new ones. Preferring to forget about the Mexican War, the Whig papers took advantage of Scott's service in the War of 1812 to inject the details of that war into the campaign with a vengeance. In July, a great "Lundy's Lane Celebration" was held at Buffalo. From all over the middle West, crowds trooped to hear the speeches and probably to get a glimpse of Niagara Falls as well. During the campaign both parties made determined efforts to swing the Irish vote to their side. A time-honored formula for accomplishing this end went under the name of "twisting the lion's tail." The *Gazette* did not spurn such tactics. It informed its readers that "The *London Times* is laboring as zealously as any other Locofoco paper in behalf of Pierce and King [*the Democratic candidates*]....Pierce is the British candidate, and if British gold and British influence can secure his election, he will be elected...." [8]

Even White must have realized the hollow pretense of the Whig predictions of victory. People were in no mood to become excited about the tariff and "British iron." Allegheny County, Whig to the core, turned in a plurality of 2389 votes for Scott, but the state went Democratic by twenty thousand. All over the country, the election represented a landslide for the Democrats. Riddle, Whig editor of the *Pittsburgh Daily Commercial Journal* thought the Whig party ought to be dissolved on account of the treachery of the southern Whigs. The election results of the year 1853 were even less promising. The *Gazette* talked valiantly of the disorganized state of the national organization, of the stay-at-home vote, of the unfortunate consequences of introducing the prohibition question into the election, but those were feeble excuses. Plainly in the year 1853 the Whig party of the North was caught in the treacherous grip of a political undertow that was carrying it out to sea.

The cross-currents were becoming very confusing. White looked anxiously about in all directions for a party banner, but for the time being he was disappointed. The party system was in a state of flux. At this juncture, the pother was intensified by the beginnings of the Kansas-Nebraska agitation. The *Gazette* at once sprang fiercely to the support of the threatened Missouri Compromise. It spoke feelingly of the "great outrage" impending. It encouraged protest meetings, letters, petitions, resolutions. It warned the South of the danger that lay in violating the solemn compact of 1820. And when the threatening bill hurdled the Senate, White exclaimed in language reminiscent of the Communist Manifesto:

> Workingmen of the North, arouse! You who expect to go, or send your children to obtain your portion of the fertile lands of the great West, look to it that you are not robbed of your inheritance.... tell the slaveholding conspirators that this outrage upon justice, humanity and freedom shall not be![9]

It was of no use. On May 24, 1854, the *Gazette* acknowledged sadly, "The deed is done." All that remained was to print the names of the free-state representatives who had voted for the bill in a black bordered box reserved for the "Black List of Traitors" or "Nebrascals," as the paper chose to term them.

White's attention was directed to other matters by the emergence of a third party movement that promised for a time to supply a unifying principle for the demoralized elements of the Whig party of the North. The Know-Nothings were an added proof of the inscrutable workings of the American political system. As a product of the anti-Catholic feeling that had been strongly evident in the forties, their organization had some reason to expect coöperation from the *Gazette*, for White had taken part in several controversies with the local Roman Catholic bishop over the schools question and once had gone so far as to denominate negro slavery and the Roman Catholic Church "the two great systems of oppression in the civilized world." But the fact that the Know-Nothing Party traced its origin to a secret society, the Order of the Star Spangled Banner, cost it whatever sympathy it might have evoked from the *Gazette*. In 1845, White expressed his conviction that all secret oath-bound societies were "wrong in principle, immoral in their tendencies, and injurious to the community." Returning to the same point of view five years later, he dwelt with regret on the multiplication of secret societies in the country, marking out as especially dangerous the Protestant Association, calculated as it was to produce bigotry, prejudice, and class hatred.

In the latter half of June, 1854, the *Gazette* first began to notice the Know-Nothings and the uneasiness of the politicians about this mysterious order. Almost immediately White made strenuous efforts to link Know-Nothingism with the Democratic party and to warn the old-time Whigs away from it. His opposition was not diminished by an anonymous letter that came to him with a ticket for a certain Professor Tiffany's lecture—"an American talk on Americanism, by which we may judge of your...future course, the past being involved in so much mystery that those interested outside of politics, find it necessary to look to that future, for a satisfactory explanation of the past." [10] When shortly after, a deputation from the Know-Nothings came to him and invited him to join their organization and make the *Gazette* their party organ he refused. As time went on, he became more certain that he had acted with discretion, even though he had not taken the popular course.

The pressure to which he was subjected was not light. On January 31, 1855, he appealed for increased circulation to offset "active attempts ... to proscribe us and break us down." He was resolved to yield no ground.

> *We* stand where we always have stood; in determined opposition to all secret political organizations. Nothing can tempt us from this position. Dearly as we love the anti-slavery cause, not even the prospect of doing *it* a benefit could induce us to yield one inch in this regard.[11]

What this must have cost him is suggested by the fact that Samuel Haight, who had been associated with the *Gazette* for some years, withdrew in March, 1855, instead of allowing his political views to be "misinterpreted." Hundreds of subscribers likewise signified that the *Gazette* need no longer be left at their doors. Many ridiculous stories were told at the *Gazette's* expense. The *Butler American* spread the rumor that, having taken over Haight's interest in the paper, Bishop O'Conner had become a silent partner of White's. Another yarn contained the information that the editor of the *Gazette* had applied for admission to the order and had been kept out by "blackballing."

The paper continued to scorn the blandishments and threats of the Know-Nothings. Was it through with party politics? The Whigs were no more. To whom should it turn? An answer to the question was provided by the new Republican party, come out of the West to challenge the Know-Nothings for the right to throw down the gauntlet to the Democrats. In a letter written many years later, White recalled his part in founding the Republican party in western Pennsylvania:

> For fifteen years, I had been giving it [*the Gazette*] an anti-slavery bent, and I was satisfied the time had come to strike out on a new political path....

I resolved then to start a new party in Allegheny county, and in the State, if possible—not the Liberty party or the Free-Soil party, but one free from all entangling alliances—the *Republican party*.[12]

On May 29, 1854, the editor, who had realized for some time that the Whig party, as a national organization, was defunct, suddenly asked why it should not be replaced with an anti-Nebraska ticket. Quickly the influential *New York Tribune* seized upon the idea, which was by no means original, and recommended it as the sentiment of the great majority of free-soil newspapers in the North and West. On June 21, returning to the position that the national Whig party was destroyed past all remedy, White prophesied that a re-grouping must soon take place and advised an harmonious fusion of the northern Whigs and the Free-Soilers based on the principle of steady resistance to all further encroachments by the slave interest. As the movement got under way the *Gazette* did its best to smooth away all obstacles. The following summer, White, according to his own account, drew up calls for a county convention and a state convention to promote the organization of a state branch of the Republican party. Both calls were published in the *Gazette* on August 15, 1855.

These efforts did not escape the notice of the Republican party chieftains outside Pennsylvania. When Salmon P. Chase of Ohio visited Pittsburgh in November, 1855, he requested White to call upon him at his hotel. There plans were laid to make the movement in Pennsylvania part of a nation-wide movement to contest the field with the Democrats.

On January 23, 1856, there appeared at the head of the *Gazette* editorial column a notice signifying the general desire that an informal convention of the Republicans of the Union should meet at Pittsburgh on February 22, 1856, to perfect the national organization of the party and make plans for a nominating convention to be held subsequently. To this notice were subscribed the names of the chairmen of the state Republican committees of nine northern states, Pennsylvania among them. There was great excitement in Pittsburgh as the day approached. Both White and Craig were on the reception committee to greet such notables as Horace Greeley, Francis P. Blair, Owen Lovejoy, Joshua R. Giddings, Abraham Lincoln. The lobbies of the new Monongahela House buzzed with political gossip.

The national nominating convention of the Republicans for that year was held at Philadelphia. Early in June the *Gazette* began to advertise half-fare excursions to that place. Already the paper had committed itself to furthering the aspirations of Salmon P. Chase for the presidency. Probably shrewd old "Deacon" White recollected the conference he had enjoyed with the politician from Ohio and allowed his mind to dwell on the possibilities that a rise to eminence on the part of Chase might offer. Either William H. Seward or Judge John Maclean of Ohio as the party nominee would be acceptable as well. All three were passed over, and White had to resign himself to the choice of John C. Fremont, a representative of "Young America."

It had been decided two weeks earlier that James Buchanan of Pennsylvania would be the choice of the Democrats. White himself attended, as a reporter, the Democratic convention at Cincinnati. Hotel rates there were high—ten dollars a day for very indifferent quarters! As if it was not bad enough to quarrel with the officials for tickets and to see northern Democrats selling their souls to the southern wing for the privilege of naming the nominee!

The chief newspaper foe was, as usual, the *Post*. The two papers came to grips over the Kansas question; quarter was neither asked nor given. Indicative of the fire that the *Gazette* flung at the "Kansas iniquity" was an editorial called "Let us Alone," which likened the attitude of the *Post* and its friends to that of the evil spirits who cried out when encountered by Christ. "Blessed be Sharp's rifles!" said White on another occasion. "They are the only peacemakers which such villains can understand or respect." [13] Another inning was allotted to the tariff as well. The Republicans went around talking about "Ten Cent

Jimmy," a nickname that had been fastened on Buchanan, the *Gazette* explained, for his stand on the tariff in 1840.

The paper reflected the exciting incidents of the campaign. In neighboring Wheeling a Frémont club was put to rout by a mob. In Birmingham the sponsors of another such club worded their call to appeal to the friends of "Free Soil, Free Speech, Free Men, and Frémont." On September 17 a great mass convention was held in Pittsburgh to which Sumner, Wilmot, Corwin, and other Republican lions came to appeal for Republican votes. The town was alive with banners, floats, and parades. A picture of the "Sin Sin Naughty Platform" drew special comment. The result of the election was at once heartening and disappointing. The surprising majority of 4900, the largest of any county in the Union, was rolled up in Allegheny County by the Republicans; in the western part of the state generally they were successful, but Buchanan carried Pennsylvania and won the election.

The campaign had proved too much for White. At the height of the excitement, he was compelled to drop his newspaper work and dispose of the *Gazette* to a new firm, S. Riddle & Co. Along with Samuel Riddle, the chief owner, were associated Russell Errett, the new editor, and James Mecrum and Daniel L. Eaton, editorial assistants. With some additions and subtractions, this firm continued to issue the *Gazette* until well into the Civil War era.

From 1856 onward, the *Gazette* became constantly more responsive to the rising tide of sectional passion. Its incisive comment on the brutal assault directed against Charles Sumner in the United States Senate showed the temper of the times: "These cut-throat Southrons will never learn to respect Northern men until some one of their number has a rapier thrust through his ribs, or feels a bullet in his thorax." [14]

The paper extracted some satisfaction from the Lincoln-Douglas debates. At first it thought that Lincoln lacked the aggressiveness and impetuosity to carry away the laurels. The reports of the debate at Freeport, Illinois, convinced the editor, however, that he had underestimated this man Lincoln. The

"Little Giant" had been fairly cornered. The masterly way in which Lincoln had undermined Douglas's position was a pretty thing indeed! Furthermore, Lincoln's demeanor at Jonesboro was convincing proof that his success at Freeport had been no happy accident. When it was announced the next year that Lincoln was to follow Douglas on a speaking tour through Ohio, Errett took notice with an editorial, "Lincoln after Him," and eagerly asked the question, "Could he not be induced to come to Pittsburgh too?"

In far away New Orleans, the antislavery utterances of the *Gazette* were not overlooked. Around June 1, 1857, the *New Orleans Commercial Bulletin* referred to some remarks in the *Gazette* concerning a national crime wave and asked why this "abolitionist paper" did not pay more attention to such things in the North and take its mind off slavery. Errett replied to this by advising the *Bulletin* to remove the beam from its own eye and by printing a list of crimes of violence culled from various issues of the *Bulletin*.

For all his sympathy for the unhappy slaves, Errett would not admit that he was an abolitionist. He subscribed to the position of the Republican party that it had no intention of interfering with the domestic institutions of the southern states; and when the news was flashed in by telegraph that old John Brown of Ossawatomie had run amuck at Harpers Ferry, Errett at first leaned over backwards to deny any intention of fostering such a raid. It was, he said, "a foolhardy adventure of a handfull of monomaniacs ... a purposeless and senseless riot." Soon, however, his gorge rose at the language of the southern papers, and he commenced to laugh at the mighty efforts put forth by the courageous Virginians to capture nineteen fanatics! When Brown was finally hanged for his deed the *Gazette* declared that, Samson-like, he had dragged down the pillars of slavery in his fall and that his victory was complete.

The battle for the presidency in 1860 promised to enlist the utmost efforts of the partisans. Some could detect an ominous undercurrent of feeling that this might be the last such election.

The unfortunate Buchanan was ruled out from the start. "Old Buck," as the *Gazette* called him, presented a pathetic figure drifting helplessly about, as if unable to comprehend his position. On the Democratic side Stephen A. Douglas seemed to have the first call. Of the aspirants for the Republican nomination, Simon Cameron, a favorite son, was most pleasing to the *Gazette*. Errett was discreetly jubilant when he perceived a split opening in the Democratic party. At last the fate that party had so long tried to avoid had overtaken it.

The Republicans went to Chicago in 1860 with high hopes. Errett advised those in Pittsburgh who were disposed to make the journey that the hotel rates in Chicago would not be exorbitant, and they might purchase round-trip tickets for only fourteen dollars. Among those who trooped down to the railroad station was "R," a special correspondent for the *Gazette* with instructions to report all political gossip at the convention to his paper and its readers. Pittsburgh received the news of Lincoln's nomination with high spirits. Flags were hung out from the *Gazette* office window in honor of the result. The words of the *Gazette's* correspondent at Chicago were not without interest:

> The nomination of Lincoln, judging from the enthusiasm here and the responses received from all parts of the country, will prove a popular one. He has in him all the elements of popularity. A man of the people, he has worked his way from the lowly position of a wood chopper to that of an eminent attorney, solely by his own energy and industry.... It is plain that we are to have a repetition of the enthusiasm of 1840. The old fence rails in Sangamon county, mauled by him thirty years ago, will find endless repetitions in this country of worm fences. We shall have rails in all possible shapes—rail houses, rail rostrums, rails horizontal, rails perpendicular, rails in all possible positions; and the Rail Mauler of 1830—the representative man of honest labor—is to be to us what the Log Cabin boy of 1840 was. It needs no prophetic vision to see the victory in store for us. Honest old Abe will be the next President, depend on it.[15]

The prediction proved accurate. After the favorable outcome of the October election, the *Gazette* set up before itself the goal of a plurality of ten thousand votes in Allegheny County. Curiously enough, when the returns of the national election were tabulated it was discovered that Lincoln's plurality in the county was precisely that figure, the highest for any county in the Union. As a result of this, Allegheny County was long afterwards known as the "State of Allegheny." From the rest of the country came tidings that made Lincoln's election certain. The Republicans might well surrender to the intoxication of the hour.

Before the election Errett had treated lightly the threats of the southern leaders that a Republican victory meant the dissolution of the Union. After the election he still remained fatuously blind to the real temper of the South. Give the southern hotspurs a chance to retreat gracefully, he advised, and they would soon forget about secession. Gradually the depth of his mistake began to dawn upon him. The attempt of a New Orleans mob to lynch several citizens from Pittsburgh for supposed abolitionist tendencies was an eye-opener. In December the *Gazette* discovered a plot on the part of the secretary of war to remove the cannons from the United States Arsenal in Pittsburgh and ship them south to New Orleans and Galveston. The publicity focused on the scheme and the excitement induced by it finally caused it to be abandoned.

With mingled relief and anxiety the paper regarded the preparations of the city to receive the president-elect as he stopped off on his journey to the nation's capital. Great crowds milled about in the rain to hear him speak from the balcony of the Monongahela House on the eve of his arrival and returned the next morning for a more lengthy exposition of his views on the crisis. The next few weeks were a fevered dream, disturbed by visions and shapeless rumors of the plight of the garrison at Fort Sumter, of the intention of Louisiana to close the Mississippi, of Buchanan's lamentable state of mind, of treasonous plots, with perhaps the assassination of the president-elect as the objective.

On the feverish public mind Lincoln's inaugural address descended like a draught of cooling water. The *Gazette* was quick to respond to its firm and conciliatory tone and to commend its author to the country. It stood squarely behind the president in his determination to enforce the laws: "It may cost the nation a war to maintain itself against this mad rebellion. To yield to it must not for a moment be thought of." [16]

To some it seemed that the new administration was temporizing with its foes, but the crisis was at hand. On April 6 Errett was of the opinion that a struggle was imminent unless the secessionists receded soon from the fearful position in which they had placed themselves. On April 9 he painted in dark hues "The Impending Crisis." Three days later the blow struck. At ten o'clock on the evening of April 12 the telegraph instrument at Pittsburgh began to tick out the news that the batteries in Charleston harbor had opened fire upon the federal garrison at Fort Sumter. In the streets men gathered in knots and circles to discuss anxiously what effects might follow. At the theater a large crowd listened attentively to the reading of the fateful news dispatches between acts and cheered loudly for Major Robert Anderson, the hero of the hour. "The War has Commenced"—the words stared out from the editorial column the morning after.

> With a swift and cruel contradiction of its message last night, the telegraph now brings the stern tidings that the cloud of war so long gathering around Anderson and the brave men with him, who have faithfully guarded their country's flag within the walls of Sumter, has burst upon their devoted heads at length....
> The secessionists have drawn upon their own heads the fearful responsibility of inaugurating civil war, and a tremendous war it is likely to be.[17]

It was a far-sighted prediction. The war was to work an economic and social revolution in the land. Its close would date a new period in national history. But who could predict that? All that men could hear at the moment was the muffled roar of the guns at Fort Sumter. The signs pointed to boom times ahead for the newspaper men, but probably Errett gave that only a passing thought. Temporarily, motives of individual selfishness must be put aside. The call was for united action, and the traditions of the *Gazette*, tinged with national feeling as they were, inclined it to respond generously. There was an insistent sound about the booming of those guns at Sumter that spelled "Reveillé." Errett bent to his task.

CHAPTER XII

THE BATTLE CRY OF FREEDOM

The Pittsburgh landscape sparkled with blue; the martial sound of bugle notes rang out cheerily from Camp Wilkins, where the local boys were drilling. It was the eager springtime of 1861. The suspicions stored up in men's minds for many a year had been released for an airing, and the tension had been broken. The government at Washington had called for volunteers. From Pittsburgh's mills, shops, and residential districts they streamed, thrusting out their hands for muskets in answer to "Father Abraham's" call. For the first time in its history the *Gazette* beheld a war that it could in all conscience approve. It did not welcome bloodshed, but the editor was convinced, along with most of his friends, that the action taken by the administration had been unavoidable. The authority of the national government must be sustained. Many of the *Gazette's* employees volunteered their services to the government. Russell Errett himself was soon called to Washington to assist with the enormous correspondence that had deluged the war department. Before the end of the year he had seen considerable service with the army as a major on the Port Royal expedition in South Carolina. In the summer of 1862 the *Gazette* was fairly apologetic for the handicap placed upon its operations by the absence of a number of its men, who had volunteered.

S. Riddle & Co. was still publishing the paper at the outset of the war. The conflict had hardly begun when another newspaper, the *Commercial Journal*, was merged with the *Gazette*. For nearly two years the paper labored under the ambitious title, *The Daily Pittsburgh Gazette and Commercial Journal*. Early in 1864 it was transferred to new owners led by Josiah King, E. H. Irish, and Robert Ashworth. The Gazette Publishing Association, as they called their organization, continued to publish the paper until after the war.

153

Shortly before the war the *Gazette* experimented with separate morning and evening editions. Throughout the conflict the evening edition specialized on latest news bulletins, and the morning editions gave more attention to the discussions of public problems. In response to the unprecedented demand of the community for news, the proprietors addressed every effort to expanding their facilities. Already in January, 1861, the paper had added special reporters in Washington, D. C., and Harrisburg. Within three weeks after the war began the *Gazette* had appointed two correspondents to visit the volunteer Pennsylvania regiments and to write daily letters from the camps as long as the war lasted. The *Gazette's* office in Washington was located on Fourteenth Street opposite Willard's Hotel. In the latter part of 1862 the *Gazette* made plans for a battery of assistants to aid its correspondent there in the collection of news. With certain Detroit, Cincinnati, Louisville, Indianapolis, and St. Louis papers the *Gazette* formed a Western Associated Press to supplement the service of the Associated Press, a combination of New York dailies. All of this involved expense: the *Gazette* boasted that the cost of its special correspondence exceeded by some hundreds of dollars that of the entire news department before the war began and that it paid more for news per week than all the other Pittsburgh dailies combined paid per month.

Such expenditures involved no little anxiety for the firm. In November, 1862, the *Gazette*, the *Evening Chronicle*, the *Dispatch*, and the *Post*, the four English dailies of the city, announced a new schedule of advertising rates necessitated, on the one hand, by the depreciation of the currency, the operation of a new tax bill, and the greatly increased cost of everything used in the printing business; on the other, by a shrinkage in advertising—in some cases as much as fifty per cent. Paper, ink, telegraphic dispatches, gross revenue—each carried a tax. The scarcity of cotton rags was driving the cost of paper up. Labor was expensive and hard to procure. During 1862 the cost of publishing the *Gazette* approximated fifty thousand dollars.[1] In December of that year the annual subscription price of the morning edition was raised from six dollars to eight dollars and that of the evening edition from three dollars to four dollars and a half. The entire income of the *Gazette* from state, county, city, and borough advertising in 1862, however, did not pay the cost of the paper's special telegraphic service for three months. Later in the year the compositors at the *Gazette* office combined with their brethren in the other city offices to strike for higher wages, and before the war was over they were being paid as high as twenty-five dollars a week for their work. In the summer of 1864 the *Gazette* was forced to raise its subscription rates again. The price of the morning edition mounted to ten dollars per year; that of the evening edition to six and a half. At these levels they remained until after the war.

There were other difficulties for the business office to ponder. At intervals the iron hand of military censorship was felt. Early in 1862 the *Gazette* remonstrated at an order from the war department forbidding the press to publish any except officially authorized military dispatches. At the time of the battle of Antietam definite knowledge of what had transpired was held up several days by the action of the military authorities. Now and again the editor complained of the conduct of the Associated Press: its favoritism, its illegibly transcribed dispatches, and its fragmentary reports. The delivery of newspapers outside of the city was another problem. The movements of troops and munitions along the railways choked up the shipment of other articles. As a result newspapers had to take their chance along with other commodities of a non-military nature. Then again, the *Gazette* had to be alert to prevent its compositors from profiting at the expense of its own news-gathering. The *Chronicle* was an habitual offender. On repeated occasions it drew censure from the *Gazette* for borrowing news without acknowledgment.

One thing the war improved—circulation. Thomas Costemagna, the *Gazette's* bookkeeper, was busy with caring for the accounts of the new customers that came to the paper. In 1863 it claimed to have the largest circulation of any of the city papers;

in May, 1864, it reported that the circulation had nearly doubled since the previous December. To take care of this increased demand the management installed at this time one of Hoe's four-cylinder presses, which cost about twelve thousand dollars and was capable of printing ten thousand issues per hour.

It was the policy of the paper to strengthen the hand of the government by all possible means. To this end it interested itself in promoting recruiting. During the first months of the war advertisements for recruits and notices for the sale of military supplies and information about pistols, cartridges, and bayonet scabbards, even red, white, and blue neckties, were to be found in the paper. About the middle of 1862 there were abundant signs that the first enthusiasm had waned. Losing its earlier optimism, the *Gazette* warned its readers that unless the North aroused itself the war was lost. A great mass meeting to inspire recruiting was held on the west common in Allegheny; lists of names of subscribers to volunteer bounty funds were published; a warning was sounded that the draft was imminent. While deprecating the practice of conscription, the *Gazette* could not conceal the pleasure it obtained from witnessing the application of the draft to the noisy anti-war men.

> A certain class of men in this community have been taught to despise and disregard the conscription act, as a tyrannical and unconstitutional measure.... It is this class who endeavor to dodge the enrolling officers by every mean device, and it is this class who threaten violence and bloodshed. We are glad to observe, therefore, that the Provost Marshal of both these districts deal promptly and severely with every man who offers the least obstruction or resistance to the enrollment.[1]

In view of these remarks the community must have found something humorous in the fact that one of the proprietors of the *Gazette* himself fell subject to the draft and was the recipient of grave congratulations from the editor of the *Post* for the good fortune that had befallen him. The *Gazette* did not fail to notice the terrible draft riots that took place in New York City. With a thrust at the "Satanic *Herald*" and the remainder of Gotham's Democratic press, the editor spoke his mind:

> Paris gave law to France in the era of her great revolution, because Paris *was* France. New York, thank God, is not America, and cannot be allowed to give the law to this great country. Woe to her, if there is not conservatism enough in her midst to save her from her own canaille![3]

The *Gazette* also did its part in advertising Cooke's bond drives and encouraging the good work of subsistence committees, sanitary committees, and the United States Christian Commission. Between July 26, 1861 and April 3, 1862, over forty-three thousand soldiers passing through Pittsburgh on the way to the front lines were fed and otherwise cared for by the Pittsburgh subsistence committee. In June, 1864, the Pittsburgh Sanitary Commission undertook to hold a sanitary fair to replenish its exhausted treasury. Full publicity to the opening was given by the *Gazette*. From all around Pittsburgh came large crowds to admire the fair exhibits: Floral Hall with its miniature mountain, Monitor Hall with its miniature lake and Monitor at anchor, the Ladies Bazaar with its children's play house and Chinese pagoda, the art gallery, and the old curiosity shop.

The loyalty of the *Gazette* to the government was not blind loyalty, however. At first it expressed displeasure with those "parlor soldiers" who cried "Forward to Richmond." As time went on it grew more critical of the military leadership of the Army of the Potomac. Regarding McClellan as especially objectionable, the *Gazette* complained bitterly of the "divinity that doth hedge—a General." Reflecting upon the mistakes that had cost the lives of many soldiers, the paper said, by way of admonition: "We tell those in authority that if they will not fight the enemy they shall not murder our men.... many of us have sons and brothers and husbands in the ranks, and it is horrible to think that they are in the hands of a set of incompetent blunderers." [4]

The engagement at Fort Donelson was the first victory of any consequence noted in the paper. With headlines—"Glorious News! Great Victory! Fort Donelson 'Captured!"—the *Gazette* told the story of the long awaited success. The city received the news with open joy. The steamers at the wharf hoisted their colors, thousands of happy townsfolk thronged the levees, and bells rang everywhere. Men stood in the drizzling rain to read of the hostilities in the account that the *Evening Gazette* provided.

At the outset of the conflict the *Gazette* said: "There can be nothing truer than that Slavery was the cause of this war." Acting on this hypothesis, the editorial policy of the paper was exerted in behalf of negro emancipation. In the summer of 1862 it was more insistent than ever on this point. "It is Time"—one editorial fairly besought the president to issue his proclamation at once and strike a mortal blow at the heart of the rebellion. When in September President Lincoln finally announced his intention of taking such action the *Gazette* rejoiced that the country was "out of the wilderness."

Several times during the war the Pittsburgh community was startled by reports that an invading army was approaching. The first scare came in September, 1862, at the time of Lee's first invasion of the North. That it was no chimera of an editor's imagination was demonstrated by the fact that a successful raid on Chambersburg, Pennsylvania, took place at the time. The "rebels" had simply chosen to strike in another direction. In the summer of 1863 the threat became much more real. The North watched with apprehension as Lee moved up the Shenandoah Valley in June. Behind the screen of the mountains he could mask the direction of his blow. If he chose to cross the Pennsylvania border west of the mountains Pittsburgh would most certainly be his first objective. Earlier in the year rebel raiders had penetrated as far as Morgantown. Who could tell? Perhaps Jeb Stuart and his command were already spurring madly in the direction of the Point. Inspired by a sense of public danger, the merchants clubbed together and raised a half million dollars for adequate military defenses. The *Gazette* for its part lost no time in saying:

> Let our entire male population, of town and country, who have sufficient strength to endure a short campaign, rush to the rescue. There is not a day to be lost.... Let the corn take care of itself; let the shop be closed; let that half-erected house stand; let the goods lie on the shelf; in short, let us have a universal Sabbath as to all work except the one of saving our homes from these ruthless invaders.[5]

The appeal was hardly needed. Everywhere men turned out to work on entrenchments. When at length it became manifest that the main body of the Confederates was descending on Gettysburg, the grime-smeared workmen could drop their spades and return to their occupations. For the time being Pittsburgh was safe.

As a strong Union paper, the *Gazette* tirelessly played upon the spirits of its readers to keep their *morale* high. It advised the formation of Union Leagues to counteract the influence of the seditious Knights of the Golden Circle. It recommended a policy of taking no prisoners in retaliation for the treatment accorded negro prisoners by the Confederates. It even accused the chivalrous Lee of beating a female slave and pouring brine upon her wounds. War-time passions ran high: in October, 1863, Pittsburgh was stirred to the uttermost by a newspaper controversy between one of the *Gazette's* readers and the respected Dr. Pershing, the head of the Pittsburgh Female College. Accusing Dr. Pershing of being a "copperhead," the complainant demanded that he be removed from his official position. Pershing replied with a long vindication of himself that satisfied most people that the charges were unfounded. Several heated exchanges ensued, however, before the matter was allowed to die.

The climax of the *Gazette's* political activities came during the presidential election of 1864. During the early stages of the war the editor had looked with contempt upon attempts to replace the Republican party with a Union party that should be broad enough to comprehend the war Democrats. Now that McClellan

was the presidential candidate of the peace Democrats, the *Gazette*
regarded him even more unfavorably than before. As the campaign got under way the atmosphere was burdened with charges
and counter-charges. The *Gazette* regaled its readers with the tale
that McClellan had been found hiding in a gunboat at the time of
a battle. More than that, he had even offered his services to the
Confederacy at the outset of the war! To the soldiers the information was conveyed that the copperheads were in the habit of
alluding to them as "Hell-Hounds." On September 30 a mass
convention of the Union men was held on the west common in
Allegheny. General Negley, Pittsburgh's valiant son, led the
procession thither, and Simon Cameron, the speaker of the day,
recited the issues of the campaign.

The *Gazette* was almost frantic in the warnings it broadcast on
the eve of the election. The vote that would be cast on election
day was the most important that had ever been cast—"more important than was ever cast by man since the world began, and for a
thousand years there may not be the like of it again." [6] It promised
that the result of the morrow's election would determine whether
the government was to survive or perish, and it ventured the
prediction that if McClellan were successful, a period of disorder
would ensue that would make the Reign of Terror in France pale
by comparison. These forebodings were dispelled by the news of
the election. Allegheny County had gone in the right direction
by eight thousand votes. The country had been saved for Lincoln
and the cause of the Union.

Throughout the war the *Gazette* watched anxiously the state
of American foreign relations. While viewing Louis Napoleon, the
emperor of the French, as the country's most dangerous enemy, it
bestowed more attention upon the policies of the British cabinet.
With a hope that goodwill between the two countries might still
continue, the editor permitted himself to feel that the hostility of
the British press was not representative of British opinion as a
whole but only of that of the "cottonarchs." Even at the time of
the Trent Affair, the tone of the *Gazette's* editorials remained

surprisingly moderate. Later, in the face of repeated depredations by British-built cruisers flying the Confederate flag, the *Gazette* changed its course and advised the government at Washington to break off diplomatic relations with Her Majesty's government.

The approaching end of the war was viewed with relief. The long lists of wounded, the descriptions of the bad treatment afforded Union prisoners in southern prisons, the mourning advertisements had been very depressing. Probably a popular song advertised for sale by the *Gazette* in the spring of 1863, "When This Cruel War Is Over," expressed the unconscious yearning of the people. On November 19, 1864, the editor was confident that he was witnessing "The Beginning of the End." Atlanta had fallen, and Sherman was on his way to the sea. Farther north, Grant was striking one sledge-hammer blow after another against the receding line of gray. On April 4, 1865, came at last the news for which the country was waiting; Richmond had fallen; Lee was in full retreat. On April 7 the *Gazette* printed a false rumor that Lee had surrendered, a pardonable slip, considering the state of the public mind. (The *Gazette* had reported the fall of Vicksburg one whole year ahead of time.) Fortunately the event followed hard upon the heels of the rumor.

For a moment Pittsburgh disposed itself to join in the national celebration of the return of peace. Its joy was short lived. The *Gazette* of April 15, 1865, brought tidings of the greatest tragedy yet: "Most Startling News!—President Lincoln and Secretary Seward Assassinated—The President Dying!—The Secretary Will Probably Die!—The President Shot in the Theatre!—Seward Stabbed in his Bed!—Narrow Escape of Gen. Grant—Escape of the Assassins—Wild Excitement in Washington." The headlines went on and on, recounting the sickening details of the sad story.

Adopting the assumption that assassination was the child of slavery, the *Gazette's* editor moved swiftly to lay down the course of action that ought to be followed. There was no element of softness in it, only the spirit of retaliation and reprisal, the product of four years of struggle baptized in bitterness.

The lesson which the hour teaches us is that of stern-
ness. There must be no further thought of mercy to rebels
and traitors. There must be no more pandering to Southern prejudices, no more concessions to southern pride.
The South has provoked its doom, and it cannot be
averted. We must wipe out every vestige of Slavery,
wherever, or in whatever stage it exists. We must teach
the rebellious people of the South that there is nothing for
them but submission or expatriation—that there is no
door open through which they can come back and be as
they were before. If they choose to fight on until they
are wiped out, so be it; if they choose to submit, let them
do it with a full understanding of what is to follow—the
halter to all who have earned it, and disfranchisement to
all who have followed them.[7]

CHAPTER XIII

MID-CENTURY STRIVINGS

> We are not aware of any city in the West where the means of living cheaply, yet comfortably, and even luxuriously, are more abundant than in Pittsburgh.[1]

These were the words of David N. White, the editor of the *Gazette*, in 1844. Pittsburgh had been in the past, if the reports of travelers were to be believed, an expensive market place for those who came to buy. In 1844, however, flour was selling at an average price of $3.75 per barrel, potatoes at 31–31¼ cents per bushel, the best beef at 4–5 cents per pound, chickens at 15–25 cents per pair, eggs at 5–6 cents per dozen, fresh print butter at 10–12½ cents per pound. A new seven-room brick house could be rented a half mile from the center of town for one hundred dollars per year. Armed with information of this kind, the editor felt free to say that the "Birmingham of America" presented lively advantages to eastern men in search of manufacturing sites.

> Our manufactures are in a most promising condition, and so soon as we have the Tariff question settled, which will now soon be, they will increase with unexampled rapidity. We have the whole Southwest, West and Northwest, with their almost illimitable territories, fast filling up with sturdy consumers of our products. The faster they grow the greater will our manufactures expand.... Entrenched behind a barrier which saves us in a great measure from the competition of the unfortunate, half-paid, ill-fed operatives of Europe, we can develope the exhaustless resources of which Western Pennsylvania is possessed.[2]

The *Gazette* was very proud of its position as spokesman for the city—on the one hand giving expression to municipal interests, on the other counteracting the incorrect impressions of Pittsburgh created by alien presses. Even the *Wheeling Times*, an old antagonist, was willing to give the *Gazette* credit for "standing by Pittsburgh through thick and thin." [3]

Only in the midst of a heated political campaign did the editor of the *Gazette* permit himself to forget the commercial character of his paper. At other times he hewed to the line, counseling and encouraging the business men of the community. He might be heard to criticize the policy of maintaining agencies in other cities for Pittsburgh-manufactured articles, because people might not then go to the city; or again, he might conceal his satisfaction in the city's acquisition of a new market house by lamenting the fact that Pittsburgh was the only commercial city of its size in the Union that did not possess a merchant's exchange. In the latter case his criticism had the wholesome effect of inspiring the formation of such an organization within less than a year and a half.

The panic of 1857 brought only a temporary interruption in the uprush of Pittsburgh's trade and business. Widespread were the evidences of war-time prosperity. During the Civil War new capital poured into local manufactures at a great rate. Iron foundries and cotton mills were busy meeting war-time wants. A new business, the oil refining business, was drawing newspaper attention as well. The *Gazette* was troubled by the mad behavior that this inspired. It beheld everywhere "the disposition ... manifested by those who have money, to spend it lavishly in the gratification of personal vanity, their appetites, love of display, etc.... Fashion rules the hour, and extravagance ... the market."[4] Taking the view that economy was a necessity, the editor urged everyone to get out of debt before it was too late, and to invest only in prime necessities and to anticipate the "harder times to come."

The *Gazette* was embarrassed by the rise of organized labor. It opposed the introduction of the ten-hour day into the Allegheny cotton mills until the eastern mills were ready to take an equivalent step, and so when in 1845 and again in 1848 factory riots arose over this issue, the *Gazette* was very severe upon the "infuriated Amazons" who led the way to the destruction of property. The

Post, on the contrary, rallied to the side of the strikers and defended their resort to force. Withal the *Gazette* tried hard to remain fair to the strikers, even though it could not sympathize with their aims. Indeed it went so far as to say to them on one occasion:

> One of the charges alleged against your employers is, that they have gone into the newspapers with their statement, while you are precluded from doing the same on account of the expense! Now we promise you that, while we will make your employers pay for every line published in our paper, we will publish your replies, of equal length for nothing.[5]

The newspaper business itself was not exempt from the pressure of labor difficulties. In 1852 the newspapers were greatly hampered by a general strike proclaimed by the printers' union. The *Gazette* made no complaint until some months later, when it printed an advertisement asking for the services of five or six journeymen compositors. The editor explained that he had been abandoned by his help after he had refused to surrender the management of his office to the control of the printers' union. Only the commercial reporter, the local news reporter, and three apprentices had remained. The editor also intimated that if the worst came to the worst, he might be disposed to employ women compositors!

The traditional interest of the *Gazette* in transportation persisted. During the forties the merits of plank roads were considered; for local traffic the editor considered them superior to railroads. The early enthusiasm for canals had waned, but river news was a conspicuous feature. The river brought raw materials to Pittsburgh's factories, and carried away to downriver ports Pittsburgh-made tools, glassware, and a hundred other accessories. Steamboat explosions and the brawls of boat gangs; low-water stages at various points and the petty meannesses of the Wheeling merchants—all were noted in the *Gazette*. In the latter part of 1852 Congress passed a new steamboat law requiring lifeboats on all river craft. The boating fraternity along the Ohio River was greatly annoyed:

> Imagine, they say one of our little "dinkies," drawing 18 inches water, "wrecked" on a "bar" in the Ohio.... The stout-throated captain ... cries, "Man the Life Boat!" and presently the passenger-saver cleaves the roaring billows which lash the sides of the ill-fated "dinkey...." in a short time the affrighted passengers are landed on the shore, blessing Congress for having thus interposed to save them from the horrors of shipwreck. After the "life boat" has thoroughly performed its mission, the Captain probably wades ashore, without taking off his boots.[6]

The editor of the *Gazette*, however, did not adopt the same attitude, and he commented that "Too much protection cannot be afforded to passengers on steamboats.... Thousands of lives have been lost on the western waters for want of such means of deliverance as life-boats afford." [7]

Before the end of the period it became apparent that changes were in process that might reduce river navigation to a position of secondary importance. Dwelling on the importance of western trade in the year 1859, the *Gazette* called attention to the fact that business firms were no longer willing to wait through periods of drought until river navigation could be resumed. A steadily increasing railroad traffic between Pittsburgh and Chicago supplied their needs.

It was an ingrained habit born of business tradition and state pride for the *Gazette* and its merchant friends to look to Philadelphia for guidance in undertaking transportation projects. Consequently the reluctance of the Quaker capitalists to unloose their purse strings promptly and liberally in support of a railroad irritated the expectant Pittsburghers beyond measure. With many a taunt directed at Philadelphia's strange apathy, the *Gazette* began in 1845 to direct attention to the Baltimore and Ohio Railroad, now slowly creeping west. Pittsburgh, Wheeling, and Parkersburg were all rated as eligible locations for the western terminus of the line. Might not the possibility of Pittsburgh being chosen frighten Philadelphia into building a feeder line to join the Baltimore line and so promote its rapid construction to Pittsburgh? It was essential that the Baltimore and Ohio Railroad be given a liberal right of way across Pennsylvania. Turning to the Philadelphia press, the *Gazette* asked in challenging fashion: "What say you, gentlemen of the United States Gazette, North American, Inquirer, and Ledger?" [8]

The replies were not reassuring. The *North American* thought better of a line built directly from Philadelphia to Pittsburgh. The *Gazette* scowled at this, for such a project would consume a decade at the very least. The *North American* seemed to be in no haste to take action. The *United States Gazette* was even less desirous of making itself agreeable. Exhibiting a haughty mien toward these gibbering Pittsburghers, it dourly predicted that Parkersburg, Virginia, must be the eventual western termination for the Baltimore and Ohio. Pittsburgh might even count herself lucky to be on the line of a western railroad from Philadelphia.

Such words carried no message of good cheer for the *Gazette*. As Philadelphia's opposition to the right of way became manifest in the legislature at Harrisburg the editor complained that the state capitol was filled with "borers" against the road from Philadelphia. He went on to declare:

> If the bill is defeated through the machinations of Philadelphia, the sudden upheaving of a volcano on the Allegheny mountains would not astonish them more than the demonstrations—the moral earthquake—they will hear of from some twelve to fifteen counties in this section of the State. The excitement is indeed most intense. Nothing like it has been known for many years.[9]

When the Right-of-Way Bill was defeated by one vote in the state senate, the excitement was redoubled. White advised a fresh submission of the bill:

> We now warn Philadelphia, that if she persists in her course, and succeeds in defeating the bill, she will call

down upon her head the hearty and permanent *dislike*—
to use a mild word—of the whole community of Western
Pennsylvania, a dislike which will not die away in a few
weeks or months, *but will exist as long as the effects of the
injury inflicted.* This dislike—we may call it *hatred*—for
it will lead to that, will manifest itself in a thousand
ways,—in business, in social relations, in the legislative
halls. Opposition to Philadelphia will become a part of
the settled policy of the west, overriding even state
partialities and party lines.[10]

During the next few days, western Pennsylvania broke out in a
rash of public meetings. A blaze of excitement "very near akin to
a revolution," in White's words, swept over the region. At a
meeting in Allegheny on April 8, 1846, Walter Forward was
reputed to have declared that no earthly power had a right to say
that the people of western Pennsylvania must trade alone with
Philadelphia. To forbid a railroad connection with Baltimore,
New York, or any other place was "to usurp our natural rights
and render us serfs and slaves to Philadelphia." Derisive fun was
had at the expense of the "Celestial City" and the "Mandarins
of Philadelphia."

About this time an investigation disclosed the fact that in
1843 the legislature of Pennsylvania had chartered a railroad line
to be known as the Pittsburgh and Connellsville Railroad. Why
should not this line be constructed to join the Baltimore and Ohio
at the state line and continue to Pittsburgh? When wails arose
from the Philadelphia press at this "fraudulent" evasion, White
observed calmly that the Philadelphia brethren had simply been
caught napping. With considerable elation, he urged the opening
of subscription books for stock sales. Just when it seemed that at
last a complete understanding between Baltimore and Pittsburgh
had been reached, the Baltimore capitalists suddenly began to
display an unaccountable coolness. In view of this, the Pittsburgh
directors decided to call a halt on the enterprise for the time being.
Assuring himself that Baltimore was a heartless flirt, White concluded that Pittsburgh must turn elsewhere. There were indica-

tions that Philadelphia was now at length awakening from her deep sleep.

In November, 1846, White began to see the possibilities of a western railroad (perhaps to St. Louis). Indeed, he said, it was now ten times more important for the eastern cities to have railroad connections with Pittsburgh than *vice versa*. If, moreover, Pittsburgh succeeded early in garnering the trade of the West by a chain of artfully planned railroads, she would have a weapon for bargaining that might be used on the East. According to White the amount of agitation in Pittsburgh for a western railroad was increasing every day. For a time the *Gazette* interested itself in drumming up sentiment for a Pittsburgh-Cleveland line. Finally it identified itself with the movement for a great central railroad extending from Philadelphia to St. Louis. To the north, the Erie Railroad was threading its way across New York state to Dunkirk; to the south, the Baltimore and Ohio was forcing its way up the mountain grades toward Wheeling. Already men were saying that St. Louis was destined to be the eastern terminus of a transcontinental railroad. A letter from one of the *Gazette's* readers in Canton, Ohio, indicates the undercurrent of feeling:

> Some may sneer, and others may say, "well, it will do to talk about, but you and I never shall see a railroad to the Pacific ocean." So I once heard people talk about "De Witt Clinton's Big Ditch," and where now are such croakers? Mark it, sir, ten years will not pass by, before there is a good portion of the great National railroad from St. Louis to the Pacific in use, and if so, who can set bounds to the value of the stock of your great central railroad from Pittsburgh to St. Louis, through the heart of Ohio, Indiana and Illinois.[11]

The *Gazette* was in full sympathy with the views of its correspondent. Loudly it shrilled:

> If the people of Allegheny are not stark blind they cannot fail to see the effect of longer procrastination.... *Action*, action, ACTION, is what we want now....
> Let not then the golden opportunity about to be pre-

sented to us be lost. Let the aid asked be given, and a
subscription be made for prosecuting our share of the great
Road now in course of construction.[12]

The force of these words sank deeply into the public mind. On
May 30, 1848, a meeting of Allegheny County's taxable citizens
placed the resources of the county behind the central railroad.
There had been so much empty talk about railroads that existed
only on paper that a real sense of surprise must have been occasioned when the news drifted into the *Gazette* office one summer
day in 1851 that something was doing over on the Ohio and
Pennsylvania line. The story concerned the first excursion trip
over the line out of Pittsburgh. As an invited guest of the railroad
on the occasion, White reported:

> This is a novel announcement in a Pittsburgh paper,
> but one which is to become common hereafter, as much
> so as a steamboat trip. On Saturday afternoon, the first
> railroad excursion ever made from the city of Pittsburgh,
> took place on the Ohio and Pennsylvania Railroad from
> here to Rochester, at the mouth of the Beaver.... Al-
> though we stopped frequently, from various causes ...
> we made the trip, of 25 miles, to Rochester, in one hour
> and forty-five minutes. Returning, it was necessary to
> run slowly, as it was quite dark part of the way, and we
> had the locomotive behind us, pushing us along—not a
> very safe way of travelling; but we arrived safe at the
> Federal street station about nine o'clock, having been
> absent about four hours and a half. We found the road in
> excellent order, considering that the laying of the iron is
> just finished, and the track is not brought into proper
> running order. We have travelled over the best roads
> east, and seldom have found one smoother than this in
> its present unfinished state.[13]

Ten days later the "Grand Opening" of the road was celebrated. Drawn by the locomotive, "Salem," the first train, with
four hundred guests on board, puffed out of Pittsburgh in sight
of cheering thousands, outstripping some young gallants on horseback, and scuttled along to New Brighton, the point to which the

road had been built at that time. There was a dinner at the Merrick House; there were many toasts and speeches. On the way back to Pittsburgh that evening the engineer decided to show his guests what a speed demon they were riding on, so he opened the throttle wide and let his engine thunder along at the awe-inspiring rate of twenty-five miles per hour! A regular schedule of train service between Pittsburgh and New Brighton was thus inaugurated. One train left the Federal Street station at 10 A. M. each day, and set out from New Brighton for the return trip at "2½ P. M."

With almost the interest of a proprietor, White followed carefully the reports of the westward progress of the Ohio and Pennsylvania Railroad. Flattered by his attention the railroad did its best to reciprocate. When in April, 1852, service was resumed on the line after an interruption caused by floods, S. W. Roberts, the superintendent, took pains to address a letter to White apprising him of the fact. In the autumn of that year, White was asked by the railroad to act as its delegate to an important railroad convention in Warsaw, Indiana. He also promoted the development of the Connellsville line to the South. In the spring of 1853 he even took the trouble to accompany several of the directors on a trip to Baltimore in order to obtain more substantial backing for the road. The journey had its unpleasant side: when the editor and his companions arrived in Martinsburg at breakfast time they trudged into a tavern only to find a scarcity of seats, food, and conveniences of all kinds.

> What [food] there was, was only half cooked, and was served up in a slovenly manner. I secured a cup of a dirty looking liquid they called coffee, to which the addition of some sky-blue milk gave the appearance of dish-water. For this and a small piece of parboiled beef, and a piece of bread, I was charged 50 cents. Many got nothing. This mockery of a breakfast over, we again started at our old slow gait, and finally arrived at this city about 4 o'clock this afternoon having been 20 hours in the cars between Cumberland and Baltimore.[14]

In the East, Philadelphia had at last fallen under the railroad spell and was building to Pittsburgh. On December 11, 1851, the *Gazette* noted that except for a brief distance supplied with stages the entire route to Philadelphia was open for railroad traffic. It was not until a year later (November 29, 1852) that the first railroad train from the East, making use of the inclined planes as did the canal boats, reached Pittsburgh. In 1854 the inclined planes were abandoned, and a tunnel was substituted. Complacently the *Gazette* remarked, "Fifteen hours from Pittsburgh to Philadelphia ought to satisfy the fastest of this fast generation." [15]

The *Gazette's* advocacy of railroads caused stories to be passed about that financial inducement had secured its support. Both White and Errett snapped back that such accusations were ridiculous. White rejoined that the railroads had even been slow to settle up for paid advertising in the paper, and Errett demonstrated by his criticisms of railroad rate discriminations against Pittsburgh that the paper was by no means wedded to the railroad interests.

In many ways the *Gazette* taxed its energies to make midcentury Pittsburgh a better city in which to live. At the time of the great fire of 1845, it showed its capacity for public service. Beginning in an old frame shed on the east side of Ferry Street, the fire picked up momentum from a high wind and swept through the heart of the city on April 10, 1845. At six o'clock that evening in the midst of all this, editor White sat down at his desk "with a sad heart," to pen the details of "the most fearful calamity which ever befell any city the size of Pittsburgh."

> While we now write, an awful fire is raging, consuming the fairest portion of our city, and no human being can tell where it will stay its ravages. It has now been burning for six hours, and confusion reigns extreme, and it cannot be expected we shall give anything like a particular statement of a calamity so extensive and involving such fearful ruins. [16]

Before the fire was checked it had converted fifty-six acres of city into a smoking mass of ruins and caused a property loss ranging between three and four million dollars.

Once the shock was over, the *Gazette*, relying on "the indomitable energy and spirit" of the merchants, began to preach recovery. The city's natural resources, manufactures, and markets were not destroyed. "All we want is capital. Give us a sufficiency of capital to develop and keep in activity all our resources, and the late fire will be remembered ... only as some disagreeable dream."[17] Ingenious rumors must be combatted as well. The *Gazette* was quick to undeceive editors from far and near who looked upon Pittsburgh as a "doomed city." Grocers and commission merchants had resumed business as rapidly as possible, new stocks were substituted for burnt ones, hotel accommodations for travelers were more abundant than before. Everywhere was the sound of hammers, the rattling of timber, and the laughter of Irish workmen. A Cleveland newspaper man who visited the city three years after the disastrous fire frankly marveled at the "energy and enterprise" evinced by "a people who can build a city desolated by fire as this was three years ago." To ward off a future calamity of the kind the *Gazette* stressed the necessity of precautionary measures. Wooden structures were a perpetual fire hazard. The new buildings should be made fireproof by arching with brick. The fire-fighting facilities of the city had not been very efficient. More apparatus, new fire plugs, and larger water mains would go far to remove future danger.

The paper also recognized the need of public sanitation. In an article on the housing situation written in 1846, White declared:

> We wish to call the attention of those about to build tenements to one thing which is totally neglected. We mean *Baths*. How many out of the thousands of houses in and about Pittsburgh, are furnished with this indispensible necessary to health and the enjoyment of life? ...
> The working people need them more than others....
> Just convince them that by the free use of the Bath,

they could save many a dollar that goes for Patent
Medicines and Doctor's bills, and they would pay a little
more rent with a hearty good will....

We are surprised that three large Hotels have been
built since the Great Fire, without any provision of this
kind, that we know of. A suite of Baths should be just as
much a part of a Hotel in a city like this, as a suit of
Parlors.[18]

With impartial vigor, the paper attacked such public nuisances as
the imperfectly ventilated Allegheny County Courthouse and the
droves of hogs infesting the city's streets and alleys. In April,
1856, the paper conducted a campaign for cleaning up the public
streets and was rewarded for its enterprise by a round of public
applause.

During epidemics of diseases such as Asiatic Cholera the
Gazette did its best to keep up the public *morale*. In the absence of
a board of health, it attempted to furnish case statistics; it ran
series of articles on cholera treatment; it warned against intemperance and careless diet. Sometimes its own facilities were
impaired by the panic. Once in 1854, for example, after several
frightened hands had "taken to the woods," the paper had to
apologize for a sparseness of news. The havoc wrought by the
destroyer was swift and severe. Without exaggeration, the *Gazette*
spoke of one visitation:

> When the plague raged most fearfully in London, that
> town could not have worn a more pestilential appearance
> than Birmingham did yesterday. The people gathered in
> knots of four or five, round the huge fires which were
> burning in the streets, some built of coal, others of tar
> and rosin, while the streets wore almost a wintry aspect,
> in spite of the fire and smoke, owing to the quantity of
> lime scattered all around....
>
> Several instances have occurred in which men, while
> walking through the streets, have been attacked, and
> dropped down as though struck by lightning. Whole
> families have been carried off, and there seems no end to
> this deplorable state of things.[19]

Comic relief was offered by a story told of a man whose body was found lying in front of the Allegheny Market House. Convinced that he had fallen victim to the cholera, the curious crowds preserved a respectable distance. After some hours the supposed corpse stirred, flopped around a bit, and at length teetered unsteadily away, evidently little the worse for the drunken stupor.

Crime was still looked upon by the editor as a cancerous growth upon the body politic rather than as news:

> We avoid giving the details, generally, of the numerous murders and fearful crimes which take place in our country, except when we think there may be some good effect produced by the fearful example, or when there is some circumstance connected with the tragedy of an extraordinary character.[20]

Thus spoke the *Gazette* in 1846. Many papers had cast such ideals to the wind. When in 1857 the *Gazette* returned to a statement of similar views, the *Journal*, a sister paper, resented what seemed criticism of its own course and by its retorts created a controversy among the city newspapers as to the respectability of crime news.

Certain it was that crimes of violence were on the increase in Pittsburgh. The whole gamut of human depravity from petty thievery to murder was run in the news column. One reads of horse and buggy thieves and confidence men, of wild fights among the boatmen on the Ohio River, and of affrays between members of the local fire companies rushing to the scene of a fire. In 1853 White observed with grave concern: "The frequency of riots, broils, stabbings, shootings, and murders, is really appalling; but not more so to us, than the indifference with which these things are looked upon by the community." [21]

Naturally the police came in for some share of the blame. "A Householder" who wrote to the *Gazette* in 1844 enlarged upon the fact that in the days when the city was without police of any kind, robbery and burglary were almost unheard of, but now, with these officers added, a succession of such crimes took place every week. Perhaps the small number of the guardians of the law was the cause of their inefficiency. In 1848 the local editor of the *Gazette* freely expressed the opinion that the police force of Allegheny was "scarcely sufficient to guard a country village." In March of '61 the paper suggested a measure to improve the situation:

> There are many reasons why the Night Police should be uniformed. Strangers arriving in the city after night, and others who are not familiar with the streets and localities, would feel much safer in making application to a person whose clothing clearly indicated his position, than to an ill-favored individual with a club in his hand, who might or might not turn out to be an officer.[22]

The *Gazette's* interest in the cause of social reform in general was selective and preferential. It had little regard, for example, for the schemes of Fourier, Robert Owen, and the other Utopian socialists: socialism was visionary, unfitted for men, dangerous in its effects, and impossible. For the cause of women's rights the paper evinced somewhat more enthusiasm. White was willing to grant that women were regarded by the law as having little more capacity for caring for themselves than children or idiots; but he asserted that it was wrong to drop all distinctions between the sexes.

Temperance and penal reform were much nearer the heart of the editor. He had good words for the results of the periodical visits of John B. Gough, the famous temperance lecturer; and when the prohibition movement of the fifties reached Pittsburgh, the *Gazette* enlisted under the banner of Neal Dow, its leader. The *Post* took the opposite side. In both the elections of 1853 and 1854 the prohibition question was prominently featured. During the latter election Pennsylvania conducted a statewide referendum on the issue of prohibition. While the reformers were defeated only by a narrow margin, the *Gazette* had to admit outright defeat, for the majority against prohibition in Allegheny County had been greater than the majority against prohibition in the whole state.

The paper's efforts in behalf of penal reform were more productive. When Dorothea Dix, the famous reformer, visited Pittsburgh in 1845 she cast a searchlight upon the unspeakable treatment accorded the inmates of prisons and poorhouses. White admitted that Miss Dix's "truly painful account" was enough to make him blush for humanity's sake. At the time, Pittsburgh was without an asylum to house the insane. While directing publicity to the need for such an institution, the *Gazette* conducted a further examination into the conditions of local penal discipline. A masterpiece of description came from the pen of Russell Errett in January, 1858:

> As soon as you enter the jail, there is a cell, gloomy and bare, with a thick grated door.... An object is lying on the floor at the further end which ... we discover to be—*a man*. Yes, a maniac.... This man, stalled like a *wild beast*, this naked and chained maniac, this fellow being who has committed the crime of losing his reason, this creature chained in a cell like a tiger, walked out to the cell door and peeped from his glaring eye-balls upon the crowd. His whole bare body was covered with filth. ... When his convulsions would possess him, or his quick wild fancy conjured up from the darkness of his prison, the devils with which he protested his cell was swarning, his very flesh would creep up into knots on his limbs as if it were full of serpents and his eyes glared with an expression of intense terror superadded to the madness which tore his brain and kindled it into rapt fury. In this cell we could see no clothing, no bedding, no utensil of any sort—there the bare wall and the stone floor, the chain and the manacles, were the luxuries of this poor man, bereft of reason....
>
> In the name of Heaven why is that poor maniac, whom they call "George," in that jail? ... Why is he not taken from his torments and placed under the kind hand of the physician ... We have done our duty in the premises, and we ask the public, the benevolent, those whose duty it is to take cognizance of such matters, to look into this terrible case and right it.[28]

As a sequel to this impassioned editorial the poor man was removed from the jail by order of the prison physician and given special care. Three years later Dixmont, a special hospital for the treatment of the insane, was opened near Pittsburgh.

As before, the *Gazette* continued to reflect the paramount interest of its readers in religion and morals; to sanction the blue laws and the spirit that brought them into being. When the stockholders of the Pennsylvania Railroad voted to run Sunday trains, White was convinced that they had decided unwisely, and he hoped that after the road was finished they would reconsider the decision. To the irreverent there must have been some humor in the fact that in 1846 J. Heron Foster, editor of the *Dispatch*, sued White and Harris for violating the statute against Sunday labor by employing typesetters on that day. White was very angry at what he termed a malicious prosecution:

> It is probably known to most of our readers that it is customary to work on the Sabbath in the offices of nearly all of the Morning Daily papers in the country.... It is done, we believe, in every morning office in this city, except ours—Certain it is that it is done by the prosecutors in this case.[14]

On March 13, 1844, a letter was printed in the *Gazette* that posed an interesting problem:

> Mr. Editor:—
> I was glad to see in your paper, a day or two since, a brief notice of the Mercantile Library of Philadelphia and New York ... why is it that, as a city, we are so far behind in all those things which tend to elevate and refine the public taste? We have no public library, no Gallery of Paintings, no Museum, no Cabinet of Minerals, in fine, nothing of a public character to which the citizens generally can resort, either for amusement or instruction; Will not some of our wealthy men set themselves to correct these evils? In the East it is a common thing for men of rather moderate abilities to give from $1000 to $10,000 for public libraries. Where is the man among us who will make a beginning? Where is the citizen of this community who will come forward and lay the foundation of some public institution which will remain as a monument

of his munificence long after he shall have been gathered
to the generation of his fathers?

One wonders if the youthful Carnegie read those lines. True it
was, as the editor of the *Gazette* admitted, that the pursuit of
material wealth had caused the busy populace to overlook the
possibilities that lay in the realm of arts and letters. In 1849 the
reviewer of one of Fleming's performances of *Hamlet* took it upon
himself to say:

> We are positively ashamed of Pittsburgh. Night after
> night, for weeks in succession, a company of minstrels
> with their burlesque exhibitions of negro eccentricities,
> will draw crowded houses, but when a truly intellectual
> feast is presented to our citizens, the performer finds be-
> fore him a "beggarly account" of empty benches.[25]

Music seems to have been the favored art in the city during
these years. The excellence of Pittsburgh's musical authorship
was a matter for newspaper comment, and many concert musicians
of note included Pittsburgh on their itinerary. Probably Pittsburgh's greatest musical event during this period was the visit of
Jenny Lind in 1851. The *Gazette* had been full of references to her
ever since her arrival in New York the year before. The fact that
Phineas T. Barnum was her sponsor promised excitement for all.
The Pittsburgh concert was very pleasing. The "Swedish Night-
ingale" responded to her audience's wishes by trilling her famous
Bird Song and *Home Sweet Home*. Unfortunately, at the end of the
concert a disturbance agitated the modest Jenny, and she made a
hasty departure from the city. Soon the story was going around
the country that Jenny Lind had been terribly insulted by the
people of Pittsburgh. The *Gazette* went lustily to work to stop
this slander. It explained that the crowd had simply wanted to
obtain an unobstructed view of the singer. A few inconsiderate
youths, it was true, had cast pebbles against her windows, but no
glass had been broken. A French newspaper had magnified the
incident by alleging that "the gamins of Pittsburgh" had stoned
the singer's carriage and had even carried their want of decency

as far as to throw stones at her "*bed-chamber windows*." This, said the *Gazette*, was unequivocally false.

In 1858 the city of Pittsburgh celebrated the fact that it had become a centenarian—in the words of the editor, a great city with "stately edifices and sumptuous mansions," with huge factories and seventy "Temples of the Living God." Yet it still had some of the characteristics of a small town:

> The society of Pittsburgh is of a social, genial, cast, the stiffness and formality of large cities not being felt in our more hospitable community. Our people resemble, in some respects, more those of a borough than a city, there being the same free and candid interchange of feeling and sentiment.[26]

There were those, nevertheless, who were troubled by the social requirements prescribed by an hastening urbanization. In 1859 the editor was appealed to by a certain "Mary Jane," a self-constituted representative of the young women of the town. Mary Jane lamented that considerations of propriety restrained her and hundreds of her kind from going unescorted to lectures and other worth while entertainment in default of an invitation from a member of the other sex. The editor assured her that in his opinion it was no more improper for her to go unescorted to a lecture than it was to go to church in similar fashion. But "William," a self-confessed admirer of Mary Jane, altered the basis of the discussion by explaining in a letter to the paper that it was the expense of hiring a carriage (from three to five dollars) that discouraged him and his acquaintances from offering chivalrous attentions to the fairer sex. The average annual income of a young man, said William testily, ranged from eight hundred to one thousand dollars; the conventions of the time would fain bankrupt him.

Already the bugles of '61 were sounding, and William was soon to rush away to the battlefield, whence he would write back vastly different letters to his Mary Jane. Pittsburgh's metropolitan period was about to begin. The Age of Steel was in the near future—a future that was to see poured into the city's lap such wealth and power as it had never known before.

PART IV—1866–1900

THE STALWART

CHAPTER XIV

THE REIGN OF REED

One May morning in the year 1866 four men of varying ages walked into the old *Gazette* office at 86 Fifth Street and looked over the plant with the appraising eyes of new owners. They had just purchased the establishment—lock, stock, and barrel—for the surprisingly moderate sum of ten thousand dollars. Within a month's time they were to sell enough discarded machinery and supplies scattered about the press and composing rooms to reimburse them in full for their outlay. F. B. Penniman, the senior partner, was known to be a veteran newspaper man. Josiah King, the builder of the old Eagle cotton mills, was reputed to be one of Pittsburgh's leading merchants, having made successful ventures in the wholesale grocery and oil business. For two years he had been directly connected with the paper as president of the Gazette Publishing Association. Thomas Houston and Nelson P. Reed completed the quartet of men, all highly respected in the community for their business ability and native acumen.

With the passage of years the composition of the firm was subjected to many changes. When Penniman retired from the business in 1870, the firm name was altered from Penniman, Reed & Co. to King, Reed & Co. Henry M. Long, D. L. Fleming, and George W. Reed, the last a brother of the junior partner, were all newcomers in the business during the seventies. But Long and Fleming were only briefly connected with the paper. Houston himself died in 1875, and his interest passed into the hands of the surviving partners. In 1877 the *Gazette* proceeded to add another to the long list of Pittsburgh papers that it has absorbed. This time it was the *Commercial*, a sound morning competitor started during the dark days of the Civil War by C. D. Brigham and widely known for its outspoken Republicanism and distinguished editorial page. After the acquisition the paper adopted the title of the *Commercial Gazette*.

Early in the next decade the *Gazette* firm was again reorganized. At the time of Josiah King's death in 1882 a new publishing group was formed—Nelson P. Reed and Company.—It included the three Reed brothers, Nelson, George W., and Joseph P., as the chief proprietors. From that time until 1900 the *Gazette* remained substantially in the hands of the Reed family. Frank W. Higgins, for a brief time the head of the composing room, held a part interest in the paper from 1883 to 1887, but this was reabsorbed after his death.

It should be clearly understood that by this time a new era in newspaper management had been reached. No longer was the editor practically supreme in control. The impersonal and commercial journalism characteristic of the times had done away with that. Although a succession of editors found employment with the *Gazette* after 1866, one man, irrespective of the changes, continued at his desk—the business manager, Nelson P. Reed. No longer was the *Gazette* the personal venture of a cruising editor. It was now an expanding business concern, which required an able executive to oversee the many details of news gathering and newspaper distribution.

From the very first, young Reed had fitted into his position beautifully. When he first became connected with the *Gazette* he was looked upon by the editor of the Pittsburgh *Leader* as "a young man of extraordinary energy and resources." He was born in Butler County on August 14, 1841, and after a preliminary education at Butler Academy he started to work for his father, Major George Reed, who was county treasurer at the time. Then came the Civil War. Would "Nelse" Reed join the local company of volunteers that was being formed? It was easier to say yes than no. Private Reed marched away in answer to the president's call and saw considerable service before a shot laid him low at Antietam. He was trundled back home to recover from his wound. There the fancy to take up a business course struck him. Soon he was in Pittsburgh, where he enrolled in a bookkeeping course at Duff's Commercial College. He speedily obtained employment at the provost marshal's office. From there he went to the Pittsburgh *Dispatch* as business manager and built up the prosperity of the paper considerably before participating in the deal with the *Gazette*.[1]

Reed occupied his first years with the *Gazette* in coöperating with King and the others to administer tonics to their debilitated patient. The old *Gazette* was far from being in a prosperous condition in 1866. The war had impressed upon local citizens a sense of the value of a daily newspaper as a medium for news, but Pittsburgh business men were still woefully indifferent. It was Reed's aim to make the *Gazette* a thoroughly equipped and reliable business journal. In this he succeeded so well that in the course of time the paper came to yield him a princely income. From 1883 until he was stricken by a fatal attack of grippe in 1891, he was the actual head of both the business department and the editorial page of the paper, and every division felt the impress of his control. It was his forte to bear responsibilities with unruffled poise and unshaken nerve. Yet his manners were simple and frank, and his kindness of heart was proverbial. At all times he conversed freely with and was closely in touch with all members of his staff. An excellent judge of men, he kept around him a continuous corps of trusted employees, who enjoyed his remarkably keen sense of humor and liked him all the more for his hearty booming laugh that echoed and reechoed through the office corridors.

His nephew and son-in-law, Alfred Reed, was his immediate successor in the control of the *Gazette*. The younger Reed, after graduating from the University of Pennsyslvania in the late eighties, started in at the newspaper office as reporter and typesetter. From this he matriculated into the field of writing "minion" editorials. Having served his apprenticeship, he was prepared to succeed his uncle in the management of the paper and to exercise a controlling interest in it, which he did until its sale in 1900. On at least one occasion, his earlier experience proved very serviceable for at one time, during a printers and typographers' strike in the middle nineties, the newspaper was put out for several days by the lone efforts of Mr. Reed, the foreman of the printing office, and one other helper.

Notwithstanding the fact that the *Gazette* was not the vehicle of expression for a great editor's personality in these years, it enlisted some able editorial talent. Penniman was chief editor at first, "the ablest and most polished writer on this side of the Alleghenies" according to one journalistic contemporary.[3] After his retirement, Josiah King took over the duties of editor-in-chief and remained in that capacity, at least nominally, until his death in 1882. Most of the actual work of writing editorials was probably performed by others. Houston acted as associate editor with King, even as he had with Penniman. Henry M. Long and the Reverend Jonathan Vannote also took their turn at fashioning editorials during the seventies. When the *Commercial* was taken into camp, Russell Errett came over from the office of the *Commercial* to supervise the editorial work of the *Commercial Gazette;* but after his re-election to Congress in 1878, he had to put down his editorial pen because of the pressure of political duties. This defection was unfortunate, but happily about the same time William P. Anderson joined the staff of the *Gazette* and remained the chief editorial writer of the paper throughout the Reed *régime*.

The life of a newspaper editor in the eighteen seventies hardly conformed with modern conceptions of what it should have been. The conveniences of arrangement to be seen in the newspaper office of today were for the most part unknown. The large egg-shaped stove, the ample coal box, and the equally ample wood box half filled with sawdust and toby stumps were the familiar furnishings of the composing room, which, as the one place in a morning newspaper office that was always occupied, was in winter the most comfortably heated room in the building. Not infrequently Vannote, while associate editor, would enter a city pulpit on Sunday morning and then, after the sermon, make his way to the *Gazette* office to write a leader for Monday morning's paper. Since the fire in the sanctum was likely to be unlighted, he would, if the morning were frosty, go to the composing room; there, seated in a sagging split-bottom chair with his feet on the coal box near the stove and a pad of paper across his knees, he directed his thoughts to the editorial blast for the morrow.

When Reed took over the entire direction of the paper in 1882, he delegated the task of writing editorials to others, although he insisted that their policy agree with his own. In one instance, however, he encountered a will as strong as his own. James F. Hudson, for a short time managing editor of the *Gazette,* was reading copy one morning, when the chief owner dropped a poem from a Butler County friend on the desk with a note directing its insertion in the paper. Hudson looked it over but, failing to detect any merit in the verses, rejected it. The next day Mr. Reed with characteristic bluntness demanded of Hudson, "Jim, who's running this paper, you or I?" "Well if you put it that way," replied Hudson, "I should say you are," whereupon he reached for his hat and coat and left the office, never to return.

The post of managing editor in the *Gazette* organization seems to have been specially created by Reed. Its first tenant was Frank M. Higgins, a native of Huntingdon, Pennsylvania, and a graduate of Bucknell. Higgins, after a try at the ministry, turned to journalism. His ability was demonstrated by his excellent record with the *Genius of Liberty*, a Uniontown newspaper published in 1882 and 1883. He moved to Pittsburgh to step into his new post in 1883, but his death in 1887 terminated his promising career. A successor was found in Henry Jones Ford, who came to the *Gazette* with the most cosmopolitan experience of any newspaper man since the days of Erastus Brooks. Ford was born in Baltimore in 1851. After graduating from Baltimore City College he became an editorial writer on the Baltimore *American* in 1872. As city editor of the Baltimore *Sun* and later managing editor of the *American* he added to his journalistic experience. In 1879 he went off to New York to enter the office of the New York *Sun*, one of the best schools of journalism the country has ever known. For four years Ford wrote editorials under the tutelage of the great Charles A. Dana. After further experience with the Baltimore *Sun* he invaded the Pittsburgh newspaper world and was rewarded with the post of managing editor of the *Gazette*. He remained in that position until 1892, when Nelson Reed's death brought Alfred Reed to the fore and induced a change of managing editors.[3]

Robert Simpson, his successor, once referred to as "one of the best known newspaper writers in western Pennsylvania," was a Canadian by birth. During the oil-boom days of the early seventies, he made his way to Oil City and took a job in the composing room of the Oil City *Derrick*. In 1886 he became attached to the staff of the Pittsburgh *Dispatch*. Shortly afterwards he undertook to act as political writer and legislative correspondent for the *Gazette*. During several legislative sessions at Harrisburg he made a notable record in that rôle. From 1892 to 1900 he acted as the *Gazette's* managing editor, subject to general directions from the chief owner, Alfred Reed.

A great many other interesting personalities were identified with the *Gazette* in the twilight years of the century. There was Josiah Copley, a connection of the Thaw family, whose career as editorial writer and contributor to the *Gazette* extended, except for long interruptions due to ill health, over the period from 1838 until 1885. As a young man he had been a partner in a printing business in Kittanning, Pennsylvania, and he was one of the editors of the Kittanning *Gazette* for eight years. In later life he wrote several books of a religious nature. *Gatherings in Beulah* (1878) is probably the best known.

John N. Hazlett, later the very forceful city editor of the *Dispatch*, served his apprenticeship as a reporter on the *Gazette* for some years, beginning in 1866. In the early eighties three Pittsburgh newspaper men of the first rank contributed their formative years to the service of the *Gazette:* Arthur G. Burgoyne, John S. Ritenour, and William H. Davis. Burgoyne, an Irish immigrant who had graduated from the University of Dublin and then turned up in Pittsburgh to teach languages for a living, wrote musical critiques for the *Gazette* for several years before transferring to the *Leader* in 1885. Ritenour, one of the founders of the Pittsburgh *Press*, was on the staff of the *Gazette* as late as 1882. At the time, he was generally recognized as one of the best

reporters in the city. Davis was city editor of the *Gazette* from
1883 to 1885. On all sides it was said that he was probably in
closer touch with municipal events than any other newspaper man
in the city. Two other *Gazette* men of note were Frank Jenks, the
city editor during the early nineties, and James Blaine, Jr., the
son of the distinguished party leader and a reporter for a few
months around 1890.

Far and away the most prominent personality with the *Gazette*
during the period was Erasmus Wilson: Ohio farm boy, Civil War
veteran, country doctor, and the modest owner of a nation-wide
reputation, won for him by his newspaper column, "The Quiet
Observer." [4] He started in at ten dollars a week with the Pittsburgh *Leader*, then shifted to the *Gazette* for the three years from
1877 to 1880. He picked up further experience with the *Telegraph*
and *Dispatch*. It was on the last paper that he finally discovered
his own peculiar talent. According to the story that he always
loved to tell, sometime during the year 1884 he submitted a report
of a political gathering that the managing editor wrathfully denounced as neither news nor editorial. Wilson was dismissed with
the words "your head is off" ringing in his ears, but fortunately
friends intervened with such effect, that, as he whimsically put it,
"I was permitted to go around town with my head off for several
weeks." He was permitted to continue writing the type of article
that had drawn the grim sentence. Eventually his random remarks
took the form of a special column, selections from which provided
the material for a book called *Quiet Observations on the Ways of
the World* (1886). It had an extensive sale, which, in all likelihood,
recommended him to the attention of Reed; for in January, 1888,
"Ras" Wilson was prevailed upon to come back to the *Gazette*
and pen his famous column for its readers.

For nearly twelve years he kept up his daily column of comment, delighting thousands of readers with the keen vision and
gentle humor of his paragraphs. Once, when it was hinted that
his feature might be discontinued, the *Gazette* was deluged with so
impressive a flood of indignant letters that the idea was hastily

dropped. "Manners and events," his self-chosen field, permitted him to discuss such widely removed subjects as the obnoxiousness of male flirts, the public attitude toward bachelors, politics in the public schools, and the intricacies of social etiquette. That he did so with appreciable success is revealed by the fact that he was widely copied in other newspapers. His work as dramatic critic and book reviewer brought him scarcely less attention.

He was also rarely happy in his friendships, not simply with Pittsburgh newspaper men, who uniformly liked him for the kindly greeting that he extended as naturally to the cub reporter as to the owner of the paper; but also with a wider circle. "Marse Henry" Watterson, Strickland Gilliland, Arthur Brisbane, Ella Wheeler Wilcox, Elbert Hubbard, Sol Smith Russell, and Joseph Jefferson were among the friends with whom the "Quiet Observer" carried on a regular correspondence. It is likely that during his newspaper career, Erasmus Wilson, through a wide itinerary of lecture tours, visits to old soldier conventions, and other journeyings, came to know intimately a greater number of celebrities than any other man in Pittsburgh. One of his most prized friends was James Whitcomb Riley, who showed the strong attachment between the two by writing a special poem in honor of his friend. In part it reads:

> 'Ras Wilson, I respect you, 'cause
> You're common, like you allus was
> Afore you went to town and s'prised
> The world by gittin' "reckonized,"
> And yit perservin', as I say,
> Your common hoss-sense ev'ryway! . . .
>
> You're common, as I said afore—
> You're common, yit oncommon *more*.—
> You allus kindo' 'pear to me,
> What all mankind had ort to be—
> Just *natchurl*, and the more hurraws
> You git, the less you know the cause.[5]

Such a tribute spoke volumes.

One crisp January Day in 1890, a special train, chartered by the New York *World*, chuffed briskly into Pittsburgh from the West. Aboard was a battery of *World* reporters and a brisk little woman called Nellie Bly, who was on the last leg of a spectacular seventy-two-day trip around the world. A crowd of Pittsburgh newspaper men were on the platform to greet this feminine disciple of Jules Verne, but gay Nellie had no eyes for them. Where was the Quiet Observer, she asked. He was the newspaper man she wanted most of all to see. A representative of the *Commercial Gazette* came forward and mollified Nellie somewhat by promising to convey a special message to the man who wasn't there. There was a warning blast from the locomotive, a premonitory rattling of the couplings, and a chorus of cheers as the train picked up momentum for the journey to New York. The incident occupied hardly more time than it takes to tell; yet it deserves to be mentioned for the light it throws on Wilson's strangely assorted collection of friendships. In 1885 "Nellie Bly" was Elizabeth Seaman, but recently a little country girl from Armstrong County, Pennsylvania. A badly written letter from her to the *Dispatch* somehow caught the attention of the managing editor, George Madden, and Erasmus Wilson, who was then with the *Dispatch*. Wilson advised that a note asking her to call at the office be dropped in the mail. Elizabeth Seaman answered the note and found the Quiet Observer to be a "great big, good-natured fellow" instead of the little "gray-haired, sharp-nosed sour-visaged fellow who could look clean through you" that she had pictured him to be. Ever afterward they remained friends even though the spectacular newspaper career of Nellie Bly, as Madden christened her (with the aid of Stephen Collins Foster's song) soon carried her to New York and greater opportunities in the field of metropolitan journalism.[6]

Still the *Gazette* was more than a galaxy of personalities whom the public infrequently saw. Daily, weekly, the paper glided from the press to its faithful circle of readers. The issue of both morning and evening editions seemed patently unnecessary now that the war had died away, and the evening edition was abandoned. The *Gazette* office was moved several times. From 86 Fifth Street it was shifted to the corner of Sixth Avenue and Smithfield Street in 1870, then back to 70 Fifth Avenue in 1877, to 76 and 78 Fifth Avenue in 1890, and at length to 318 and 320 Fifth Avenue in 1897. The subscription price was also successively raised and modified. The price of the daily started out at eight dollars per year, three cents per copy, in 1866 and vacillated between that figure and ten dollars per year until 1876, when it was fixed at eight dollars. In 1894 the price was dropped to five dollars per year, two cents per issue; in 1895 to three dollars per year and one cent per issue. Although the *Gazette* was out frankly to increase its circulation, other newspapers were impressed by the seeming fact that only strong advertising revenues could warrant such sacrificial prices. At first the annual charge for the weekly fluctuated between one dollar and a half and one dollar and seventy-five cents for single copies (with appropriate reductions for club subscriptions). Then in 1888 a flat rate reduction to one dollar and a quarter per year occurred, followed by a further reduction to one dollar in 1890.

Meanwhile the mechanical equipment of the paper was steadily improved. In 1882 the *Gazette* directed public attention to its large new press, capable of printing fifteen thousand impressions per hour instead of the six thousand of the discarded four-cylinder Hoe press. Both sides of the paper could be printed at once, and each complete issue was cut, pasted, and folded before leaving the press. For those who were unaware of the new process of stereotyping, the publishers took pains to provide information about it and about the advantageous use to which it was being put in the *Gazette* office. In 1894 the management introduced equipment for setting type by machinery. With the use of the new "Mergenthaler Machine" or linotype as it came to be called, a more economical system of newsprinting was made possible.

At sundry times, the paper was subjected to changes of size and format. In 1866 its sheet size measured 26 x 20 inches. It was also a folio, or four-page, edition eight columns wide. Two years later the sheet size was cut to 23 x 15, while the number of pages was doubled. Each page was, however, only six columns wide. Evidently the public did not react well toward the new quarto edition, for in 1869 the *Gazette* became a four-page journal, swelling to even greater proportions than before. The fondness of the newspaper readers for those blanket-sized editions is hard to explain. Perhaps it was the result of habit, but even so the business man of that era, jolting along to work in a crowded horse car, must have found it far from convenient to pass the time poring over the sizeable columns of his morning paper. In November, 1882, King, Reed & Co. saw fit to experiment with a smaller eight-page edition, this time with success; for never again was the paper forced to depart from this policy. Withal, the standard edition remained at eight pages. About 1885 the *Gazette* instituted the practice of running its Saturday edition into twelve pages, sometimes more, but the week-day edition continued to conform to the conventional figure.

At first the proprietors of the *Gazette* abstained from a lavish use of display. Double column heads and scare heads were not in vogue. For display effect the compositor often elected to run the heads in a series down the column. On special occasions whole columns of headings were utilized to emphasize the appended news story. Illustrations were used very sparingly. Technical improvements in the field of photography had been slow to make their appearance, and the *Gazette* was far from being a picture paper at this time. In 1884 it plumed itself on "a feature new in Pittsburgh journalism" when it announced that, beginning with a "picture gallery" of local common pleas court judges, it would print from time to time portraits and sketches of outstanding community leaders. Cartoons were not much evident until late in the period. As early as 1876 a drawing of a boat filled with Democratic leaders adrift on a river of "reform" was shown on the *Gazette's* front page. Not until the decade of the eighteen nineties did regular cartoons, usually borrowed from other newspapers, become the paper's stock-in-trade.

There were signs that the front page had emancipated itself from its earlier bondage to advertising. The first page of the *Gazette* of January 1, 1870, contained no advertising at all. Instead, a column of "religious intelligence," a short story by Horatio Alger, Jr., a letter from the famous missionary, David Livingstone, and some news articles of both foreign and domestic origin interested the reader in the news of the day. In 1900 the front page was different only in detail. Short news summaries called ears had appeared at either side of the masthead, and illustrations and bolder headlines dressed up page one.

It could not be gainsaid that the editorial no longer conveyed a forceful message of opinion to an indifferent public, and the editorial page had greater space for small featured columns. One of regular issue in 1885 bore the alliterative title "Paragraphic Pencilings of Passing Events Pertinently Put." "Terse Telegrams," "Near-Town Notes," "The Quiet Observer," "Capital Chat," "Assorted Oddities," and "Jocular Jottings," are also representative of the departmental divisions of the editorial page.

There were other signs of a wider audience whose varied tastes the newspaper felt bound to respect. For the first time the *Gazette* was setting aside space for concerns that it had long ignored. The feminine newspaper reader was recognized. In 1884 the *Gazette* took the bold step of promising a résumé of current society events every Friday. Before the dawn of the mauve decade, it had installed a full-fledged editor, Cara Reese, whose "Cara's Column" came to serve as the women's department of the *Gazette*. The paper was beginning to take note of the sports lover as well. Shortly before 1882 the *Gazette* began to print box scores for baseball games. Before the end of the century the great national pastime was well reported—league standings were posted, and local pride in the exploits of "Our Own," as the Pittsburgh baseball club was commonly known, was developed by the attention that the *Gazette* bestowed upon those exploits.

Styles of reporting differed very radically from those common today. Criminals were seldom "hung." They usually "expiated their crimes upon the gallows." There were few "alleged" fires, robberies, etc.; the reporter was ordinarily less cautious. Conceptions of news value were also less strongly developed. Accounts of petty wrongdoing were printed in profuse detail to the exclusion of stories of greater consequence.

One of the most interesting fields in which the newspaper's makeup differed during these years from that of today was in advertising. The quantity of advertising in the *Gazette* increased steadily during the years from 1866 to 1900. In the latter year, however, a smaller percentage of space was devoted to advertising than in the earlier year. Granting this, it still can not be denied that both the character and makeup of advertising had been completely transformed by 1900. The most startling revolution was in department-store advertising. In 1866 such stores rarely made use of more than two or three squares of space. By 1900 Joseph Horne and Company, Kaufmann's Grand Depôt, Gusky's, Campbell's, and other well known firms were resorting to full-page advertising spreads, illustrated as never before, and prodigal of space in a way that would have struck their predecessors to the heart. The advantage of placing advertising matter in a contiguous position to news was being fully appreciated by both the newspaper and its customers. Advertisers also showed themselves willing to pay handsomely for such arrangement.

The *Gazette*, did not have at this time the reputation of being a "stunt newspaper." Nevertheless it was not at all reluctant to draw the public eye by a featured performance. In 1867, for example, it sent Josiah Copley to represent it on a tour of the West sponsored by the Union Pacific Railway. As one of a large party, which included several members of Congress as well as some representatives of large Eastern papers, he traveled as far as Fort Harker, the western terminus of the Union Pacific at the time, and made the trip the basis of twenty-two letters to the *Gazette* describing the topography, mineral resources, towns, and educational facilities of Kansas and enlarging upon the imperial possibilities of the transcontinental line then building. The letters were later published by their author in a separate volume.[7] In 1885, at the time of President Cleveland's inauguration, the *Gazette* congratulated itself for sending out a special train from Pittsburgh to carry its edition to out-of-town customers, the first time this had been done in the history of Pittsburgh journalism. Leaving the Union Station at 2:50 A. M., the train occupied solely by *Gazette* men and the railroad employees raced two hundred and twenty-five miles into Harrisburg to place the story of the inauguration there in advance of any other Pittsburgh newspaper.

The *Gazette* paid its *devoirs* to popular memories of the Civil War by printing on September 8, 1894 a special edition of the paper in honor of the annual national G. A. R. encampment at Pittsburgh. The same year it undertook the distribution of *The Century War Book*, with nine hundred illustrations from the war—in the words of the *Gazette*, "the most superb and valuable work ever offered by an American newspaper."

Such efforts met with the popular encouragement they merited. From 1870 to 1900 the circulation of the *Gazette* advanced progressively. For the year 1870 an estimated circulation of 9000 for the daily *Gazette* and 14,000 for the weekly edition was reported. At the turn of the century the respective figures were 35,267 and approximately 17,000. Practically the only serious interruption of the climb in circulation took place after the panic of 1873, when the average sales of the daily skidded from 7500 in 1872, to 4500 in 1873, to 4000 in 1874, and finally reached bottom at 3500 in 1875. Happily, the *Commercial* was absorbed by the *Gazette* soon afterward and brought with it 6000 subscribers to refresh the flagging subscription lists of King, Reed & Co. Until the very end of the period the daily circulation of the *Gazette* was considerably in arrears of its weekly circulation. At first the *Dispatch* and the *Leader* were the *Gazette's* principal competitors in the city field, but after 1880 the *Times*, the *Press*, and the *Chronicle Telegraph* forged ahead in the contest for subscribers. In 1900 the *Press* had the largest daily circulation of any of the Pittsburgh newspapers.[8]

As early as 1864 Pittsburgh was the home of a Sunday paper,

the Sunday *Leader*, founded by John W. Pittock in that year. During the seventies its circulation ran between 12,000 and 15,000. The *Dispatch* decided to enter the field in 1885, and proposed to put out an edition that should redeem Sunday papers from the bad reputation under which they generally labored at the time. It was an immediate success. Within fifteen years its subscribers had increased in number from 20,000 to approximately 70,000. With Sunday newspapers the *Gazette* would have nothing to do, however. In 1888 it advised church going people to boycott all newspapers that profited by Sunday editions, and in 1893 it took a conspicuous part, along with the Philadelphia *Ledger*, in a controversy at Harrisburg that was provoked by the introduction of a bill to legalize the publication of Sunday newspapers. Behind this policy were to be discovered the religious convictions of Nelson P. Reed and his family. Reed, a stout Presbyterian, was often heard to say that as long as he lived his Sabbatarian scruples anent the subject of newspapers must be strictly observed.

His attitude was perfectly consistent with the conservative pattern of the *Gazette's* policy, which may be described as a discriminating type of non-yellow journalism. The feverish public excitement created during the Civil War by the long rows of war bulletins begot a taste for sensational news articles, which the *Gazette* was loath to gratify. And so it remained aloof for the most part from the "parade of vice and crime" that it saw spread across the columns of rival journals. Perhaps because of this, the *Gazette* was always held in high respect by its contemporaries. On numerous occasions its fellow journals denominated it the leading Republican newspaper of western Pennsylvania; its high editorial caliber, its varied and excellent correspondence, and its faithful local news coverage entitled it to widespread recognition at home and abroad.

CHAPTER XV

TALES FROM THE HEADLINES

The great Charles A. Dana, journalist *par excellence* of the post-Civil War generation, once said: "The first thing which an editor must look for is news. If the newspaper has not the news it may have everything else, yet it will be comparatively unsuccessful." [1]

Like Dana, Reed and his associates reached the height of their careers in a post-war world, a world of rising cities, of clashing industrial armies, a world of restless change. The craving of newspaper patrons for news was greater than ever before. Within the first three years after Penniman, Reed & Co. was established, the *Gazette* had three news stories of the first magnitude to set the imagination of its readers to dancing: the completion of the Atlantic Cable uniting the Old World and the New by wire, the opening of the Suez Canal, perhaps the most important artery of world trade in the nineteenth century, and the insertion of the last spike at the junction point on the transcontinental railroad. The public's craving for news could never be stilled. The *Gazette* had a commodity to sell; the public would buy if sufficiently interested by the paper's view of the drama of events. The task of the *Gazette* was cut out. It must furnish news, more news, scour the country for it if necessary, have special correspondents everywhere, and, toward the end of the period, pay a good price for the use of Associated Press facilities.

In wartime the newspaper market is especially lush. Rumors are more easily believed; false reports are more easily magnified; the very atmosphere of dread and uncertainty, of patriotic fervor and utter selflessness lends itself to creating an abnormal appetite for news. During the last years of the century, two wars aroused the American people. With the one the United States had no connection; in the other it was actually involved. Both brought unsolicited business to the door of the *Gazette*.

From the very outset of the Franco-Prussian War, in July,

1870, the sympathies of the *Gazette* were with Prussia. Everywhere it was believed that France was the actual aggressor. Remarked the *Gazette:* the educational and religious features of the Prussian government were like those of the United States; during the dark days of the Civil War the Prussian government, in marked contrast to the "wily emperor," Napoleon III, had been a staunch friend to the Lincoln government; finally, there was a large number of Germans who had come to America and assumed the responsibilities of citizenship. In Pittsburgh, where sympathy for the Prussian cause was said to be nearly unanimous, the *Gazette's* position was very popular. The *Commercial* was almost the only local paper that ventured to adopt the side of the French, embroiling itself in the process with *Der Freiheits Freund*, the leading German newspaper of Pittsburgh.

The *Gazette's* first concern in the war was of course the news. But reliable news was difficult to secure. Often the editor fell to complaining peevishly about the "unintelligible, contradictory, and even absurd dispatches" which he and his readers were asked to assimilate. All went reasonably well as long as dependence was placed upon the services of the New York *Tribune.* As the demand for war news became more keen, however, the *Gazette*, with questionable wisdom, chose to patronize instead the New York *World* and the New York *Herald.* Unfortunately both papers inclined to the side of the French; worse than that, as tidings of French victories failed to come in, the special correspondents of the *World* and *Herald* were apt to rely on their fancy to counteract the effect of Von Moltke's successes.

The news of the great Prussian victory at Sedan in September, which the *Gazette* hurried to its readers, brought transports of joy to most Pittsburghers. So too did the long account of the fall of Paris, which came through in January, 1871. The editor of the *Gazette* could not help feeling glad that the war was over. The whole world, with the exception of that "arrogant people," the French, would welcome the return of a general peace he thought. And so it proved.

The interest of the *Gazette* in the Spanish-American War was of a different kind. Like most administration newspapers, it was prone to look upon the Cuban disorders with an air of resignation and to frown on the efforts of the *Post* and the rest of the Democratic press to force the hand of the McKinley administration. Even the booming explosion that sent the U. S. S. Maine to the bottom of Havana harbor did not rock the *Gazette* out of its studied calm. True, it provided an excellent news story: the front page of the *Gazette* on February 17, 1898, full of pictures and news of the disaster, was evidence enough of that. But the editor would not have it that the ship had been destroyed by any agency known to the Spanish authorities. For the "vicious journalism" practised at the time by the New York *Journal* and the rest of the yellow press, the *Gazette* had only the utmost loathing. The editor saw in it "partisanship and sensationalism run mad." "Compared with the promotors of such journalism," he impatiently observed, "the vultures wheeling above the sunken Maine may command admiration." ₃

The *Gazette* proceeded, nevertheless, to print rumors of impending war and military preparations. When on March 25 the official report of the American Court of Inquiry attributing the explosion to an external cause was published, the paper seemed prepared for what was to follow. Six days later a picture of the body of Lieutenant Jenkins, the lone Pittsburgh member of the Maine's martyred crew, was shown lying in state at the courthouse rotunda. Firmly the *Gazette* stood behind President McKinley in his well-meant efforts to avert hostilities, desirous of shielding him from the "vile abuse" heaped upon him by the yellow press. On April 22 the news for which the country had been anxiously waiting came over the wires. A streamer headline six inches deep was spread across the front page of the *Gazette:* "WAR WITH SPAIN NOW ON." The next day the blockade of the Cuban ports was a matter of public information, and the *Gazette* broke out in a rash of streamer headlines such as its readers had never seen before. The compositors ransacked their cases for larger and larger type

EXTRA—LAST EDITION · ALL THE WAR NEWS

Pittsburgh Commercial Gazette.

...TH YEAR. ONE CENT A COPY. PITTSBURGH, MONDAY MORNING, JULY 4, 1898. SIX CENTS A WEEK. NO. ...

A Glorious Fourth!

Cervera off the Earth!

CERVERA'S FLEET DESTROYED BY SAMPSON

Gen. Shafter Demands the Surrender of Santiago and Expects Demand Will Be Complied With.

WASHINGTON, D. C., July 3.—Admiral Sampson's fleet to-day engaged the fleet of Admiral Cervera and entirely destroyed it. The following dispatch was received at the war department:

"PLAYA DEL ESTE, July 3.—Siboney office confirms statement that all the Spanish fleet except one warship destroyed, and burning on the beach. It was witnessed by Captain Smith, who told operators. No doubt of its correctness. ALLEN, Signal Officer."

Later the following cable dispatch was given out at the White House:

"PLAYA DEL ESTE, July 3.—The destruction of Cervera's fleet is confirmed. ALLEN, Lieut.-Col."

The following statement was also to-night given out at the White House: "General Shafter telegraphs from Playa del Este, July 3: 'Early this morning I sent a demand for the immediate surrender of Santiago, threatening to bombard the city. I believe the place will be surrendered.'" This contradicts the report that Gen. Shafter has fallen back.

SANTIAGO A RUIN.

Terrible Execution Done in the City By American Shot and Shell.

THE SPANISH LOSS IS 1,000.

Gen. Linares, Commander of the Spanish Forces, Seriously Wounded—Reinforcements Will Be Immediately Sent to Enable Shafter to Complete His Work.

SHAFTER LOST 1,000 KILLED AND WOUNDED,

WASHINGTON, D. C., July 3.—The following dispatch from Gen. Shafter was received to-day and made public from the White House:

"PLAYA DEL ESTE, July 3.

"To Secretary War, Washington:

"CAMP NEAR SEVILLA, CUBA, July 3.—We have the town well invested on the north and east, but with a very thin line. Upon approaching it we find it of such a character and thoroughness of defense so strong it will be impossible to carry it by storm with my present force. Our losses up to date will aggregate a thousand but this has not yet been made, but little sickness outside of exhaustion from intense heat and exertion of the battle of day before yesterday and the almost constant fire which I kept up on the trenches. Wagon road to the rear is kept up with some difficulty on account of rains, but I will be able to use it for the present. Gen. Wheeler is seriously ill and will probably have to go to the rear to-day. Gen. Young also very ill; confined to his bed. Gen. Hawkins slightly wounded in foot during verde convex made last night which is being hastened upon. The behavior of the troops was magnificent. Gen. Garcia reported he holds the railroad from Santiago to San Luis and has burned a bridge and removed some rails; also that Gen. Pando has arrived at Palma and that the French contact with about four hundred French citizens came into his line yesterday from Santiago. Have directed him to treat them with every courtesy possible. SHAFTER, Major-General."

Secretary Alger sent the following reply to Gen. Shafter:

"To Gen. Shafter: The President directs me to say that you have the gratitude and thanks of the nation for the brilliant and effective work of your noble army on Friday, July 1. The steady valor and heroism of officers and men thrills the American people with pride. The country mourns the brave men who fell in battle. They have added new names to our roll of heroes. "W. A. ALGER, Secretary of War."

Secretary Alger, when asked what course was to be pursued in view of Gen. Shafter's report of the condition at Santiago, said that the government did not intend to make any of its plans public and give the enemy an opportunity of knowing what was intended. It is understood that Gen. Shafter will at once receive instructions. War department officials have been in conference at the White House and War Department.

All of Gen. Shafter's dispatches were not made public for reasons of expedience. It is understood he will withdraw to the hills near the sea and await reinforcements which will be sent as soon as possible. Assistant Secretary Mickiejohn is now busy arranging for the reports.

Gen. Miles says the result at Santiago appears to be a drawn battle. He also said that the withdrawal of Gen. Shafter to the highlands of Sibaney near the sea would be temporary, enabling the troops to rest and prepare for future work. Gen. Shafter would probably give up El Caney and the gains not far from Santiago.

BLANCO'S ADMISSION OF AMERICAN SUCCESS AND SPANISH LOSS.

MADRID, July 3—10 A. M.—Captain General Blanco reports to the government under date of July 2, as follows:

"At noon to-day the enemy vigorously attacked Santiago and succeeded in taking the advance position of Lomes and San Juan after a vehement resistance lasting three hours on my part. We were able to save our artillery, though half the troops were placed hors de combat. Gen. Linares was severely wounded in the left arm and relinquished his command to Gen. Toral. The enemy in considerable force attacked the village of El Caney this morning, but were repulsed by Gen. Vara. The night was resumed this evening and ended in El Caney itself, after a vigorous resistance on our part. Our losses were heavy. I have no news from the Cuartel and Cervera squadrons, with which I found it impossible to communicate against all efforts to do so."

6 P. M.—The government has received cipher dispatches from Cuba. Our contents of which have not been made public. It is stated, however, that the Spanish naval forces, considering the American troops which made an attack upon the Spanish entire position at Santiago, Gen. Vara de Rey, who commanded at El Caney, fought with the greatest courage, setting his men an example by losing the advance. It was under similar conditions that Gen. Linares was wounded.

According to official dispatches received the Spanish troops fell back upon the city of Santiago in order to await reinforcements.

The dispatches do not mention the death of Gen. Vara de Rey, which, it is rumored, has occurred.

Reinforcements for Linares.

They Are Said to Have Effected a Junction and to Be Among for Shafter's Right Flank.

Pittsburgh Post-Gazette

Consolidation of The Daily Post and Gazette Times

PITTSBURGH'S ONLY MORNING NEWSPAPER
PRESS SERVICES
The Associated Press, The United Press, The Chicago Tribune, The New York World.

POST EST. 1842—GAZETTE EST. 1786.   TWENTY-FIVE PAGES.   TUESDAY MORNING, AUGUST 2, 1927.   THREE CENTS A COPY.

CHAMBERLIN FIGHTS WAY THROUGH FOG, LANDING MAIL FROM BIG LINER

Hop From Deck of Leviathan Is Success

POUCH IS TAKEN TO NEW JERSEY

CURTIS REFUSES TO JOIN DEMAND ON COOLIDGE FOR EXTRA SESSION

But Robinson and Edwards Favor Early Meeting.

ALL SEE FLOOD CONTROL URGENT

Decides Romance By Toss of Coin

Girl Pastor Quits 'Cause She Preached "Much Too Strong"

PITTSBURGHERS READY TO GIVE COL. LINDBERGH WARM WELCOME

Complete Final Arrangements For Fete Tomorrow.

CITY POLICE TO PATROL FIELD

LEADERS IN BIG ARSON RING TRAPPED AFTER PLOTTING TO FIRE MILLINERY ON NORTHSIDE

Millicent to Try Matrimony Again

Two Women Play Important Part In Capture

ALL CONFESS, OFFICERS SAY

COOLIDGE SEEN AS 1928 CHOICE DESPITE THIRD TERM TRADITION

Business Interests to Decide Issue, View.

AWAIT ANSWER OF PRESIDENT

GIBSON ORDERED BY WASHINGTON TO END NAVAL MEET THURSDAY

Failure of British To Meet U. S. Viewpoint, Cause

MOVE COMES AS SURPRISE

Rail Company Sued After Millions of Bees Die in Transit

GUNMEN KILL MAN IN STREET

PILOT, STUDENT KILLED IN FALL

Chicago's Aerial Death Toll Mounts to Seven in Eight Days

CORNWELL UNDER KNIFE

PLANE FOR HOME HOP READY SOON

CONFESSIONS IN AS EVIDENCE

ROBINSON SEEKS PARTY HARMONY

FIVE CONVICTED FOR FLOGGING

NINE AIRPLANES IN OCEAN RACE

MARINE FACES COURT MARTIAL

MISS KELLER'S TEACHER DIES

AIMEE, MOTHER AT PEACE AGAIN

LLOYD GEORGE SEES FRIENDSHIP

Woman Who Lured Arson Gang In Trap Tells Part She Played

FEARED FOR LIFE PENDING ARREST

Sacco-Vanzetti Presiding Judge Questioned by Governor Fuller

FINAL DECISION DUE TOMORROW

ANNOUNCEMENT

Effective today the proprietorship of this newspaper passes from the present owners to Paul Block. Mr. Block has also bought The Pittsburgh Sun. The new owner will combine the publication of The Pittsburgh Post from the present publishing.

It is with keen regret that we make this announcement of our retirement from the newspaper publishing field in Pittsburgh.

Paul Block
President and Publisher.

THE FIRST ISSUE OF THE POST-GAZETTE

with which to astound and edify the news-hungry public. It mattered not that a large amount of space was wasted in the process.

Apparently the *Gazette* was content to rely upon the Associated Press and the news services of the eastern papers for war reports. Still there was no deficiency in that respect. While the local national guard contingents were hurrying off to training camp at Mount Gretna, the appetite of the public was being whetted for the tidings of Dewey's great victory at Manila. The latter event provided the opportunity for an important news story. Of local interest was the minor detail that the armor plate for Dewey's flagship, the "Olympia," had been forged by the Carnegie Steel Company at Homestead. In time Dewey's own story of his victory found its way into the *Gazette*.

Other reports came thick and fast, depicting in deep colors the impetuous trip of the "Oregon" around the Horn, the bottling up of Cervera's fleet in Santiago harbor, and Hobson's daring attempt to sink the "Merrimac" across the harbor mouth. Hobson's conduct was the subject of a highly laudatory editorial in the *Gazette* of June 6, 1898; as later noted, it won for him as well an honorary degree from nearby Washington and Jefferson College.

In the middle of June, the *Gazette* gave currency to rumors that another Spanish fleet piloted by Admiral Camara was about to sail for some unknown destination. From the wild forms that these rumors assumed, the news-writers could not help extracting some humor. At the announced time of the fleet's departure, the *Gazette* carried headlines: "Camara's Fleet Sails,—It May Bombard Boston or Turtle Creek or Go to Manila." [3] Happily the never very real threat of Camara's fleet vanished away in the ocean mists, and on July 4 came great news: Admiral Cervera's fleet had been put out of commission while attempting to escape from Santiago harbor. The *Gazette* spared no effort to stress the importance of the happening. A stately picture of the American eagle flanked by captions "A Glorious Fourth" and "Cervera Off the Earth" filled the upper part of the front page. Below was a full account printed in bold-faced type. The same day a crowd of one hundred and fifty thousand people gathered in Schenley Park to celebrate the news of the victory and listen to addresses arranged for by George T. Oliver, the chairman of the day.

Suddenly realizing the importance of world geography, the *Gazette* hastened to prepare a war map of Cuba, the other West Indian islands, and the Philippines, and to distribute it among its readers for a small sum plus newspaper coupons. Pittsburgh responded nobly to the appeals of the *Gazette* for public support of the war. It furnished large quotas of volunteers, and its relief contributions made through the medium of the local Red Cross auxiliary were second only to those of New York City.

The end of the war was in sight, however. Victories on land and on sea presaged it. On August 13, 1898, the *Gazette* announced the happy news of peace to its readers with editorial thankfulness for the fact that the war had been so quickly and painlessly won. The outcome of the war might well be pondered by the editor with some misgivings. In the early stages of the conflict he had stated explicitly that "There need be no fear that this country is about to enter upon a land grabbing policy and become a competitor of old world nations in that kind of imperialism. It is not the sentiment of the nation and will never find expression in action." [4] Moreover, within ten days of the end of the war, he put himself in agreement with the general tone of Andrew Carnegie's current article in the *North American Review*, which expressed opposition to the acquisition of the Philippines on ethnological grounds. After the war the *Gazette* editor had to practice some mental gymnastics to reconcile such statements with the support that he extended to a peace treaty embodying the annexation of the Philippines. None was more aware of the contradiction than he; and when the Philippine insurrection broke out early in 1899, the *Gazette* could not but admit that the sooner an honorable withdrawal from the archipelago was arranged the better for all concerned.

While the *Gazette* was far from being a sensational journal it was not averse to finding material for news stories at the scenes of notable crimes and disasters. Probably the leading murder cases featured during the period were the assassination of President Garfield (1881), the Jimmy Nutt case (1883–84), and the Lizzie Borden case (1893).

The *Gazette* seems to have been the first newspaper in the city to bulletin the shocking news of the assassination of President Garfield. According to one story, a Western Union Telegraph Company employee took the first dispatch concerning it and rushed breathlessly over to the *Gazette* office with the news. The staff was incredulous at first but, gambling on the chance that the story might be true, put out a bulletin laconically stating that the president had been assassinated. The crowd that collected before the window began to mutter as it was bruited about that the other newspaper offices had no intimation of the happening. The men at the *Gazette* were just about to tear down the rash bulletin when their informer came running over again with full information about the shooting. The *Gazette* also scored a "beat" with this second bulletin and then hurried to get out an extra edition.

When in early autumn the president succumbed to his wound, the *Gazette* described the last scene with an air of sad deference befitting the occasion. Most mortifying at the time was the inability of the paper to put itself in mourning by the simple device of turning the column rules upside down. This was made impossible by the peculiar construction of the paper's Hoe four-cylinder press. Consequently the heavy black lines that customarily bordered the columns on occasions like these were unavoidably absent. This was amply compensated for, however, by the *Gazette's* description of the way Pittsburgh received the account of Garfield's death.

A City's Grief

It were hard to convey an adequate idea of the spectacle presented in the Smoky City when the sun rose on yester morn. The somber trappings of woe hung on every hand, and our streets and avenues were shadowed with all the sable panoply of gloom. In the still hours of the night, broken only by the mournful music of the bells which tolled the grievous tidings, many citizens began the work of draping their homes and places of business with crape and other ebony hued symbols of sorrow. Around the most imposing business structures on Fifth avenue and cross streets, were twined black drapery mingled with evergreen, and flags that were shrouded or fringed with crape hung at half mast on the public buildings. In the early morning a mist swept down over the city and added to the gloom. With the break of day came the knowledge to thousands whose slumbers had not been broken by the tolling bells, of the death of the President, and instant and almost universal preparation was made to imitate the example of those who had worked in the night in decking the city in black.[5]

The Nutt case involved the murder of a certain Nicholas Dukes of Uniontown, Pennsylvania, allegedly by the defendant, Jimmy Nutt. Interest in the case was heightened by the fact that young Nutt had taken the law into his own hands to avenge the seduction of a female relative and the killing of his father by the same Dukes. A change of venue from Fayette County was applied for, and the case was tried in Pittsburgh from January 14 to 22, 1884. For a week Pittsburgh was the focus of national attention, much of it fed by the exhaustive reports to be found in the *Gazette*, ten to fifteen columns of them on the average each day. A Johnstown newspaper man openly declared that it was more satisfactory to read the *Gazette* than to be in personal attendance at the trial. Sympathy for Nutt's predicament ran high in the community. It was commonly agreed that the law had been remiss in securing justice for the youthful defendant. His father had been the Republican leader in Uniontown and Dukes the Democratic chief there—which made the affair resemble a political vendetta. As the result of a suggestion from the *Gazette* a fund was raised to be used in behalf of the defense, and notable contributions to it were received from Uniontown. The *Gazette* scored a scoop on the acquittal, placing its extra edition on the street three minutes after the outcome became known and fully fifteen minutes in advance of the other Pittsburgh papers. Delighted with the verdict, the *Gazette* printed congratulatory statements from prominent individuals all over the country, including President Arthur himself, and one of its representatives even entered the home of James G. Blaine to secure from him a statement praising the jury for its fine work.

The double murder for which Lizzie Borden was tried occurred at Fall River, Massachusetts. Probably more widespread popular interest was created by the murder and the trial than any since the famous Webster trial of the fifties. Like other American papers, the *Gazette* threw open its columns to the case and exploited the possibilities for human interest that it contained.

One of the great catastrophes of the period that made the front page of the *Gazette* was the spectacular Chicago Fire of 1871. On the morning of October 9, 1871, Pittsburghers took up the *Gazette* and picked their way through the descriptive headlines: "Chicago—Great Fire—24 Blocks Burned!—Most Awful scenes!— Human Efforts Powerless!—Thousands Homeless!" On and on they read. They scurried to the city hall, where a large public meeting had been called. Among those in charge of the meeting was Josiah King of the *Gazette*. As a first expression of sympathy, the citizenry immediately subscribed sixteen thousand dollars for the relief of the sufferers, and William Thaw headed the list with a five thousand dollar donation. The next impulse was to tender the services of the Pittsburgh and Allegheny fire departments to the hard-pressed Chicagoans. The offer, first refused, was later accepted, and all tracks were cleared ahead on the Fort Wayne road for the departments to proceed to the fire. In due time the city council met and pledged a donation of one hundred thousand dollars to speed the recovery of Chicago. Meanwhile the *Gazette* did a land-office business. The newsboys were kept busy supplying the demands for information about "The Great Fire," and bulletins were changed freely to satisfy the morbid curiosity of the crowds that thronged the streets before the office. It was more than a week before flashes from Chicago ceased to be front-page news. The *Gazette* did not allow the occasion to pass without warning the city council that Pittsburgh's fire department needed many improvements before it would be able to cope with a similar emergency at home.

Hardly less spectacular than the Chicago Fire was the Johnstown Flood. On the morning of June 1, 1889, the front page of the paper carried a headline two columns wide: "Extra—A Stupendous Calamity—The Conemaugh Valley Scraped Bare and the Town of Johnstown Wiped Out by an Overwhelming Deluge from a Mountain Lake." The rest of the page was devoted almost entirely to a more detailed account of the tragedy. The news had reached Pittsburgh the evening before at 7 o'clock, with the *Gazette* and *Post* managing to scoop their morning rivals by placing the first telegraphic news accounts before the public. The rainy season of the past few weeks had practically suspended railway service east of Pittsburgh, but nevertheless the *Gazette* managed to charter a special locomotive, and, with some of the paper's most able and intrepid reporters aboard, including Alfred Reed, the train pulled out of the Pennsylvania Station at 9:15 P. M. Several anxious Pittsburghers were aboard, among them Mr. Durbin Horne, junior member of the firm of Joseph Horne and Company, who had three relatives in the disaster zone. The train was unable to penetrate beyond Bolivar, some twenty miles from Johnstown, as the railroad bridge at that point had been washed away. There was nothing for the reporters to do but continue their journey by other means. They got through, however, and sent back an account of what they had been told. What a tale of horror it was! A tale of white-faced messengers giving the alarm, of panic-stricken folk fleeing to higher ground, of the terrible scenes that ensued when the hill of water rolled into the town, of the last telegraph dispatch from Johnstown at 6 o'clock the evening before: "Must leave, the water is coming in. Good-bye." One paragraph left an unforgettable picture in the reader's mind:

> With pallid cheek and hair clinging damp to her cheek, a mother was seen grasping a floating timber,

while in the other arm she held her babe, already drowned.
With a death grip on a plank, a strong man just giving up
hope cast an imploring look to those on the banks. An
instant later and he had sunk beneath the waves. Prayers
to their God, cries to those in safety rang above the
roaring waves.[6]

The lot of the unhappy sufferers preyed upon the sympathies
of every one in Pittsburgh. Gusky's, a well-known Pittsburgh
department store, purchased two columns of advertising space
from the *Gazette* and then with telling effect left this space bare
except for a small card in the center conveying the feeling of sorrow of the management. In the emergency the *Gazette* advised
that the unfortunate survivors most in need of attention should
be removed at once from Johnstown to Pittsburgh, where they
might be better cared for. On June 5 four train loads of them were
accordingly brought into the city, where they were the recipients
of open-handed hospitality on the part of everyone. Yet something more was needed. This was, said the *Gazette* editorially, the
most appalling disaster in the history of Pennsylvania. For that
reason the *Gazette* would willingly take charge of all money contributions for the benefit of the sufferers and forward them at
once. The community responded generously to the appeal, none
more so than Carnegie and Westinghouse, who gave liberally of
their means to relieve the suffering. The *Gazette* subscribed three
hundred dollars on its own account, and then a few days afterward placed a pledge for five thousand dollars at the head of a
subscription loan that it asked western Pennsylvania to raise.
To create added incentive the paper published what it called a
roll of honor, including the names of those who were willing to
respond to the appeal. This subscription loan plan was given up
when the Philadelphia banks came forward with funds and made
unnecessary loans by private individuals.

Some other newspapers were not as public spirited as the
Gazette. A Pittsburgh evening paper printed a fictitious narrative
about riots in Johnstown that the *Gazette* was prompt to label a

manufacture and to cite as an example of the "shameful prostitu-
tion of the press." As ever, the *Gazette* refrained from conscious
exaggeration. It insisted on correcting the first sensational reports
of the death roll. It intervened to protect the Pittsburgh members
of the South Fork Hunting and Fishing Club from the condemna-
tion that was freely showered upon them by the outside press.
The *Gazette* was proud of the good work that it and the other
newspapers had performed in accurately reporting the situation at
Johnstown and in stirring up the country to a realization of the
vital need for organized assistance. It had its reward in the shape
of an enormous demand for its editions, a demand so great that
the supply of paper on hand was fairly exhausted. The regular
size of issue had to be reduced temporarily and an express order
for additional supplies sent in.

Labor troubles in an industrial area such as western Pennsylvania was becoming bade fair to supply the *Gazette* with news
stories of first-rate importance. The great railroad strike of 1877
was a case in point—the result of a period of hard times dating
for some years back. There had been wage cuts and resultant hard
feeling between employer and employee. A little after the middle
of July, 1877, the *Gazette* began to take notice of disturbances on
the Baltimore and Ohio Railroad that threatened to spread to the
Pennsylvania Railroad. The paper's attitude was mildly critical
of the "violent and incendiary conduct" of the strikers but hardly
one of concern until, on July 20, it awoke to the fact that the
"railroad war" had broken out in Pittsburgh—the greatest "lock-
out" ever seen in the city. That day the *Gazette* bulletin board
was continuously watched by dense crowds that gobbled up an
extra edition as soon as it appeared, providing what the editor
called a "newsboys' harvest."

The next day (Saturday morning) the storm broke. For a few
hours, a veritable reign of terror existed in Pittsburgh. The
Gazette came out on the following Monday with an exhibition of
headline artistry: *"Riot Law Triumphant—The Reign of Anarchy
in the Smoky City* ... Men Women and Children Fall Victims to

the Bullets ... The Incendiary's Torch Leads to Fearful Destruction ... Over Thirty Lives Lost and Ten Millions of Property Destroyed ... The Magnificent Union Depot Goes Down" With this introduction the tale of destruction proceeded eloquently:

> Few could have imagined, on Saturday morning, when we closed our account of the strike, that a civilized city would be subject to such scenes as Pittsburgh has passed through the last forty-eight hours.... It was as though the French Commune had suddenly been vomited over us, and all the scenes characteristic of the Commune were re-enacted in the city of Pittsburgh befored our unresisting population. Streets were filled with persons, generally of the lowest type, rolling barrels, carrying parcels, and in all ways bearing off plunder, taken from cars before they burned. Other were playing the part of fire fiends—deliberately setting fire to valuable property until from $6,000,000 to $7,000,000 have been given to the flames.... It was a case appalling in the utter disregard displayed as to property or life....
>
> Yesterday was a black day for Pittsburgh, and one that will forever remain a disgrace to her.

At once the *Gazette* began laboring to restore quiet. Editorials with such titles as "Let Order Obtain" and "Let Reason Prevail" were addressed to the warring sides. The strikers were admonished to surrender up the railroad property they had appropriated; the railroads on the other hand were advised to settle their differences with the strikers. The opinions of various large city newspapers condemning the resort to violence were printed *en masse.*

It is likely that the sympathies of the *Gazette* were mainly on the side of the railroads although, aware that public sentiment in Pittsburgh was generally in favor of the strikers, it managed to steer a fairly successful middle course. The editor pointed out, on one side, the fact that dividends on the Pennsylvania Railroad had been cut to six per cent, the legal interest rate, thus placing a hardship on the investor; yet he was willing to grant that the ten per cent wage cut should have been graded to protect those in the lowest wage brackets.

The position of the *Pittsburgh Post* was somewhat different. From the beginning it was definitely on the side of the laborers. Only when the strikers began to destroy property did the *Post* swing about and then, interestingly enough, because the strikers' destruction of property was not harming simply the railroad but the general public, which depended on train service for food and indirectly for employment. J. P. Barr, the publisher of the *Post*, even went so far as to write personally to the president of the Pennsylvania Railroad, Colonel Scott, demanding that he act promptly to terminate the difficulties that had arisen.[7]

By some the Pittsburgh newspapers were criticized for having in one way or another contributed to the outbreak. The Chicago *Inter-Ocean* deliberately censured the *Pittsburg Dispatch* for making light of the strike on the very eve of the riots and for opposing the muster of the militia. The *Gazette* itself during the first excitement declared that certain Sunday papers (referring, it would seem, to the *Globe* and the *Sunday Critic*) had encouraged the work of vandalism "in a spirit as fiendish, and in language as pointed as that of the worst papers in Paris during the Commune."[8] Later the editor rallied to the defense of the Pittsburgh press generally against wild and unfounded charges from outside. To the relief of all, rumors of a settlement began to multiply. On July 31, they were confirmed: The strike was over.

Not until the nineties did Pittsburgh provide any newsworthy labor disturbances to match the riots of '77. When more trouble came, it developed in Andrew Carnegie's steel business in Homestead up the Monongahela. The issue was the wage question. Both sides stood firm. The labor leaders talked of a strike. Henry C. Frick, acting for Carnegie, said nothing, but gossip had it that he was erecting a nine-foot palisade around the steel company works and putting them in such a state of defense as to be prepared for the strictest siege. The *Gazette* was anxiously watching these preparations. On June 30, 1892, it reported the discharge of the entire labor force at Homestead. Soon it observed that the old employees were thoroughly organized and determined to forestall any invasion by "black sheep from Pittsburgh."

Just before the *Gazette* went to the press on the morning of July 6, an exciting dispatch fell into the hands of the news editor. According to the information, a barge headed upstream, with three hundred detectives from the Pinkerton Detective Agency aboard had passed Lock No. 1 on the Monongahela River at 2:15 A. M. At 2:30 watchers reported the circumstances to the pickets at Homestead, whereupon alarm bells were sounded, and thousands of men, women, and children streamed down to the bank of the river to catch sight somewhere in the gloom of that barge full of Frick's hirelings. About 4:45 A. M. their curiosity was rewarded. Wonderingly they stared at the barge nosing through the early morning blackness to the shore; watched the Pinkertons prepare to disembark. At this point a pitched battle ensued. The *Gazette* was sure of that but knew little more.

The next day the story of what had happened was all over the front page. "A Bloody Fight—Strikers and Pinkertons Do Battle at Homestead—16 Men Are Killed ... Hordes of Angry Workmen Line Both Banks and Rain Bullets at the Barges." In that manner was the event headlined. There were illustrations of a kind, too, but the account of the happening was enough. The Pinkerton men had been trapped on the barge like rats in a cage. After presenting a pitiful resistance, they had surrendered themselves up to the strikers, whose promises of good treatment were lost sight of in the excitement. At length the Pinkerton men were permitted to return to Pittsburgh, frightened out of their wits, according to the *Gazette* reporters who interviewed them, and only too glad to board outgoing trains for points far distant from the hornet's nest at Homestead. Meanwhile the tumult in the city was intense. All up and down the street in front of the *Gazette* office was a closely packed throng of citizens asking each other the latest news from Homestead.

On July 7, the *Gazette* took editorial notice of the affray. With some attempt at a balanced view, it blamed the company, on one hand, for the "grievous blunder" of importing the Pinkerton men. Simultaneously it criticized the workers for taking possession of

the mill property and resisting the attempts of the constituted
authorities to take possession. They ought to remember, the
editor chided, that every dollar's worth of destroyed property had
to be paid for by the taxpayer. Interviews with advocates of both
sides were printed: Frick was willing to explain his side of the case;
Carnegie, still somewhat in the dark about the whole episode,
refused to be quoted; Benjamin Butler, speaking for the strikers,
indulged in a violent tirade against the policy of the company.
For the time being, Homestead was the rendezvous of the *Gazette*
newsmen, who found good copy in Hugh O'Donnel and the other
chief strikers. Swarms of other news representatives flocked to the
scene, until finally the townsfolk became suspicious of so many
strangers about and ordered several of the reporters to leave. On
July 11 came welcome news. The governor of Pennsylvania had
at last decided to call out the national guard. On the thirteenth
the *Gazette* announced their arrival at Homestead. The end of the
strike was at hand.

One of the most humorous stories that the *Gazette* printed
during the period treated of the journey of "Coxey's Army" to
Washington, D. C.[9] "Coxey's Commonweal Army of Jesus
Christ," as it proclaimed itself, was an outgrowth of the period of
economic distress that followed the financial panic of 1893. In
1894 Jacob D. Coxey, a native son of Massillon, Ohio, hit on the
idea of leading a mass movement to the national capital to coerce
Congress into enacting legislation for the benefit of the unemployed.
As the army slowly defiled up the valley from Canton, Ohio,
toward Pittsburgh, press notices of its progress increased in
extent. The *Gazette* was rather inclined to be contemptuous of
the movement and looked on it as a gang of hobos rather than the
band of crusaders that it affected to be. Many of the characters
on the march were likely butts for the ridicule of the newspaper
reporters, who drew from Coxey such uncomplimentary epithets
as "the subsidized hell-hounds of the press" and "the Argus-eyed
demons of Hell." Nothing could have been more pleasing to the
demons in question, who sported their names with all the mock

pride warranted by the situation. Among the more widely touted marchers was "The Unknown," whose identity was sufficiently mysterious for the reporters. Much comment was circulated about his "military bearing," the "sinister glint of his steel blue eyes," and the "firm compression of his lips." Every day some new theory as to why he remained unrecognized was manufactured. Others of note were "the Weary Idler"; "Cyclone Kirkland," the astrologer of the expedition; Jasper Johnson, the colored standard bearer; and his yellow mongrel, "Bunker Hill."

When the "army" encamped at Sewickley, a certain Judge Stowe, the president judge of the Allegheny County Court, attempted to inspect the camp of the "soldiers," only to be warned off the premises. The *Gazette* printed a description of the happening under the headline: "Bounced A Judge—The Unknown Orders Hon. Edwin A. Stowe Out of Camp Duss." [10] It is said that Alfred Reed, the principal owner of the paper at the time, was very much agitated by this way of referring to the bench and subjected the offender to a firm reprimand.

From Sewickley the Commonweal Army tramped along the dusty way to Allegheny, where it was met by the Allegheny director of public safety and compelled to follow a different route into the city from that already planned. A night of sleeping on wet ground at the Exposition Park in Allegheny did not improve the dispositions of Coxey's men. With much grumbling they marched on into Pittsburgh. There along the Monongahela wharf an afternoon meeting, which twenty thousand curious Pittsburghers attended, was held. The same evening Coxey aired his grievances before a large company at the City Hall. Over at Harry Davis' Eden Musee an unusual entertainment was in progress. For ten cents apiece the citizens were privileged to look upon the features of the worthy and much-famed Jasper Johnson, Bunker Hill, and Cyclone Prophet Kirkland—but not with Coxey's consent. For this display of exhibitionism Coxey ordered the "freaks" read out of the association that had brought them their fame.

The army trailed wearily on to an enthusiastic reception at Homestead and then prepared for the perilous passage of the Alleghenies. Walter Christy represented the *Gazette* on the journey and sent back interesting tales of the quarreling and privations that the army had to undergo as it moved on to Washington. The departure of the army from Pittsburgh was viewed with content by the *Gazette's* editor, whatever the reporters might think. Little good could be expected from this "motley aggregation of homeless wanderers" whose singular movement was essentially "a mixture of absurdity and blasphemy." Coxey's army marched on, leaving behind memories strangely compounded of mirth and bewilderment.

CHAPTER XVI

THE HERITAGE OF A WAR

Long after the grass had grown high on the graves of the soldier dead the painful memories of the Civil War scarred the recollections of those who had lived through the days from '61 to '65. The Republican party had fairly been baptized in the blood of Chancellorsville and Gettysburg. The stern experience of the war was burned into its very fiber. These early impressions deepened as the party ripened into maturity, for war veterans were the political leaders of the generation. And so the war did not really end in 1865: the batteries were stilled by the scene under the apple tree at Appomattox, but the issues that had been created by the war did not die. During each succeeding political campaign they were brought down from the shelf, carefully dusted off, and shaken fiercely in the face of opponents.

As a radical Republican newspaper the *Gazette* proudly cherished its memories of the war. Into the political struggles of the Reconstruction Era it entered with a will, serenely confident that the party of the right must continue to triumph in the elections as it had on the battlefield. Jefferson Davis lolling in his ease at Fortress Monroe was contrasted pictorially with the Union prisoners suffering unspeakable tortures at Andersonville. Andrew Johnson, once an object of high regard on the part of the *Gazette*, speedily lost caste with it when his clement leaning toward the unrepentent rebels became apparent. When the "dictator," as the *Gazette* termed President Johnson, visited Pittsburgh on his famous "swing around the circle" in 1866, he was fairly howled down by the disorderly crowd that he attempted to address. The old *Gazette* quite forgot for the time being that Johnson was the president of the United States, for it lost no time in justifying completely the unpardonable behavior of the crowd. Later it stalked him to the very precincts of the impeachment chamber. When it was discovered that Johnson had been saved from forced

retirement by the narrow margin of one vote, the *Gazette* proclaimed the Republican senators who had decided for acquittal
to be false to their personal honor as well as to their party affilia-
tions. It did not even hesitate to insinuate that a reputed "whiskey ring" stood behind the acquittal.

With vigor the paper extended its support to General Ulysses
S. Grant, the military hero of the war, in the presidential campaigns of 1868 and 1872. In the latter campaign it placed squarely
in the foreground the necessity of keeping the "rebel" element
submerged. This could best be done by advancing the candidacy
of Grant, for the secessionist views of his opponent, Horace
Greeley, in 1861 left no doubt on that score. A national convention of old soldiers held in Pittsburgh during the campaign was
even turned into a demonstration for Grant by the watchful
Gazette, and a special supplement was brought out for the occasion. Again in 1880 the paper put itself behind Grant's third-term
ambitions and cheered on the group of "stalwarts" who stood
immovably for Grant in the Republican Convention that year,
even in the face of certain defeat.

In 1876 the *Gazette* disclosed for the first time its leanings
toward the presidential candidacy of James G. Blaine, a native
son of western Pennsylvania and long the idol of the Republicans
of that region. With speechless wrath, the editor saw Blaine
"done out" of the nomination by the machinations of the Pennsylvania state "ring." Indeed it was with reluctance that the
Gazette's editor brought himself to uphold the national ticket of
Hayes and Wheeler that fall. Probably it was the suddenly militant bearing of the Democrats, with the gleam of victory in their
eyes, which swung the *Gazette* into line. The *Post* was the only
paper in Pittsburgh to support Slippery Sam Tilden, as its arch
adversary called him, but it made up in aggressiveness for its
lack of newspaper allies. The *Gazette* for its part labored to mini-
mize the sorry story of corruption that was smeared across Grant's
second administration. It regarded the "reformers" with fine
contempt; it attacked Tilden's war record; and it warned its

readers of the economic dangers to which the return of southern supremacy in the national government would give rise. Accompanied only by the *New York Times*, the *Pittsburgh Gazette* stood apart from the remainder of the national press in denying the accuracy of the first reports of Tilden's election. The next morning after the election it printed a list of the states to be counted in his favor. When months later the Electoral Commission certified the returns, it was found that the list of states that had gone for Hayes deviated in no one instance from the list that the *Gazette* had published.[1] But there were numerous signs in evidence at this time to convince almost anyone that "waving the bloody shirt" was an outworn formula. Hayes's margin of success had been very slim indeed. Even the customary large Republican majority in Allegheny County had been whittled down to about nine thousand. New issues must be found to win the passing fancy of the voter.

The *Gazette* had long been recognized as a "business paper." Not simply did it enjoy the confidence of the substantial commercial element of the city, but it was also regarded elsewhere as an authority on the Pittsburgh markets, particularly iron and petroleum. At the time of the alarming financial panic of 1873 it stood forth as a prophet of hope, minimizing the stress from which Pittsburgh suffered acutely and calling upon the public to stand by the banks. After the panic had subsided, the *Gazette* championed the Congressional act of 1875, which provided for the resumption of specie payments in order to restore the faith of business in the government. So ably did the *Gazette* sustain the policy of John Sherman, the secretary of the treasury, that some of the other local newspapers accused it of having John Sherman on its editorial staff. The editorials, in reality composed by Jonathan Vannote, were widely copied by other newspapers throughout the country.[2] The *Gazette's* position as a leader of Pittsburgh business partly explains why it was inclined to emphasize the tariff issue to a greater degree than the Republican press did generally, up to the time that President Cleveland's ringing message to Congress in 1887 made the tariff a national issue of prime importance.

The presidential campaign of 1880, as far as the *Gazette* was concerned, was to be remembered for more than a growing emphasis upon the tariff issue, for it marked the first general use by the paper of the figure of the coon as a Republican insignia. Furthermore it denoted a high point in the campaign warfare of the *Post* and the *Gazette*, the doughty champions of their respective parties. With a flourish the *Post* related to all and sundry the fact that a wealthy merchant from Georgia had come to Pittsburgh in 1879 to buy a large order of nails. While stopping at the Monongahela House he was shown a copy of the *Gazette* that was so abusive of the South that he boarded the first train for Wheeling and made his purchase there.[3] The accused journal did not receive such thrusts meekly. In return it made the *Post* smart for its Civil War record and even went so far as to advise General Garfield, the Republican standard bearer that year, to sue the *Post* for libellious statements concerning him. Toward the end of the campaign, the *Gazette* remarked: "The *Post* has voluntarily ranked itself among the most unscrupulous Democratic papers in the country. It has reached the lowest stage of journalistic depravity, and should not hereafter be permitted to enter a Republican dwelling or house of business." [4]

It might have been surmised that the *Gazette* would lose no time in toasting the victory of Garfield in the election. Large illustrations of the Republican coon and the Democratic rooster were displayed on the front page of the paper the morning after the election, together with a legend reading "The Hurricane Strikes the Office of the Pittsburgh *Post* and Scatters Its Poultry in All Directions." Elsewhere on the same page was the figure of a boat adorning a mock notice, "For Salt River—the Rotten Boat Democracy Left its Wharf Tuesday, Nov. 2, 1880 bound up Salt River in search of the late lamented Samuel J. Tilden." [5]

Four years later, the *Commercial Gazette* donned its war paint anew for the most spectacular national campaign that the country had seen for years. The memories of many who are yet living will hark back to the thrilling Blaine-Cleveland contest of 1884. Again the tariff figured strongly—"The paramount issue of this campaign" the *Gazette* called it. Significantly the local campaign was opened at LaFayette Hall by none other than Pig Iron Kelly, the arch foe of free trade and in the estimation of the *Gazette* "one of the most notable men of contemporaneous history." [6] The prohibition question was injected into the campaign, too. The Prohibition party met in national convention at Pittsburgh that year, but the *Gazette* simply looked on it as "a sideshow for the benefit of the Democratic party" and dismissed its candidate for the presidency, John P. St. John, as a "crank."

The campaign fairly crackled with personalities. Charges against the moral character of both Blaine and Cleveland were freely bandied about. The *Gazette* exerted itself to refute the one and explore the other. Finally it came to the point of advising the Democratic leaders to withdraw Cleveland on account of his "moral impurity." No "confirmed debauchee," it averred should be placed at the head of the American nation. If Cleveland's own party were deaf to these considerations, then the religious press of the country must speak out with one voice against the infamy of elevating Cleveland to the highest position in the land. For those who cried persecution the *Gazette* had evidence to show that Cleveland was still "sowing his wild oats."

From beginning to end, the campaign was not unlike a continuous Fourth of July celebration. The city was treated to a plethora of torch-light processions, and marching to the sound of fife and drum were thousands in campaign regalia—cape, cap, leggings, and torch, all specially ordered for the occasion. At such times the leading hotels were ablaze with flags and Japanese lanterns at every window. On the night of October 14, 1884, a large crowd collected in front of the *Gazette* office to hear the returns from the October election in Ohio. As it became fairly obvious that Ohio had been "redeemed," the crowd commenced yelling, "Bring out the Coon," "Show up the Coon." This was done amidst great cheering and shrieking of tin horns while the sky was illuminated with a display of Roman candles. The *Post*, still the lone Democratic daily in western Pennsylvania and having no good news to offer, consoled itself according to report with a series of stereoscopic views that only a handfull of easily fascinated schoolboys gathered to watch.

It was well that the *Gazette* had its jollification thus early, for the November election told a different story. At first the stalwart newspaper, with memories of 1876 still fresh, claimed the victory for Blaine and Logan. Allegheny County was safe by eighteen thousand votes (official count 14,458), Pennsylvania had gone Republican, and New York, it was said, would furnish a margin of ten thousand votes for Blaine. Doubts arose, however, as the days passed and a careful check on the returns proceeded. The *Gazette* began to waver in its position. Finally, twelve days after the election, it yielded up its claims and admitted that Blaine was beaten. "That Same Old Coon" returned to his hole, and the *Gazette* prepared, with the best grace possible, to undergo the first Democratic national administration since the days of James Buchanan.

The national campaigns of 1888 and 1892 had very little of the spectacular about them. Benjamin Harrison, the Republican candidate for president both years, was not the kind of candidate that reporters love. Perforce the *Gazette* discoursed long and earnestly about the tariff and delineated its many advantages to the manufacturer and the working man. At this time the tariff views of William P. Anderson, chief editorial writer on the *Gazette*, and James Mills, who had the corresponding position on the *Post*, created a rivalry that became well known in the Pittsburgh newspaper world. In the campaign of 1892 the *Gazette* printed what was probably its ablest editorial on the tariff question during these years, for it met with great skill the Democratic attacks on the McKinley Bill and provided an excellent perspective of the background of the tariff issue in American political history.[7] It was during the same campaign that political cartoons first began to appear in the *Gazette* as regular features, although usually they were reprints from metropolitan newspapers in New York or Chicago.

The labor question never attained the rank of a political issue during these years. The *Gazette* essayed to handle it somewhat gingerly when election contests were not in the offing. For the most part the paper looked benevolently upon trade unions, although not for a minute would it temporize with lawless and violent procedure on the part of the workingmen. As far back as 1877 it viewed with some apprehension the growth of the "pernicious doctrines of communism" in the nation. When in 1886 Haymarket Square in Chicago became the scene of a bloody riot fomented by anarchists, the *Gazette* lost no time in making its position understood. In loud tones it thundered:

> These pestilent wretches, who flaunt in their parades the red ensign of murder and arson, cannot long presume upon the forbearance of any American community. The feeling is not dead which Gen. Dix roused to fervor when he gave the command:—"If any man pulls down the American flag, shoot him on the spot." [8]

At the time of the attempted assassination of Henry C. Frick in 1892 the editorial policy of the paper was more moderate. Although placing indirect responsibility at the door of the Amalgamated Association, the *Gazette* reëmphasized its friendliness to organized labor in the abstract.

In the course of Cleveland's second administration the *Gazette* sat in judgment upon both his domestic and foreign policy. The former had to do with the great panic of 1893, which made business magnates and government officials alike appear sadly impotent until the worst of the gale had passed. In February, 1893, the *Gazette* gazed complacently upon the rising price levels for rents, seeing in them an evidence of prosperity in Pittsburgh. The East End was gaining ground over the North Side as a favored spot for residences, and a building boom seemed in prospect. In May there was a flurry on Wall Street, but, as before, the *Gazette* spoke cheering words. "The legitimate business of the country is in conservative hands and is being conducted within safe and prudent limits," it advised. By midsummer, however, there was no further disguising the truth. The country was in the grip of the worst industrial depression it had known since 1873, and Pittsburgh was feeling the pinch along with its sister cities. From Chicago came fifty carloads of salvaged merchandise from the defunct firm of James H. Walker Company, the "largest commercial house of the West," to be placed on sale at Kaufmann's. From points not so far distant came armies of tramps to add to the city's already crying unemployment problem. Two iron and steel firms were unable to continue; a number of mercantile houses closed their doors; the spectre of public soup kitchens came floating through the air. Ruefully the *Gazette* witnessed the repeal of the Sherman Silver Purchase Act, which was freely blamed for the country's financial ills. For the time being it refrained from making capital of the panic at the expense of the national administration, quite content if some way might be found to rediscover the fountains of prosperity that the Republicans had always so carefully guarded.

The Venezuela question, which drew the United States to the brink of war with Great Britain in 1895, fixed the attention of western Pennsylvania upon American foreign policy more surely than any incident since the days of the Civil War. For once the *Gazette* could forget its political alliances and join hands heartily with the backers of the Cleveland administration. After Cleveland's famous message to Congress in December, 1895, asking for the appointment of a commission to delimit a Venezuelan boundary line, the *Gazette* in common with most American newspapers expressed its hearty approval and emphasized the duty of the United States to force the acceptance of the line by Great Britain. That this might lead to war was realized, crime against humanity though that might be. On the front page were to be seen such threats as: "The Pennsylvania Boys in Blue Could Be Sent to the Canadian Frontier so Quickly as to Make Our Blue-Nosed Cousins' Hair Curl and Make John Bull Feel That More Things Were Coming His Way Than He Bargained For." [9] In such manner the *Gazette* stood firmly for the conservation of the national honor and observed with a sense of gratification the way in which Cleveland made his protest good.

Already the country was on the eve of another of those presidential tournaments that dilated the nostrils of the old party war horses. The magic year of 1896 was in the offing; free silver—strange heresy—was being talked of far and wide. The *Gazette* stirred uneasily at this. Its preference was for sound money, but public opinion must be served. On the eve of the Republican national convention the paper conducted a straw vote on the issue of a gold standard versus a bimetallic standard, but it adopted at the same time the wise precaution of interviewing various prominent Pittsburghers whose views on the money question were generally considered "safe." McKinley's nomination by the Republicans was agreeably received, although with a feeling of regret that Quay had been passed over. For Bryan, the favorite orator of free silver, the *Gazette* had little respect; indeed it professed great sympathy for the old guard Democrats when Bryan swept the Democratic convention with his famous "Cross of Gold" speech and thereby won the coveted nomination for himself. Walter Christy, later a star political reporter for the *Gazette*, was present when Bryan made his début, absorbing his first impressions of the national political arena.

The campaign was a stirring one. Penrose and Quay were stumping the state, pelting the "Popocrats" and the "Silver Cranks." Delegations from Pittsburgh and the vicinity, eleven thousand from Allegheny County on one occasion, it appears, were making pilgrimages to Canton, Ohio, where McKinley was meeting his friends and addressing them in his reassuring way. Even Andrew Carnegie became sufficiently interested to write a letter to the *Gazette* advising the workingmen of the perils of free silver.

The *Gazette* in turn made bold to predict that McKinley's election would mean an industrial boom; for Republican success would quiet capital's fear of Bryan and his silver panacea. In one of its many appeals to the electorate to stand proof against demagogic pleas the paper urged:

> Let the possessors of this wealth—and they are
> people of small means as well as of fortunes—be told by a

sweeping majority next Tuesday, that this country will
never be a partner to a conspiracy to make the dollars
they receive in profits or their employes receives in
wages less than the value of the dollars they invest.[10]

The *Gazette's* was no lone fight. The *Post* was still the only
Democratic daily paper in Pittsburgh. The other dailies, the
Chronicle Telegraph, the *Dispatch*, the *Leader*, the *Press*, and the
Times were in accord with the wishes of the *Gazette* for a Republican triumph. Consequently the first reports of the event were
gladly received in Pittsburgh. Allegheny County had rolled up an
unprecedented majority of over forty-five thousand votes for
McKinley and Hobart. The editor was so excited that he honored
the event with a lead editorial, "The Triumph of Common Sense,"
printed in bold black type to stand out from the plain format of
the page. The result of the election represented, he felt, a striking
exhibition of the power of the press. Ninety per cent of the influential newspapers of the country had opposed Bryan, and so a
large measure of credit for the result must adhere to them. Even
the advertisers in the paper caught the spirit of festivity. On the
morning after the election a furniture store dealer, speaking for
himself and his friends, led off his three column spread advertisement with the caption: "1897–1901—Four Years of Prosperity and
Happiness—The Nation Hath Proclaimed It!" [11]

As the leading Republican organ of western Pennsylvania, the
Gazette could not entirely avoid being embroiled in the factionalism
that divided the ranks of the Republican party in the state. The
same year, 1866, that saw the *Gazette* enter the possession of
Penniman, Reed & Co. marked the entrance into power of what
one historian calls "the most powerful political dynasty in the
history of American politics." [12] From 1866 to 1921 Pennsylvania
politics underwent the domination in turn of four remarkable
political bosses, each the student of his predecessor: Simon and
Donald Cameron, Matthew S. Quay, and Boies Penrose.

Between the state organization and the local party organization there was at best an armed truce, which was preserved by a

working agreement backed up by "No Trespassing" signs. In later years, when the power of Quay, the state boss, was arrayed against that of Christopher Magee, the owner of the *Pittsburg Times* and the all powerful local boss, the *Gazette* preferred to take the side of Quay. At the time of the sensational struggle between Quay and the Magee-inspired "Hog Combine" over the state chairmanship in 1895, the *Gazette* rallied enthusiastically behind Quay, mustering in his support a straw vote that favored him for the office by a margin of thirty to one. Nelson P. Reed was of course an ardent Republican with a wide political acquaintance-ship, which he sedulously cultivated by regular attendance at the state and national conventions. With Quay, whose daring intellect and strong sense of loyalty to his friends went far to counteract the ruthlessness that he practised in party warfare, Reed was very friendly. During the Civil War Quay had braved the danger of shot and shell to drag Reed's wounded brother to a place of safety and had thereby established a bond between the two men that was never severed.[13] In after life, when political errands took the "Beaver boss" to Pittsburgh, it was his custom to stop overnight at the Reed home. Thus their political intimacy was maintained.

While identified closely with "regular Republicanism" and proud of its part in converting Pennsylvania into a private preserve of the Republican party, the *Gazette* was not insensitive to the need of political reforms. It was ever restive under the sway of the Magee faction or the "ring," as the *Gazette* chose to call it—"one of the most corrupt combinations that ever ruled a municipality."[14] In 1896, sensing a growing sentiment for a change in the constitution to permit a direct election of United States Senators, the paper proceeded to canvas the opinions of prominent Pennsylvania legislators on the subject and to print their generally favorable replies.

Through the years from 1866 to 1900, the *Gazette* spun out the heritage of the war. Not all the issues that were threshed out in the campaigns of these years were directly traceable to the war.

But they were often molded in an atmosphere of political prejudices that the war had strangely concocted. Whether men knew
it or not, the day of small business was gone. Already far distant
corners of the world were calling for shipments of steel "made in
Pittsburgh." Not unwillingly the politician hearkened to the
appeals of the business men, now national figures. As a large
metropolitan journal the *Gazette* responded to the whims of both
and identified itself with those newspapers whose creed was a
large national establishment dotted with smoke stacks and protected from the competition of the outside world by a high wall
of tariff legislation.

CHAPTER XVII

THE QUIET OBSERVER

> Yesterday morning as a drove of cattle was being driven up Fifth Avenue, one of the animals shied off and entered the hat store of Fin, Mains & Co., nearly opposite the *Gazette* office. The inmates of the establishment were considerably surprised by the appearance of this novel customer, who, however, discovering his mistake, beat a hasty retreat.[1]

The year was 1869. The circumstance was such as might have taken place in any little country town in America. Plainly this Pittsburgh was not the Pittsburgh of 1900 or 1936. Its first fire-proof building was not finished until 1871. Pittsburgh did not see an eight-story building until Fifth Avenue between Smithfield and Wood Streets became a business section about 1883. The first power elevator in 1870 began to serve the customers of Arbuthnot & Shannon, dry-goods merchants in business at the corner of Liberty and Wood Streets. An article about it in the *Gazette* at the time aroused so much curiosity that thousands of people came to see it and ride in it. In the nineties tall buildings were becoming commonplace. The office girl was no longer being subjected to the rude stares she had first elicited, though now and then "The Quiet Observer" was the recipient of complaints describing the scornful treatment accorded her by her male associates in the business world. Of a Sunday the tired business man might promenade with his wife in Schenley Park, three hundred acres given to the city in 1889 by Mrs. Edward Schenley.

When the "dog days" came in August, opulent Pittsburghers were disposed to desert the city for the ubiquitous summer resorts. Open a random issue of the 1870 *Gazette* and there might be found a letter from Atlantic City describing the beach fashions prevalent there and listing the well-known residents of Pittsburgh who were in the resort. Later in the seventies there ran in the paper at half intervals a column called "Saratoga Siftings," relaying bright

227

chitchat about high doings at the New York resort. Before the
end of the period the townspeople were spending their leisure time
in a variety of places. A *Gazette* article of 1896 described exten-
sively the merits of Atlantic City, Conneaut Lake, Cresson,
Chautauqua, Cambridgetown, Ligonier, and Saegerstown.

Sports afforded an all-year-round diversion for an increasing
number of those who read the columns of the *Gazette*. As a matter
of course, the attitude of the paper shifted. Referring to a pro-
posal for a professional baseball team in Pittsburgh, the *Gazette*
frowningly said in 1880, "That no such a plan should be success-
fully carried out should be the ardent wish of all true friends and
admirers of that noble game. Professional base-ball has always
borne a character in Pittsburgh the reverse from creditable." [2]
About the same time, it termed prize fights "muscular misde-
meanors" and "disgusting exhibitions," spoke slightingly of "the
confraternity of shoulder-hitters, gamblers, plug-uglies, and
thieves" in attendance, and, hearing that another brawl of the
kind was imminent in Pittsburgh, asked the sheriff of every county
within one hundred and fifty miles of Pittsburgh to be on guard
to arrest those guilty of such a breach of the peace. Ten years had
hardly passed, however, before the *Gazette* was reserving a good
share of space for news of professional baseball, and in 1892 the
details of the Sullivan-Corbett fight for the world's heavyweight
championship made the front page. Approximately the same was
true for other sporting activities. One evening in 1881, the new
office telephone was nearly worn out by the numbers of anxious
questioners who wanted to know the results of "the great college
boat race" between Harvard and Yale that day. During the
nineties the *Gazette* gave heed to the golf fan intent on reducing
the size of his card. Before the end of the century a woman's golf
tournament in Pittsburgh had become a matter of public record
and report.

To keep pace with the city's sprawling movements over the
hills, various modes of inter-borough transportation were introduced. In 1866 Pittsburgh was imperfectly accommodated by a

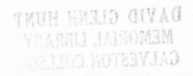

number of horse-car lines connecting the North Side and the East End with downtown. In winter, to make up for the lack of stoves in the cars, the management was accustomed to spread straw on the floor for the added convenience of the passengers. Toward the close of the eighteen-eighties, the cable car and the electric car began to appear. On June 28, 1889, the editor of the *Gazette* admitted, as his private opinion, that the old slow-going horse car had had its day and that the cable or electric car would soon supersede it on all principal lines.

Not all Pittsburghers were content to ride on trolley cars. Handsome carriages were a common sight. Nelson P. Reed himself was a great horse fancier and never more happy than when seated behind a brace of dappled greys. The *Gazette* was wont to boast that not New York, Philadelphia, Boston, or Chicago contained a finer track than the one in Schenley Park, and that the elaborate turnouts of Pittsburgh's aristocracy offered comparison to any in those cities. It was the bicycle craze, though, that offered the greatest possibilities for those who desired to ride privately to their destination. Back in 1879 the *Gazette* had printed an advertisement showing a high-wheeled bicycle, which it called "a practical road machine ... easy to learn to ride and when mastered one can beat the best horse in a day's ride.... Purchasers of bicycles taught free." Whether or not the hazardous nature of the sport discouraged the first comers cannot be answered with finality, but it was not until the peak of the nineties that the bicycle fever became the butt of the newspaper columnists. "All the world is awheel," observed the editor of the *Gazette* in amazement in 1896. Well he might say so. Everyone talked about the new wonder; everyone was affected by it. Pittsburgh hastened to introduce bicycle policemen to cope with a new kind of criminal. The world of fashions rustled as it made way for a new style of garb for pedaling women. In elegant Sewickley bicycle teas were held in honor of the new pastime. Only the tailors were dissatisfied and they because the demand for special clothing did not reach their expectations.

To the sworn friends of the bicycle it appeared that the future
of local transportation was well taken care of for some time, but
the decade was hardly more than half over when a new wonder
loomed on the horizon. Yes, it was true. The editor of the *Gazette*
was talking of nothing other than "horseless carriages" and
predicting their general use before many years had passed.[3]

Like most cities of the time, Pittsburgh often seemed in need
of a thorough house cleaning. The *Gazette* was not usually known
as a crusading journal, yet from time to time its voice was lifted
to expose cancerous conditions in the social life of the city. In
1870, for example, the editor publicly stated his regret that Pittsburgh was no longer "a well conducted, orderly, and moral city."
It had all the characteristics of a "big town," with a corresponding
share of sin and wickedness. "After night fall a respectable
woman, unaccompanied by an escort, can scarcely leave her door-
step without meeting with insult. A man's life is not safe on the
streets in daylight or darkness from thieves raised here and imported from abroad." [4] The remedy indicated for such conditions
was swift and summary justice for all offenders.

Such observations were occasional, however. Not until late in
the period did the *Gazette* give any sustained attention to the
subject of the city's moral welfare. The paper made a gallant
though unsuccessful attempt in 1892 to check the extent of the
social evil. In the face of clamor from several other Pittsburgh
dailies, the *Gazette* printed one day a list of names of persons
guilty of selling liquor without a license. "A directory of dis-
reputable houses," some chose to call it. Not content with this,
the paper proceeded to direct a withering fire of news articles and
editorials at the police, lashing them for their inactivity in sup-
pressing public vice. The community was greatly aroused by
these exposures. One of the aggrieved parties lodged a suit for ten
thousand dollars damages against the paper, but generally the
Gazette was commended for its position. Hundreds of letters
poured into its office praising it for the courageous stand it was
taking. The mayor was sufficiently impressed by this show of

public sentiment to order the superintendent of police to enforce the liquor license law throughout the city. After the wave of excitement had died down it was discovered, nevertheless, that the police had no real intention of interfering with organized vice, and the *Gazette* had reluctantly to admit itself beaten in this attempt to promote a higher standard of public decency.

With better effect, the paper exerted itself to make the city conscious of the need for better public health conditions. At the very beginning of the period, in 1866, it explained to its readers the close connection between a pure water supply and public health and alluded to the growth of population in the upper Allegheny Valley. "Year by year the waters become more unfit for drinking. Ultimately they must become prolific of disease and death." [5] Two years later the "imperative necessity" of providing an adequate supply of pure water for the city was brought to public attention. The importance of these warnings was soon proved. During the following decades typhoid fever became Pittsburgh's chief scourge, "a fearful destroyer." When in 1898 Pittsburgh's Filtration Commission decided upon a plan to filter the city's water supply, the *Gazette* rejoiced at the announcement, for thereby it hoped to see the "principal source of ill health in this city" eradicated.

All efforts of the kind to promote human health and comfort were cordially welcomed by the paper. In 1884 it bluntly demanded the prosecution of the sellers of suspicious grades of meat at the central stockyards. Four years later it took note of an offer by the Chicago packing houses to pay the expenses of a committee of Pittsburgh business men deputed to inspect the packing houses in question. Unlike the *Leader*, the *Gazette* opposed the proposition as a white-washing device. Better to inspect the meat shipments at the time of their arrival in Pittsburgh. By 1895 the *Gazette* had finally reached the point of demanding the enactment of a national pure food law in order to safeguard the public health more effectively.

The *Gazette* had an eye, too, for the cultural activities that broadened the view and stimulated the imagination of those who were too much engrossed in the pursuit of trade. For this and other reasons the paper was duly regardful of the Philadelphia Centennial Exposition of 1876. The opening on May 10 was celebrated in Pittsburgh with flag displays, the ringing of bells, the firing of cannons, and the sounding of steamboat whistles. Before the summer was over, many people from Pittsburgh had taken advantage of the special railroad excursion rates to travel to Philadelphia for one of the truly great experiences of their lives. Among the endless exhibits in Fairmount Park was a representative collection of iron and steel products from the "Iron City."

Probably that exposition was the germ of the idea that was realized in Pittsburgh the next year—the Pittsburgh Exposition, whose annual appearance from that year on was keenly anticipated by young and old. The institution was chiefly remarkable for the expression it gave to the cultural life of the city, especially in the realms of music and of the fine arts. The opening of the first Pittsburgh Exposition, described in the *Gazette* of September 6, 1877, was a truly historic occasion. The buildings, located at the corner of South Avenue and School Street in Allegheny, included a "Centennial Restaurant," a "Machinery Hall," a "Floral Hall," an art gallery, and a "Berlin fountain," the last illuminated by night. The whole constituted, in the words of the *Gazette*, "a pretty panoramic picture of the characteristic products of our mills, manufactories, looms, workshops, and general business." [6] While the Eighteenth Regiment Band and a crowd of about five thousand people stood at attention, the Exposition was ceremonially opened with a succession of songs and speeches.

In 1883 the permanent equipment of the Exposition was destroyed by fire. The annual exhibition, it appeared, would have to be abandoned for an indefinite time. In 1889, however, the institution was revived, and the Exposition came back more splendid than before. A descriptive paragraph concerning its outward appearance was printed in the *Gazette* at the time:

The sights, sounds and odors bring up the specter of the enterprise that went up in smoke and flames six years ago. The merry rattle of the corn popper is heard, and the aroma of the bursted kernels permeates everywhere. Above the murmur of the crowd is heard the tinkling of pianos and full strains of the organ until the Great Western Band drowns all other sounds in its crashing wave of harmony. The pretty girl is there and the love-sick dude, just as they used to be over on Smoky island. There is the same dazzling array of tinware and bird cages and thrifty housewives punch their fists into husk mattresses, test easy chairs and admire the tableware in house-furnishing exhibits.[7]

It was the World's Fair at Chicago that undoubtedly drew Pittsburgh people out of the daily humdrum to a greater extent than any other event of the kind in these years. The *Gazette* was at first anxious for everyone to go. That the Fair would be a brilliant affair by night was assured by Pittsburgh enterprise, for the Westinghouse Electric and Manufacturing Company had undertaken to light the area with special dynamos capable of furnishing twice as much light as was regularly consumed in both Pittsburgh and Allegheny. The *Gazette* even offered a first-class round-trip railroad ticket to Chicago to every person securing thirty new subscribers to the weekly and five to the daily edition. Frank B. McQuiston, the *Gazette's* special correspondent at the Fair, also reported after a careful survey of conditions that an entertaining week might be spent on the grounds for no more than sixty dollars. The *Gazette* became less friendly toward the Fair when it learned that the exhibits were to be kept open on Sunday. As time went on the paper became openly hostile and remained so until for financial reasons the Fair management decided to rescind the decision to be open on Sunday. Then the *Gazette* came out with jubilant headlines and editorially celebrated the "complete triumph ... achieved by the moral and patriotic sentiment of the country over the base and sordid attempt to popularize Sabbath desecration." [8]

The *Gazette* always had a good word for Pittsburgh education during this period. Once in 1872 it ventured to suggest that the study of the classical subjects was no longer of first importance and advocated in their stead a more practical curriculum. Yet on the whole it was consistently the defender of the Western University of Pennsylvania and of the city public school system against carping criticism. Its columns were also redolent with announcements of lectures by various distinguished personages whom the Mercantile Library Association and similar groups brought to Pittsburgh. Charles Sumner came to address a fair-sized crowd of Pittsburgh intelligentsia in 1870 on the subject, "The Duel between France and Prussia with Its Lessons to Civilization"; George William Curtis, the famous editor of *Harpers Weekly*, stopped for a lecture in 1873; and "Sunset Cox," the Will Rogers of his day, in 1874, and T. DeWitt Talmadge, the great pulpit orator, in 1879, also visited Pittsburgh.

An industrious examination of the *Gazette* in these years brings to light few evidences of artistic interests in Pittsburgh. The Pittsburgh Art Association was organized in 1870, but withal the prospects for local art remained drear. Three years afterward the *Gazette* sadly remarked:

> Pittsburgh has not taken sufficient interest in Art matters. It is a pity in a community of nearly 200,000 inhabitants, that an art gallery is not kept up as an encouragement to the culture and refinement of its citizens. Here certainly, where such a high order of intelligence prevails, ought Art to flourish. There is a prospect of the association dissolving. They have come out in debt since their last exhibition, and now they do not feel [able], after conducting it so long without success, to continue. Cannot some of our public spirited citizens, who are ever helping every enterprise that tends to aid this city . . . help this enterprise, which is now so sadly on the wane? It ought to be sustained, and it will prove a discredit to us, if we thus ingloriously let it drop.[9]

This was but one of many such appeals. Betimes the *Gazette* lamented that Pittsburgh artists, though possessed of more than average skill, were not generally patronized in Pittsburgh. In 1884 it scolded the community for forgetting that there were other worthy aims besides money getting. "We should look up occasionally towards the heavens," it said, "even though we have to peer through volumes of smoke to get a glimpse of the beauties beyond." [10]

Not until Andrew Carnegie came forward with his munificent endowments did art become a truly important factor in the city's education. For this and other reasons, the opening of the Carnegie Institute on November 5, 1895, was a memorable occasion. The *Gazette* reported the event with copious illustrations of Carnegie himself and his "princely gifts." For a quarter of a century the need of such an institution had been manifest. Now "The Gift is Ours." Let the community come forward and stock these benefactions with stores of books, art treasures, and the like. The following year, the first annual exhibition at the Carnegie Art Galleries was held—a turning point indeed in Pittsburgh's art history. There on the walls hung the canvasses of Meissonier, Berne-Jones, Homer, and La Farge—three hundred and twelve in all. No less significant, as the *Gazette* pointed out, was the fact that the works of nineteen Pittsburgh artists were included.

The city's musical activities were freely discussed by the *Gazette* in these years. The city was full of musical organizations of various kinds, each with its circle of devotees. It was always a great occasion when Theodore Thomas came to town, bringing with him a large concert organization of distinguished artists. The May music festivals were always well attended, too. To one held at the Exposition Building in 1879, some two thousand people came, paying one dollar each for a "secured seat" in order to hear a rendition of Handel's "Messiah" by the Gounod Club and the Symphonic Society. The *Gazette* was highly pleased, feeling that it "marked" an epoch in the musical history of Pittsburgh.[11] Another such affair, held in the Fifth Avenue Music Hall in 1884 and featured by the appearance of Madame Materna, then considered the most remarkable woman on the lyric stage, was hailed

by the *Gazette* as "one of the finest concerts ever given in the city."
Music lovers came from a radius of two hundred miles around.
The hotels did a land-office business, and on the night of the performance there was such a jam of carriages in the thoroughfares
leading up to the concert hall that the police were helpless to deal
with the situation.

The opening of another chapter in Pittsburgh's musical life
was signalized by the *Gazette* in 1896, when the Pittsburgh Symphony Orchestra gave its first concert in Carnegie Music Hall.
The paper welcomed the opportunity to hear the finest grade of
orchestra music at prices within the reach of the average man;
moreover it praised highly the quality of the opening performance,
mainly devoted to Mendelssohn's "Scotch Symphony" and
Wagner's "Rienzi," and noted that "the fifty-four men yesterday
were as one under the able baton of Mr. Frederic Archer, conductor."

These same years, to judge by the *Gazette*, saw a respectable
growth in the Pittsburgh theater. In 1866 theater notices could
be found grouped together under "amusements" in the advertising
section. As the number of theaters increased, more space was
given to these notices and to occasional reviews. The opening of
the Pittsburgh Opera House in 1871 was an event of considerable
importance to the theater goer, and it remained the principal
theater of the city for nearly two decades. The account of the
ceremonial opening that the *Gazette* set down merits quotation
because of the excellent picture it provides of the state of the
theater in Pittsburgh at the time.

> Last night, the long looked for event, the opening to
> the public of the new Pittsburgh Opera House, took place,
> and the occasion was one long to be remembered.... The
> broad door-ways opening into the elegant hall on Fifth
> avenue, which lead to the fashionable parts of the new
> temple, were besieged as early as seven o'clock by an
> anxious and excited assemblage, whose curiosity to see
> and gain place in the auditorium was wrought to fever
> heat. The street was fairly blockaded and the police had

much difficulty in keeping an open passage way for the pedestrians. While the Fifth avenue entrance was crowded, Diamond street was literally packed, almost from Wood to Smithfield street, by big and little ones, clamorous for the gallery hall doors to be thrown open. At a few minutes past seven the doors were thrown open, and a precipitate rush was made for the ticket-office, and inside of twenty minutes all the unreserved seats had been sold.... For the balance of the hour cashier Conkling was kept busy enough in selling privileges to stand in the commodious lobbies and aisles, to drive nine men out of ten out of their wits, but he was equal to the occasion, and was as bland and quick as if no unusual rush was being experienced. Before the time for the curtain to rise, the vast house, from pit to dome, was crowded with a large and extremely *Fashionable Audience*.

Those in attendance in the orchestra and parquette had accepted the occasion as one demanding full dress, and accordingly presented a brilliant appearance. Even the occupants of the gallery presented an unusually good exhibition of white shirts and good coats. When all the audience was seated the scene was grand, and the elegant house shone to its best advantage, and convinced the most skeptical that Pittsburgh had at length possession of a dramatic temple on which the largest measure of pride can be centered. Outside of New York none more beautiful can be found in this country, and but few more properly adapted or more commodious. The gorgeous drop curtain was gracefully rolled up at a given signal at eight o'clock revealing the deep broad stage ... and as its grand proportions and artistic appointments came into view, the audience rapturously applauded with hands and feet thus giving an enthusiastic manifestation of their hearty satisfaction and unqualified delight....

The stock company were formed in a graceful semi-circle on the stage, and in a delightful manner chanted that, to the American heart, grandest of grand anthems, "Hail Columbia, happy land!" Need we say that unbounded enthusiasm followed the artistic rendition? That ladies became excited and waved their handkerchiefs, polite men stamped the floor with their polished boots, and that the always explosive element in the gallery

fairly grew wild in their demonstrations of patriotic ardor
and pleasure?[13]

The reviewer went on to tell of the extemporaneous remarks of
Manager Canning, who had no idea of being made "the victim of
the inexorable audience of Pittsburgh" and of the opening address
read by the leading member of the stock company, beginning with
the lines:

> Within this toil-stained mart of busy trade,
> Where struggling Traffic's soiling hand is laid;
> 'Mid heavy hammers' din and forges' smoke,
> The anvil's echo to the blacksmith's stroke—
> 'Mid crash of iron and the toil of men,
> Where brawny muscle's mightier than the pen—
> Culture, sweet blossom of the mind and heart,
> Fruits in this temple dedicate to art.

The feature of the program was the well-known play *Ruy Blas*,
with Charles Fechter the principal actor. Such was the *Gazette's*
description of the scene on the night of this "the most important
event in our local history of the rise and progress of the legitimate
drama."

Before the century was over, the name of many another
theater crept into the advertising files of the paper: the Duquesne,
the Bijou, the Park, the Harris Museum, the Cyclorama, the Eden
Musee, the Academy, and many others. When the Alvin Theater
was opened in 1891, the *Gazette* opined that it was the finest in the
state with few equals in the entire country.

The repertoire of the several theater companies ran the whole
gamut, from burlesque shows to the tragedies of the Bard of Avon.
Irish comedies like *Finnegan's Courtship*, awesome mystery plays
of the brand of *Lady Audley's Secret*, the popular favorites, *East
Lynne* and *Uncle Tom's Cabin*, were typical of the times. Nevertheless the greatest actors of their day were accustomed to "make"
Pittsburgh on their tours. Janauschek, "the Undisputed and
Regal Queen of English Tragedy," and Laurence Barrett were
starred performers of Pittsburgh's seventies. Joe Jefferson, Edwin

Booth, and Madame Modjeska visited the city frequently in the eighties. On the list of Pittsburgh's talented actor guests in the nineties one finds the name of Robert Mantell figuring prominently. The affectionate regard in which Pittsburghers held Joe Jefferson is suggested by a review that appeared in the *Gazette* when Jefferson was doing a one-week stand at the Opera House in 1881:

> There is no actor on the American stage who has a stronger hold on the theatre going people than Joseph Jefferson.... Not to have seen Jefferson play *Rip Van Winkle* is to confess that one is away behind the age. One might about as well confess to not having read one of Dickens' incomparable stories.[18]

Booth's *Shylock* played in the course of his visit to Pittsburgh in 1889, was to the *Gazette* a wonderful piece of acting. It had good words as well for an obscure young man who had a part in the supporting cast at the time. The young man was Otis Skinner!

Still the *Gazette* did not always view theatrical entertainment through rose-tinted glasses. Once it censured the management of the Opera House severely for shutting its doors to the drama critic of another Pittsburgh daily because of a criticism "couched in the mildest terms." Another time it criticized the New York producers for their provincial way of looking at all entertainment from a narrow New York point of view, regardless of the tastes and desires of other cities. But on the whole stage productions fared well at the hands of the *Gazette* reviewer. Already it seemed a far cry to the days when an employee of the paper was threatened with the loss of his job for the crime of having attended a theatrical performance!

All the while, Pittsburgh was growing. From 1870 to 1900 the population of the metropolitan area doubled its size. The smoke clouds hung low in the sky, but beneath them a busy people labored to build a city whose spires might pierce those clouds. There were reflections of this in the *Gazette*, often indistinct and fleeting perhaps, but sometimes very clear. In 1900, the city's outlook was most promising. The industrialists were making good with their promises of prosperity. Their philanthropies seemed destined to place culture in the reach of all. Pittsburgh, for all its newspapers, was still a good newspaper field. Above them all, serene in her tradition of more than a century, stood the old *Gazette*, surveying the scene with the air of one who has observed much and scents the approach of new triumphs in the future.

PART IV—1900–1927

THE OLD LADY

CHAPTER XVIII

ENTER—THE OLIVERS

As the nineteenth century drew uneasily to a close Pittsburgh vibrated with changes and rumors of changes. The wise ones were saying that a big steel merger was in the offing. Carnegie was approached, but Carnegie wouldn't talk, and so the public continued to toss conjectures freely about. The curious were partially satisfied when in May of 1900 George T. Oliver, a familiar figure in that group of local business leaders who had built the Golden Triangle, disposed of his Oliver Wire Company holdings to the American Steel and Wire Company and, like the great Alexander, looked about for new worlds to conquer. Although born in Ireland, he had been brought up in Pittsburgh and had graduated from nearby Bethany College in West Virginia. Successively he had tried his hand at teaching, law, and the wire business. In each he had found success. Now, in the full vigor of middle age, he was ready to essay a new career.

On the morning of June 1, 1900, the old *Commercial Gazette* carried at its head the information that the paper was no longer the property of Nelson P. Reed & Co. The shareholders of the company had signed a statement that George T. Oliver was now the holder of their joint interests in the newspaper. For him they bespoke the patronage of the large *Gazette* family. The purchase price was not made known; but a reliable estimate indicates that it was around six hundred thousand dollars. The new owner assured the public that no radical change in policy was contemplated. The *Commercial Gazette* would continue to be the "clean paper" that it had always been. It would print "all the news that ought to be read by any self-respecting man or woman" and would spare neither expense nor trouble to present the news to its readers attractively and interestingly.

It was commonly believed that either George Oliver or his brother Henry aspired to a seat in the United States Senate. If this were true the purchase of the *Commercial Gazette* was a sound political move. It might very well serve as a sounding board for the virtues of an Oliver candidate. The new owner, however, maintained consistently that the transaction had nothing to do with politics. It was a business venture—no more; straightway he proceeded to demonstrate that he was in earnest.

The old *Gazette* began to sparkle with new life. Within a few weeks it contracted for the full cable and telegraphic news service of the *New York Tribune*, the peer of any in America. The paper continued to receive the full reports of the Associated Press, as well as those of an enlarged force of special correspondents. As a sign of the new epoch, the publisher adopted for his paper the motto, "Watch the Old Lady Grow Young," and broadcast it throughout the town. In November Oliver purchased another Pittsburgh newspaper, the *Chronicle Telegraph*, in order to provide himself with an evening as well as a morning newspaper.

The next year the *Commercial Gazette* moved into a pretentious new home[1] at 335–339 Virgin Alley (now Oliver Avenue) sufficiently large to house as well the *Chronicle Telegraph*, the *Volksblatt*, and the *Freiheits Freund*, all recently acquired Oliver properties. At this time the old historic title of the *Pittsburgh Gazette* was returned to the paper. To Oliver the word "commercial" in the title had always seemed a misnomer, for, although the paper had long been noted for its full and accurate commercial news, it was certainly much more than a commercial organ. There was still another reason for the change. Now that proper mechanical equipment for the purpose had been installed, the management was ready to carry out its original intention of publishing a Sunday edition—practically a necessity in view of the public demand for it. To Oliver and his associates a *Commercial Gazette* seemed singularly out of place on the weekly day of rest, with its abstention from business activity and with the leisure it afforded for reading of a less restricted nature. On November 10, 1901, the first edition of the Sunday *Gazette* streamed from the press. Each copy contained six sections and fifty-two pages, a bulky pile of reading matter for five cents!

These rapidly induced changes quickly caught the imagination of the Pittsburgh public. The Oliver family was deservedly popular in the community; its enterprise was roundly admired. Both George T. Oliver and his two sons, George S. and Augustus K. Oliver, who were associated with him in the business, were well liked for their personal qualities. The employees of the *Gazette* always spoke well of the owners. There was little uncertainty about tenure; in fact the Olivers put a premium upon a long period of service. Their generosity was equally proverbial. They did not maintain a high wage scale, but they more than compensated for this by the open-handed way in which they extended aid to the members of their organization whenever they were approached with requests. A token of the affectionate regard that the community felt for the Olivers and their paper was evinced by the popularity that a composition known as "The Pittsburgh Gazette March" enjoyed at the time. Perhaps the catchy rhythm was in part responsible, but at any event the march was a real "hit."

In 1906 the Pittsburgh newspaper world looked on with amazement as the Oliver organization chalked up another victory. In April of that year it succeeded in snatching the Pittsburgh *Times* from under the very nose of a group headed by Philander C. Knox and added its strength to that of the old *Gazette* by a merger arrangement. After the death of "Chris" Magee in 1901, the *Times* had been operated by the Magee estate and officered by one of the most efficient staffs that the city had ever seen. Like the *Gazette*, the *Times* had been conservative, relatively free from sensationalism, and ardently Republican. The circulation of the two was approximately the same: about seventy thousand. The new *Gazette Times* looked confidently forward to maintaining a circulation exceeding one hundred and twenty thousand, an amount not simply greater than the combined circulation of all other Pittsburgh morning papers but also far in advance of that of any other newspaper between the Alleghenies and Chicago. Apparently the *Gazette Times* was on the up grade. When the *Gazette* fell into the hands of George T. Oliver in 1900 the size of its daily edition was running about thirty-five thousand. In 1907 over one hundred and thirty-one thousand copies of the *Gazette Times* were finding their way into the homes and business offices of Pittsburgh. The Sunday *Gazette Times* was doing well, too. During that same year, 1907, its sale reached an average figure of over seventy-two thousand copies per week. Up to 1907 the *Gazette* was still selling for one cent per issue. At the close of that year the price was raised to two cents. The effect was immediately noticeable, for almost at once the daily circulation dropped to around eighty thousand, where it lingered for more than a decade.

The *Gazette Times* continued its efforts to lead in the morning field. It instituted the use of stars at the masthead to indicate a change of edition, an idea that was generally copied by newspapers all over the country. It went on to pick up the service of the United Press and the International News Service for supplementary use. In 1915, along with the *Chronicle Telegraph*, it moved into a new eight-story home at Gazette Square, "the finest structure for newspaper making in the United States," according to its own announcement.[2] This preëminence did not prevent it from encountering a severe shortage of newsprint supply after the World War as a result of high freight rates and labor troubles. All over the country in April, 1920, newspapers were forced to resort to strange stratagems in order to conserve their precious newsprint. The *Gazette Times* was not compelled to have recourse, as John Scull did, to cartridge paper, but it was forced throughout the month of April to condense and in some cases to omit completely its display advertising.

In 1911 the *Gazette Times* celebrated its one hundred and twenty-fifth anniversary with all the pride that such an occasion warranted. That was all very well, but the paper's owner, Mr. Oliver, was no lover of publicity. He much preferred that his own efforts be left unmentioned by the *Gazette Times*, even when they had an important bearing on the news of the day. One of the few occasions when he showed real anger over the work of his subordinates was the result of the first photograph of him ever displayed in the paper. For the greater part of one afternoon the energies of the whole office were applied to convincing him that the editor was right in publishing the picture. This attitude could not fail to be translated in some degree into the general policy of the paper. "Trombone journalism" was the name applied by the *Gazette Times* to those newspapers that were apt in proclaiming their own virtues to the multitude. Once the editor observed in satirical vein:

> We do not care to cultivate the boastful spirit, but just to show the trombone journalists that we are also some pumpkins, we are going to make some reluctant admissions of recent tributes paid The *Gazette Times*.
>
> "I enclose a want ad for a nurse maid," writes Alfonso of Spain. "Desiring to secure a most intelligent and dignified young lady for the prince, we felt sure your journal would reach that very class."
>
> "We send our scores to your paper," writes the president of the Deer Township Golf association, "because the London *Times* is too snobbish and supercilious."
>
> *Hank Wallace* of Plumbago, O., absolutely refused to die until his relatives promised to send his obituary to The *Gazette Times*.
>
> *Lemuel Tompkins*, the patriarch of McKees Rocks, always removes his hat when a newsy offers him his favorite paper.
>
> Last, but not least, the Grand Lama of Tibet cables a communication complimenting us upon having at last succeeded in getting the Pittsburgh nine into first place.
>
> We do not boast of these things, because we are not built like the New York *Herald* and some others. Besides, we are kept busy printing the news.[8]

Before the death of George T. Oliver in 1919 a new arrangement for the publication of his newspapers had been effected. Previous to the World War the *Gazette Times* and *Chronicle Tele-*

graph were published by two separate companies, even though commonly owned and housed under the same roof. In 1917, however, a holding company, the Newspaper Printing Company, was organized to control the stock in the two ventures. George T. Oliver continued to be the principal figure in the organization until his death, when his two sons stepped into the place that he had vacated. Within a few years they carried the circulation figure of the *Gazette Times* up past the one hundred thousand mark again and nursed the Sunday circulation along so well that when they disposed of the paper in 1927 one hundred and fifty thousand copies of the Sunday issue were being sold regularly.[4]

All through the period the *Gazette Times* retained the respect of the newspaper world at large. At times it encountered rough treatment at the hands of the *Dispatch* and the *Leader*, its principal local enemies after 1900; yet when it stopped to note its ceremonial birthday in 1911, it was greeted with expressions of good wishes from scores of papers far and near. The *Leader* called it the most conservative paper in Pittsburgh. The *Gazette Times* would have been the first to admit the charge, for its conservatism was an accurate reflection of the community in which it dwelt.

CHAPTER XIX

FACES AND FEATURES

One of the first tasks of the elder Oliver was to build up a large and efficient newspaper organization. Newspaper publishing by 1900 had taken its place in the field of big business. Advertising, circulation, the preparation of a twelve-to-sixteen-page issue daily—each presented a host of problems. One might have looked into the office any evening during the period and seen a corps of staff men individually intent on the task of having the *Gazette Times* on the street in the morning. From every city in the United States, from every country in the world there were lines leading to the news department, each conveying relatively unimportant bulletins perhaps, except in rare cases.

The city editor and his assistants covered the news of Greater Pittsburgh. For their purposes the entire city was mapped like a battle field. Each man had a special district to cover. If a big news story "broke," special men were detailed to work it up. After the news had been gathered the stories were turned over to the copy editors, whose function it was to condense and correct the news stories and remove all trace of personal bias from them. In a separate editorial room sat the managing editor and his editorial writers shaping and applying the policy of the paper to public questions. Elsewhere were installed the dramatic editor, the literary editor, the Sunday editor, the financial editor, the sporting editor, the society editor, each individually responsible for the department confided to him. By no means of least importance was the art department, which the *Gazette Times* proudly annexed in 1911, the most complete in Pennsylvania, with a splendid equipment of photo-engraving devices, remarkable cameras, and the like.[1]

During the Oliver régime, a representative number of expert newspaper men served the *Gazette Times*. In those years it was customary to a much greater degree than now for a newswriter to change his employment for one reason or another. So it was that many of the best men were identified at one time or another with most of the newspapers in town. The *Gazette Times* secured the services now and then of star members from other newspaper staffs. No clear distinction was kept between the forces of the *Chronicle Telegraph* and the *Gazette Times*. Transfers from one to the other were frequent. On occasions one man might work for both papers—Henry Jones Ford, for instance, was editor in charge of both from 1901 to 1905. He was a logical selection for the position, because he had been managing editor of both the *Gazette* and the *Chronicle Telegraph* for a respectable term of years. Although never very popular because of an intellectual aloofness that seemed to set him apart from others, Ford was generally accounted a man of outstanding ability and character. He was an accurate judge of human nature and one who backed his reporters and city editors to the limit. Once he worked out a style book for his employees in order to arrive at a more precise usage. The style book became something of a joke, however, and never realized its author's purpose. Perhaps Ford was too much of a scholar to be a truly successful editor. By 1898 he had already written a book in the field of political science entitled *The Rise and Growth of American Politics*. The book was of sufficient note that both Theodore Roosevelt and Woodrow Wilson are said to have drawn considerable of their political philosophy from it. In 1906, filled with the importance of the problem of controlling public expenditures, Ford went on a lecture tour to several of the eastern universities. In 1908 he accepted the position of professor of politics at Princeton, tendered him by the president, Woodrow Wilson. This was the overture to a notable career as author and public official that carried Ford to the Philippines and back again and brought him an appointment to the Interstate Commerce Commission signed by his old Princeton mentor.[2]

From beginning to end, the *Gazette Times* was ably conducted by a succession of competent managing editors. Robert Simpson, William S. Scott, Albert Farr, Robert Ginter, and Charles W. Danziger comprise the list. Simpson remained as managing editor not more than a year after the *Gazette* became an Oliver paper. Usually mild mannered, he waxed choleric enough on one occasion to throw an obstreperous visitor down the front stairway. After he left the managing editorship, he served the *Gazette Times* both as editorial writer and Washington correspondent. His stay in Washington brought to him great popularity in the Congressional press gallery and in particular the warm friendship of great, good-humored William Howard Taft, which assured Simpson of a hearty welcome at the White House in the pre-Wilson days.

Both Scott and Farr knew their business well. Farr, who took over the office in 1908 after a term on the *Chicago Tribune* under Vanderlip, was known as a great disciplinarian. The essence of dignity, he presided over the staff like a schoolmaster. Nevertheless, even those who found him arbitrary admitted that he was a good writer, strictly fair, and one who secured results from his men. Ginter was managing editor of the paper during the brief but highly important World War period. He had been with the *Gazette Times* ever since 1906, first as Sunday editor, then night editor, and finally Washington correspondent. After the war he returned to Washington and continued there until the Olivers sold the *Gazette Times*. Like Ford, Danziger worked for both the Oliver papers. An old Pittsburgh newspaper man originally from Canton, Ohio, whose first newspaper story was the result of a "tip" from a kindly police sergeant, Danziger became one of the best-loved men in the employ of the Olivers. "Dan" to everyone, he always preserved an attitude of helpfulness and understanding that went a long way toward winning the confidence of the entire staff, from owner to cub reporter.

There were good men at the city desk too: Austin Beach, Frank Jenks, Art Goshen, Dick Ferrell, Val Oldshue, Arthur Burgoyne, Jr., and a number of others. One of the most striking of them was tall, carrot-topped Frank Jenks, who was well schooled in the art of getting the most out of his reporters. Many a good newspaper man of a later generation owed his success to the training that Jenks gave him. Once Henry Jones Ford came to

Jenks with some proof to be cut between editions. "In cutting this down, be sure to preserve the continuity," cautioned Ford. "Continuity —" was the retort. "We've got to catch a mail." [3]

To list the reporters who were on the pay roll of the *Gazette Times* at various times would require an excursion into higher mathematics. There was Harry Mitchell, who one night threw the city room into confusion when he dashed in from a Sewickley assignment with a report that he had seen a girl smoking a cigarette! Another reporter named Marc Connelly, whose talents were unsuspected at the time, broke into Pittsburgh journalism with the *Gazette Times*. The future author of *Green Pastures*, a McKeesport lad, was at once assigned the task of interviewing the wife of a man who had shot another inside a ticket cage at the Pennsylvania station. While Connelly was summoning up his courage for the ordeal, Gertrude Gorden, a sob-sister reporter, went in, got the story, and then shared it with the frightened cub. [4] The chief Washington correspondents of the paper during the period were Simpson, Ginter, and Louis M. Strayer. Some of the better known cartoonists were Charles M. Payne, Ole May, Rowland Murdoch, and Billy De Beck. Payne was probably better known for his comic strips; the same was true of De Beck, who in 1916 went from the *Gazette Times* to his native Chicago and became the creator of "Barney Google." Murdoch, more of a sketch artist than a cartoonist, was a roving genius whose work on various newspapers carried him all over the world. Now he was in Arizona doing ranch scenes; again he bobbed up in San Francisco at the time of the earthquake or rushed off to faraway Manchuria to depict wartime scenes around Mukden and the Yalu during the Russo-Japanese fracas.

A tower of strength on the *Gazette Times* staff was John O. Baglin, the financial editor of the paper—a Washington County boy who had started in as a printer's apprentice. [5] How he became a national authority on finance is a long story. Steel, glass, and the other key industries of Pittsburgh were his province. With reference to the details of local street-railway finance he was probably the best informed man in Pittsburgh. Every Saturday the *Gazette Times* published his editorial on "The Business Situation" and gave it the lead position for the day. Compact, readable, and clear, it provided probably the most comprehensive view of financial conditions ever printed in the Pittsburgh area. This feature was rated so highly in the front offices of Pittsburgh's great industries that, according to popular information, it was clipped regularly and sent to firm representatives all over the world so that they might be reliably informed of the state of the Pittsburgh business barometer. When he first came to the paper early in the century, he asked the Olivers if his new position required him to "puff" the United States Steel Corporation. On being assured that he was to have a free hand in his department, he replied that that was well for otherwise he should have found it necessary to resign. This quality of independence Baglin never forfeited. His particular "pet" was the railroad business. In it he saw the elements of stability, which meant much to the industrial community in which he lived. Long before the radio business was well established he saw in it, too, the germ of opportunity. At the time of his death in 1925 his expectations were well on the road to being realized.

A fixture in the sports department for many years was John H. Gruber, who had started in with the *Post* as the city's first sporting editor. From a lifetime of experience he drew accurate conclusions that earned for him a lasting reputation as a sports oracle. For thirty-seven years he was official scorer of the National Baseball League. A picturesque character, he left an unforgettable picture in the memory of the baseball fans at Forbes Field the afternoon he stood up in the press box to throw down the baseballs for the day to Umpire O'Day and threw instead some rockets maliciously substituted for the balls by parties unknown!

With the paper again (after several years absence around 1900) was Erasmus Wilson, somewhat older now, but as philosophically quaint as ever. His friends might chaff him for being "the man who is the world's authority on kissing," but one and all they read and enjoyed his perennially popular column, "The Quiet Observer." In later life he became greatly interested in Boy Scout activities. The Scouts returned the compliment by electing him president of the Allegheny County branch for several years in succession. His interest in the historical development of the community was shown too by his publication of a *Standard History of Pittsburg*, embodying much of the lore that he had gathered in his long newspaper experience. His death in 1922 brought to a close a career that had endeared him to a multitude of *Gazette Times* readers and to a wide circle of friends all over the country.

For about a year and a half the *Gazette Times* roster included one of the best newspaper men Pittsburgh has ever seen, the brilliant Arthur G. Burgoyne.[6] One of the most versatile men alive, he attained considerable skill in almost every field he entered. Numbered among his intimates were Victor Herbert, Emil Paur, and Ethelbert Nevin, all famous Pittsburgh musicians. The all-night musical sessions held at his Bohemian retreat high in the hills of suburban Verona were the talk of the musical fraternity of the town. Victor Herbert, it is said, once asked him to collaborate on a composition with a Russian motif, but Burgoyne refused for the very good reason that he was busy with something else at the time. Burgoyne's abilities as a linguist were hardly less admired. Early in life he became very proficient in the use of the Greek, Latin, Hebrew, French, German, Spanish, and Italian languages. That would have sufficed most men, but not Burgoyne. His literary pursuits finally convinced him that Russian culture offered something unique, which he must possess. That meant learning the Muscovite tongue, so Burgoyne surrounded himself with textbooks and dictionaries, corraled all the talented Russians he could find, and within two years he was speaking Russian like a native!

From this it is evident that his interests ranged widely. He collected stamps and was an amateur photographer of note. He remained first of all a newspaper man, however, and excelled in his line. With the *Commercial Gazette* briefly in the earlier period, he became famous as the author of the "All Sorts" column in the *Leader*. These sketches were so popular that they were separately printed in 1892 under the title "All Sorts of Pittsburghers." While with the *Leader*, Burgoyne created the figure "Pa Pitt" to represent the city in lieu of the namby-pamby Miss Pittsburgh, who had done the honors on the front page up to that time. When Alexander P. Moore took over the *Leader*, however, Burgoyne became dissatisfied with the management and began free-lancing. At that juncture, George Seibel, who knew him well, advised the elder Oliver to secure him for the *Gazette Times*. On May 1, 1906, Arthur penned his first sketch for the paper under the curt heading "Short Shots," a title that was later changed to "Snap Shots." The *Gazette Times* was very proud of its new acquisition. He was at the time vice-president of the American Press Humorists Association, with a reputation equal to that of any newspaper man in the country. He with several others had stood alongside John D. Rockefeller in Cleveland, Ohio, on the afternoon when the first authentic photograph of that camera-shy individual was snapped.[7]

The new column consisted of a drawing furnished by Payne, the cartoonist, in keeping with a short poem on some aspect of the day's news. A series of short columns usually concluded the whole. Sometimes Burgoyne varied the attack by contributing a short playlet divided into "actlets," all done in a satiric vein. His topics were sufficiently cosmopolitan. Often they dealt with local politics or party activities at Harrisburg, but now and again the doings of the Tsar or the fretful outbursts of the Cubans claimed his attention. He was present in Washington during the investigation of the beef trust and at the scene of Alice Roosevelt's wedding with "Nick" Longworth. Some of his best poems treated individuals—Carnegie, for example, whose return from Scotland in the autumn of 1906 Burgoyne saluted in jingling fashion:

> From far distant Skibo, 'way over the sea,
> As blithe and as chipper as ever could be,
> The laird has run over to give us a call
> And with breezy remarks to awaken us all.

'Tis his principal pastime to stir up debate
And with novel opinions hot times to create,
So that life is no longer a dull monochrome,
But takes on a high color when Andy comes home.[8]

In October, 1907, the Olivers decided to move Burgoyne over
to the *Chronicle Telegraph* to bolster up the strength of their
evening organ. For the next day or two his column was continued
in the paper by an understudy, who was speedily called off when
the managing editor realized that the two papers were in effect
running competing features.

With the institution of a Sunday edition the *Gazette* developed
a greater wealth of features of all kinds. James Edward Leslie
came over from the *Dispatch* to edit the first issue. There was a
section for general news and editorials, another for "Special Cable,
Finance, and Sports," still another for "Society News, Women's
Clubs," a special magazine section, and finally the "Humorous
Section." This last rejoiced in six full pages of comic strips, some
of them in color. Destined to be the most popular were Payne's
diverting Coon Hollow Folks: "The Sly Fox," "The Villanous
Wolf," "Mister Possum," and "The Coon." Other artists contributed "Dr. Quack of the Lower Pasture" and "Billy Bounce,
the Hot Foot Messenger Boy of Our Town."

The first anniversary of the Sunday *Gazette* brought to its
progenitors a great sense of satisfaction. The experiment had met
with remarkable success. The Pittsburgh Sunday *Gazette* was,
they felt, one of the handsomest and best Sunday newspapers
published in the world. It was at once "clean, reliable, and entertaining," and, unlike many Sunday papers, "Its columns have been
kept free from froth of all kinds. This has excluded not only the
publication of the ghastly, but also of the absurd, the fictitious,
and the impossible." [9] This end had been gained at no small cost.
Good prices had to be paid for quality stories by quality writers,
many of whom contributed exclusively to the *Gazette*. A large
staff of artists numbering more men, the *Gazette* boasted, than the
combined staffs of all other Pittsburgh newspapers, had made the

magazine section one of the most attractive in the country. Count Leo Tolstoy, Elizabeth Stuart Phelps, George Brandes, Maxim Gorki, and Ignace Paderewski were only a few of the distinguished contributors who had helped to make the Sunday *Gazette* what it was. For the special benefit of the Sunday readers, the paper had regular fixed correspondents in London and Paris, travelling correspondents in Ireland and "Darkest Africa," occasional writers in a score of European capitals and scattered points in every continent of the world. The proudest scoop of the year was furnished by Algernon Dougherty, the Sunday *Gazette's* Paris correspondent, who put in the hands of his editors the full details of the great Humbert fraud case weeks before the Paris newspapers themselves had rushed into print with the story. Sophie Gates Kerr, later the managing editor of the *Woman's Home Companion* and a highly popular short story writer, was in charge of one of the Sunday supplements at this time. She went to the *Gazette* directly from the University of Vermont about the time Willa Cather left the *Leader*. Many years later she spoke in a reminiscent vein of the excellent training that her happy experience on the *Gazette* had provided.[10]

The Sunday editors continued to keep their educational mission in the foreground. Disregarding the assumption of many Sunday editors that "people don't want to think, they want to be amused," they introduced in 1903 a Sunday magazine of tabloid proportions and distinctly high quality. Evidently the effort was appreciated, for a year later the *Gazette*, boasted the largest Sunday circulation of any paper in Pittsburgh. In 1906 the Sunday *Gazette* came forth with what it styled "the greatest hit ever made by a Pittsburgh newspaper," a half-tone illustrated section. The first issue included "Picturesque Phases of Everyday Pittsburgh," accompanied by views of Pasadena's Tournament of Roses, and operatic and theatrical stars of the day. Evidently the demand for humor was considerable, for several contemporary humorists were among the featured writers employed by the Sunday *Gazette*. Another feature of distinctly educational interest was the one page classic, or a condensed version of a standard novel such as *Vanity Fair, Jane Eyre,* or *The Last Days of Pompeii.*

One by one, syndicated comic strips, which came to own a large following of juvenile Americans, began to appear in the Sunday supplement. Along with such half-forgotten features as "Little Nemo in Slumberland" and "Muggsby's Social Aspirations" came the better known "Foxy Grandpa," "Buster Brown," "Little Jimmy," and "The Katzenjammers." In 1910 the lugubrious "Happy Hooligan" became the joy of the *Gazette Times's* younger generation. Some of the early enthusiasm reflected by the promoters of the Sunday *Gazette* passed after the first few years of its existence, but there was no lag in publication. George T. Fleming's historical series, featured every Sunday during the years from 1914 to 1922, contained a rich store of information about Pittsburgh and its people. The rotogravure process, first introduced into America by the New York *Times* in 1914, was available to *Gazette Times* readers in the summer of 1915. During the World War a battery of competent observers interpreted the international conflict week by week: Frank H. Simonds, Hilaire Belloc, Hugh Gibson, Philip Gibbs, and Walter Duranty among the number.

Unquestionably the content and appearance of the daily edition were influenced by its Sunday sister. The amount of newsprint required for the edition became steadily greater, and the tendency toward more rigid classifications of news persisted. The front page drew the eye more than ever before. The typographer was called upon to employ larger type for headlines and captions. More illustrations of newsworthy personages and events were included. Around 1908 sober citizens along Fifth Avenue gazed in wonder at red-ink streamer headlines flung across the top of the *Gazette Times.* The explanation was that a new press with a red ink attachment had just been purchased. No other Pittsburgh newspaper at the time possessed this unique equipment, and the *Gazette Times* took advantage of the situation by illuminating its wares with a dash of color. Even the cartoons were on the front page; there was also a column-length summary of the day's news for hurried readers.

The concern for the feminine reader was more manifest than ever. The doings of society, whose queens are ever more important than its kings, were fully chronicled. About 1912, dress patterns began to be printed in the *Gazette Times*, and features like "The Changing Fashions," which first appeared in the *Gazette* about 1918, appealed highly to women. In 1916 Winifred Black's syndicated column of advice to the lovelorn commenced to provide solace for those unhappy readers who had loved and lost.

The millennium of the sports lover was at hand. By 1927 the amount of space given by the paper to sports was roughly three times that bestowed upon it in 1900. The style of sports reporting had changed, too. The public was demanding more than a plain unvarnished account of games and contests. The sports reporter was forced to ransack his vocabulary and his pocket dictionary for picturesque epithets to describe Pittsburgh's baseball heroes in the World Series of 1909 or the moleskin triumphs of "Pop" Warner's Panther protegés. James Jerpe's "Sport-Itorials" and Charles "Chilly" Doyle's "Chillysauce" demonstrated the tendency of the sports writer to invent descriptive titles for his daily round of gossip.

On February 7, 1910, the *Gazette Times* published its first daily comic strip under the title "With Mutt in Germany—By 'Bud' Fisher" with a notice that in the future the eccentric doings of Mr. Augustus Mutt might be noted every day on the sporting page of the *Gazette Times*. "Mutt and Jeff" continued without competition to divert readers from more serious considerations, until, in 1915 Cliff Stearett's "Polly and Her Pals" appeared. This was the signal for more "comics" to come streaming into the paper, until at length in 1924 an entire page was set aside for them!

The *Gazette Times* also published a number of miscellaneous features common to the newspapers of that day; Abe Martin's droll rural philosophy, Walt Mason's daily jingle, "The Young Lady Across the Way," James Montague's "More Truth Than

Poetry," Dr. Hershberg's column of medical advice, and a daily story feature.

Advertising continued to dominate the paper's format. The department stores were as good customers as ever. Household products with popular trade names were a liberal source of revenue, too. In the first years of the century, Peruna and Castoria were leaders in the patent medicine field, Coca Cola and Postum among the beverages, and breakfast foods like Washington Crisps were being urged upon the jaded housewife. During the World War advertisements for chewing gum and cigarettes began to gain momentum. The first cigarette advertisements were of restricted size and minus the copious illustrations that have since been adopted.

CHAPTER XX

THE EDITOR'S WORLD

If you had been walking along Water Street in Pittsburgh on a bright spring day some thirty years ago, you might have been stopped by a gentleman who would have introduced himself to you as "The Elusive Mr. Elliott." The opportunity would have been worth just five dollars to you, for whoever was accosted by that nebulous person might stop in at the *Gazette Times* office and cash in on his good fortune to that extent. Not all the advertising stunts that originated with the *Gazette Times* in those days were of such minor import; fortunately there were others that were more beneficial to the community in the long run. It is true that the paper claimed the doubtful honor of having conducted the first baby show and also the first beauty contest in Pittsburgh. In the latter case, a beauty editor was appointed and an appeal for photographs of the most beautiful women in western Pennsylvania was sent out in answer to a challenge that Chicago woman possessed superior beauty posed by the *Chicago Tribune*.

In 1910 the *Gazette Times* and the *Chronicle Telegraph* coöperated in holding at Duquesne Garden what they called a "Land Show," designed to interest city dwellers in a back-to-the-farm movement. Exhibits of farm products from all over the country and many educational demonstrations of phases of farm life were spread before the twenty thousand people who clicked the turnstiles the first day and those who came afterwards. In 1913 and again in 1914 the *Gazette Times* published an almanac modeled after the popular *World Almanac*, full of valuable statistical data concerning Pittsburgh and Pennsylvania. The same year (1914), the paper noted the completion of the Panama Canal by distributing a four-hundred-page book describing the feat of Goethals and his engineers. In 1924 the *Gazette Times* launched a campaign to bring about standardized traffic regulations and a system of hand signalling for both motorist and pedestrian, and the paper

presented illustrations of the approved arm signals. This campaign
was widely endorsed. Letters of approval poured in from local
firms and individuals; the director of safety ordered the police to
enforce the signals; all over northwestern Pennsylvania and
eastern Ohio, the *Gazette Times* plan was adopted by motor clubs.
By such means the *Gazette Times* demonstrated some of the many
ways by which an alert, active newspaper can benefit the community it serves.

Thus the newspaper tried to fulfill the pledge that the elder
Oliver gave when he took possession of the *Commercial Gazette:*

> The great and paramount object of the *Gazette,* to
> which all others will be subservient, will be the upbuild-
> ing and advancement of Pittsburgh—not the mere city
> of that name, bounded by any paltry municipal lines, but
> the great PITTSBURGH DISTRICT, centering at the
> junction of our rivers, and embracing within the sphere
> of its influence nearly all the territory from the moun-
> tains to the lakes.... Even we who have spent our lives
> in the midst of this great district, and have seen and
> participated in its marvelous growth, have but a faint
> appreciation of the magnitude and variety of its re-
> sources and the splendor of its possibilities. To the
> world outside they are practically an unread book. To
> the advancement of this section and to its welfare and
> prosperity we will devote our energies, subordinating all
> things else; and for the furtherance of this object we rely
> on the encouragement and support of our people.[1]

The new publisher soon found, however, that his paper had
not only to inaugurate such beneficent movements but that it had
also to battle with hostile forces that were stronger than he had
realized. A vice ring was strongly entrenched in the city of Pittsburgh and was defiant of efforts to break it. The *Gazette* conducted
several spirited anti-vice crusades, but in default of coöperation
from the city authorities the effects were short-lived. In 1901
Matthew S. Quay and the state Republican organization finally
glimpsed a long-sought opportunity to extend their control into
Pittsburgh at the expense of the Magee-Flinn "ring." In June

1900, Edward Bigelow, the director of public works, had been ousted from his position on account of differences which he had had with the Flinn organization. In his resentment, Bigelow sent his brother Tom to Quay to make overtures which resulted in the ripper bill of 1901, by which William J. Diehl, the "ring's" mayor, was thrust out of office. The *Gazette* looked on with approval while this legislation was being enacted even though the result was to create factions within the local Republican organization that lasted for more than twenty years. Flinn's machine had been broken and with it much of his influence was lost.

1906 was a banner year for the *Gazette* and for what it stood. The long fight to have the railroad tracks removed from Liberty Avenue ended in victory, and the creation of Greater Pittsburgh, a consolidation of Pittsburgh and Allegheny, marked the triumph of another of the paper's pet causes. A reform mayor, William Guthrie, was elected that year, too. Although of opposite party from that which the newspaper preferred, he gave promise of providing the city with a well-managed administration. Arthur Burgoyne demonstrated his earnest optimism by writing:

> And now right here at home we see
> The public potentates agree
> That Pittsburgh must from vice be free,
> And even now behold,
> The city dads are buckling down
> To work. They vow to cleanse the town
> And fairly win a laurel crown
> By knocking grafters cold....
> The people's will must needs prevail,
> And—graft has got to go.[2]

Civic-minded Pittsburghers who were endeavoring to effect the needed reforms were dismayed by the discovery that members of the city council had been accepting bribes from interested sources, but they were heartened by the speed with which punishment was meted out to the offenders. As before, however, the forces antagonistic to reform simply dug in and bided their time. Their patience brought its own reward, for the public soon became engrossed in other matters. The "reformers" were turned out of office, and conditions were back where they had been before the election of 1906.

In state and national politics, the *Gazette* stood by its Republican tradition. It was a Quay paper until the Beaver boss relinguished his control of local politics in 1904. Then it shifted its allegiance to Boies Penrose, upon whose sturdy shoulders the mantle of state party boss had fallen. George T. Oliver had been personally interested in politics for a long time. Twice he had been among the Pennsylvania delegates at Republican national conventions. Then in 1904, an appointment to fill Quay's unexpired term in the United States Senate loomed up, but George Oliver shook his head soberly. Five years later he was of different mind, for then, with Philander C. Knox about to move into the Taft cabinet, a senatorial seat alongside Penrose became vacant. Again the publisher was approached. This time he was not adverse and in 1909 took the winding road over the mountains to the Capitol, then the scene of angry debates over the Payne-Aldrich tariff act. The new senator entered heartily into the debates—he was expected to show special solicitude for the iron and steel interests. In 1911 he was elected to a full term. The compliment was appreciated, but Washington, after 1914 at least, was something of a hotbox. Somewhat disillusioned with national politics, Senator Oliver brushed aside all suggestions that he should be a candidate for a second term and returned to Pittsburgh in 1917. Even the cares of a newspaper publisher were less irksome!

During Oliver's absence in Washington, the political views of the paper had been well taken care of by its chief editorial writer, the forceful Morgan Gable, who came to the *Gazette* along with the *Times* in 1906. His acquisition was so satisfactory to the chief owner that the men in the office used to pass the tale around, with many a chuckle, that "George T." had purchased the whole *Times* establishment in order to get Gable. The latter was of Lancaster County birth, a product of the Pennsylvania Dutch country. A slate picker in the anthracite mines of Tamaqua at nine, he turned up as managing editor of the *Reading Herald* at the age of nineteen. In 1887 he entered the Pittsburgh field with the *Commercial Gazette*, first as telegraph editor and later as city editor. Soon the *Gazette* lost him to the *Times* where his ability earned for him general recognition as the most able editorial writer in the city. Gable's editorials were vitriolic. His adversaries were careful not to provoke him too far, for he had a searing pen, which he wielded freely in the cause of the party to which he was attached. When the Democrats were quiet he was wont to turn his guns upon Colonel Rook of the *Dispatch* whose political ambitions conflicted with those of Gable's chief.

Some of Gable's best editorials were written at the time of the sinking of the Titanic: three in particular were entitled respectively "The Tragedy of the Titanic," "The Titanic," and "For Safety at Sea." On April 15, 1912, the *Gazette Times* printed the first news of the disaster. During the next few days the paper was full of display stories and illustrations of the unhappy event. Several Pittsburghers were known to have been on board, and on April 16 the paper printed a long list of the first- and second-class passengers in bold-faced type. Editor Gable took the position that, if the steamship company was shown to have had an insufficient number of lifeboats on hand, Congress should take immediate action to compel steamship companies to be more careful in the future; that the people of both Britain and the United States were as one in demanding that never again should such an unnecessary sacrifice of human life be allowed.[3]

During the first years of the twentieth century national politics seemed to be losing the vim and dash that had once characterized it. On the eve of the election of 1904 the *Gazette* commented: "It is a common remark heard on the streets that this is the quietest campaign in history," and again in 1908, "There is no denying that the present campaign is one of the quietest on record. What does it mean? Is it an ominous quiet? And if so, ominous of what?"[4] Answering in a fashion his own questions, Gable pointed to the lack of campaign funds for party demonstrations, meetings, and parades, on the one hand, and to the abolition of railroad passes to public officials, on the other. The change of newspaper policy in reporting political speeches was still another factor. Once it had been the practice to "broadside" the leading speech and skimp on the others, but after the turn of the century few speeches were printed in full. Moreover, the extension of rural free delivery routes had promoted a greater and more rapid circulation of daily newspapers through the country districts and so had obviated the need for political meetings to spread campaign news.

After the election of 1908, the *Gazette Times* went to bat with a significant editorial calling attention to the fair attitude of the paper during the campaign. While sturdily Republican in principle, the *Gazette Times* had acted in a manner befitting a newspaper read by people of different political beliefs. No facts had been suppressed for political reasons. As far as possible, unfair coloring and needless sensationalism had been kept out of the news. In the editorial column and there only were to be found the political opinions of the editor and publisher. These statements pointed the way to a new concept of political journalism. On the day preceding the election of 1916 the *Gazette Times* accepted two advertisements advocating the reëlection of Woodrow Wilson as president of the United States—with the comment, however, that "These two advertisements cost the Democratic National Committee $734.50. *It's a shame to take the money!*" ⁵

The election of 1912, on the other hand, unloosed the greatest amount of political excitement since the days of Bryan and McKinley. Roosevelt's spectacular Bull Moose candidacy converted the presidential contest into a three-cornered race which perforated party lines. The *Gazette Times* declared for Taft, the regular Republican party candidate, and urged his choice the more when it learned that Flinn had taken over the leadership of the Roosevelt forces in Pennsylvania. The campaign soon took on the aspect locally of a fight to the finish between the *Gazette Times* and Flinn's paper, the *Leader*. Gable exercised all his rhetoric to denounce Flinn's methods, and his "slimy trail" across the records of city, county, and state. The irony of "such a creature" serving as Roosevelt's lieutenant in a crusade for "social justice" was mercilessly attacked. Stories of "Bill Moose" Flinn's flirtations with Standard Oil funds and of his attempts to buy a United States Senatorship in 1904 came out for their airing in this campaign as well. In thus combating the great popularity that Roosevelt unquestionably enjoyed the *Gazette Times* risked losing many of its patrons. Letters came pouring into the paper, taking it to task for its stand in language so warm that the editor deemed them not quite fit to reprint in a "family newspaper." When an insane man wounded Roosevelt with a pistol shot at Milwaukee, the *Gazette Times* had to defend itself against charges of having been an unwitting instigator of the attempt. The result of the election brought no comfort to the regulars at the *Gazette Times* office. Roosevelt swept the county by twenty thousand votes, and Taft came in behind Wilson. The state went Progressive, too, but Wilson went galloping on into Washington to become the first Democratic president since the days of Grover Cleveland.

The first years of Wilson's administration slipped by. It was the summer of 1914, and not a leaf was stirring. Pittsburgh's sons and daughters were conscious of nothing very exciting. Penrose was to run for United States Senator that fall in the first popular election held for the office in Pennsylvania. Mexico was having revolutionary disturbances, but that was nothing new for Mexico. There was some talk about a projected airplane flight across the Atlantic, too. The news from Sarajevo sent a flutter of anxiety around the globe; Pittsburgh's little world momentarily paused, soon righted itself, and went rotating on. But the last week of July gave the alarmists a free rein. On the twenty-fifth, war rumors flared on the front page of the *Gazette Times*. Before the week was out the news that Europe had gone berserk came whirling across the sea. The members of the alliances were at each others throats. Standing on the periphery of the conflict, Gable permitted himself a view of what might be expected:

The great war, if it comes, will not be a struggle for principle, will not be a contest undertaken in behalf of any section of humanity, will not be a fight for the advancement of civilization, but a war for territory, for more power, for the satisfying of ancient grudges and the wiping out of old scores, a war in short that will determine which of the two big armed camps is to be boss of Europe.[6]

Probably De Beck's cartoon, "Madness," on August 1, representing a number of horsemen spearing and sticking at each other in a kind of frenzy while a circle of flames shot up brightly about them, reflected Europe as it appeared to most Americans at the time.

The plight of American tourists interned abroad was suddenly realized. Mayor Armstrong was thought to be detained in London. The chancellor of the University of Pittsburgh, it was said, was marooned somewhere in Switzerland or Germany. Many school teachers from the city schools as well were trapped in the war zone.

The *Gazette Times* hastened to expand its European newsgathering facilities. On August 2, it announced that "Pittsburgh's One Big Newspaper" had closed a deal for the exclusive services of Richard Harding Davis, who was already on his way to the front. William H. Townsend, a veteran photographer of the Boer War and the Russo-Japanese War, was engaged to take war photographs for the *Gazette Times*.

Reminiscent of the severe censorship that prevailed during the Russo-Japanese War was the veil of silence with which European nations cloaked the movements of their armies. At the same time a barrage of propaganda was being laid down which the *Gazette Times*, like other American newspapers, found not easy to avoid. Early in September, for example, it printed an article by H. G. Wells inveighing against "Kruppism"; and even Richard Harding Davis, the *Gazette Times* correspondent, advised his readers that America should not remain neutral—"Germany Fights Foully—Knowing Cause Wrong." The *Gazette Times* felt obliged to explain that the opinions of Mr. Davis were his own, and not those of the newspaper nor of the great body of American citizens far removed from the scene of action.

In the face of stubborn obstacles, the paper endeavored to preserve a neutral attitude toward the foreign conflict. To some extent its owner was thinking of the large German population on the North Side and of the members of other foreign nations who had been drawn in years past to Pittsburgh's steel mills; to some extent this policy was the result of an honest desire to be fair to both sides. Danziger was particularly outspoken in his sympathy for the Germans. So it was that on August 13 the leader editorial called for "Fair Play for Teutons" and urged the country at large to discard all biased opinion on approaching war issues.

Up to the time of the sinking of the Lusitania the *Gazette Times* navigated on an even keel. It noted the essential lack of basis for most of the atrocity stories, and it sought to counteract the flood of Allied propaganda by presenting German-Americans with every opportunity to place the cause of their native land in the best possible light. The torpedo that submerged the Lusitania off the Irish coast shifted the editorial policy of the paper. Out of the 188 Americans aboard the ill-fated vessel twenty-five had booked passage from Pittsburgh. Only the first editorial reaction was mild; on the second day after the news of the disaster the editor exploded at the plaint of some people that Germany was not being treated fairly and heatedly replied that Germany was playing the rôle of a monster among nations, running amuck "with upraised hands dripping with the blood of neutrals." The sinking of the Lusitania was "wholesale murder, cold blooded, deliberate, unjustifiable." For this "unpardonable offense" Germany would have to answer sooner or later.[7]

While the submarine added to its list of victims, the *Gazette Times* raged powerlessly, calling upon the administration to force Germany to give up unrestricted submarine warfare as the price of continued diplomatic relations. For Wilson's idealism the editor revealed small sympathy. He could not see the beauty of going to war with Germany to defend the rights of mankind. If the country was to wage war with Germany, it would do so because Germany had deeply offended the American people and had failed to grant them satisfaction. Then in May, 1916, the news flashed over the wires that Germany had yielded. The Sussex pledge was in the president's hands. Germany would abandon unrestricted submarine warfare. Now was the time, the editor contended, for the government at Washington to exact from Great Britain and her allies a pledge of the full freedom of the seas to which neutrals were entitled under the law. There could be no more leniency with Germany's enemies than with Germany herself. The *Gazette Times* did not claim to be a member of the "pro-Ally American press." Its editor gazed upon the cause of Britain with cynical eyes: "She is in the war for what she can get out of it and she proposes to win the hegemony of the world in every respect through brute strength." [8]

Aside from the European maelstrom, the *Gazette Times* viewed portentous happenings on the Mexican border and girded itself for the national political tournament. Harsh words in plenty descended upon Wilson's vacillating Mexican policy. The escape of Villa from his American pursuers was no less than a national humiliation, the editor thought. Arthur Burgoyne, Jr., was dispatched to the border to report the doings of the western Pennsylvania contingent under arms there. After a perilous ride in an old army truck over desert and mountain and into the heart of the bandit country, Burgoyne scooped his competitors with an exclusive campaign story which the *Gazette Times* featured conspicuously in its Sunday edition.

During the summer of 1916, while Pittsburgh restaurants and cabarets were echoing with the strains of Hawaiian ukelele melodies, the *Gazette Times* earnestly preached the gospel of "preparedness." Rejecting Wilson for his "wobbly diplomacy" and "uncertain purpose," the paper campaigned strenuously for Charles Evans Hughes, the Republican candidate for president; he was upheld as the friend of the tariff, of the laboring man, and of "American interests." The day after the election, the *Gazette*

Times proclaimed Hughes elected and editorially congratulated the country upon its decision. This rejoicing was premature. Late returns from the West cast doubts upon the result. After three days of uncertainty, the paper, with the best grace possible, surrendered to the fact of Wilson's reëlection and four more years of Democratic rule.

The year 1917 stole quietly in, but the sound of the big guns hammering away over the water grew louder. At the end of January the submarine was unleashed again, and America moved toward war. The *Gazette Times* treated the rupture of diplomatic relations with Germany as a necessary step and stood ready for what was to follow. An air of expectancy pervaded the city. On the eve of the declaration of war a great public mass meeting was held at Exposition Hall and recruiting signs appeared over night. The greyhounds of the sea coursed madly to the rendezvous.

Foreseeing the important rôle newspapers would play in the struggle, the *Gazette Times* prepared itself for the critical period. Robert Ginter was brought from Washington to act as managing editor. One of his first acts was to suggest to the elder Oliver an expansion of the *Gazette Times* news facilities. The Associated Press was not enough. The splendid New York Times Service ought to be secured at all costs. Mr. Oliver's answer was to send Ginter on to New York, where the necessary arrangements were effected. This service brought the special cable reports of Philip Gibbs, the great war correspondent, and many others—insofar as they were not deleted by the censors. The war made it quite impossible to keep the *Gazette Times* organization intact. Before the war was over, the paper had lost about twenty of its best men, men like Oldshue and Dan McGuire. Replacements were difficult. Putting out the paper became the task of a patched-up organization of boys, women, and old men.

The paper's every effort was given to contributing to the cause of American success. It registered no opposition to the decision of Congress to extract further revenue from second-class mail, which included newspapers and other publications. It frowned on "pacifism"; it gave full publicity to the work of the Four Minute Men, an organization intent on elevating the popular morale; it distributed free of charge copies of *The Red, White, and Blue Book*, the official United States government view of the war. At the same time it sought to keep up the spirits of the doughboy in France by persuading its readers to write letters to him and send him newspapers from home. Above all the *Gazette Times* labored for the success of the Liberty Loan drives. Editorials were headed "We Must Subscribe More," "Make Our Money Talk to Germany," and "Fight On! Buy Bonds!" John O. Baglin undertook to write a series of articles explaining the financial aspects of the loans. Advertising for the drives filled the issues. John McCormack and Sousa's band both came to town to lend their musical influence to the persuasive atmosphere. The citizen was assailed from all sides with suggestions as to how he might help win the war. He might subscribe to the Red Cross, contribute to the Y. M. C. A. drives, or paper his walls with War Saving Stamps. The Jones and Laughlin Steel Company paid for a two-page advertisement in the *Gazette Times* featuring a pledge by every man in its plant to support the war. Even the method was indicated:

> A Good Day's Work Well Done
> Goes Far to Beat the Hun.[9]

At Camp Louise Carnegie, up the Allegheny River, youthful "farmerettes" from the Margaret Morrison Carnegie College were working for the government. In fashionable Sewickley wealthy gentlewomen were knitting for the soldiers (the art was explained in the *Gazette Times*). The William Penn Hotel was observing "wheatless Wednesday" with "war bread" compounded from corn meal, rye flour, and alfalfa-seed meal and garnished with "war butter" concocted in like manner from tomatoes, suet, raisins, and brown sugar. The war had settled down to a matter of grim endurance. Hun-hating was the only positive outlet. Many Pittsburghers went to the movies to cheer for pictures bearing such livid titles as "To Hell with the Kaiser." To make matters worse a national epidemic of the influenza swept through Pittsburgh. At one time nearly five thousand cases of the disease were reported from the city, and fourteen hundred saloons and one hundred and sixty-five motion picture theatres were ordered closed.

Just before the war ended, the *Gazette Times* decided to send one of its own men to France to act as a special war correspondent. Charles J. Doyle, upon whom the choice fell, went first to Washington, where he was given a uniform and special credentials through the courtesy of the war department. From there he hurried to Hoboken to take passage across the Atlantic. His special assignment was to cover the activities of the soldiers from the tri-state area, most of them in the Eightieth Division. Bozeman Bulger, Damon Runyan, Edwin L. James, and a host of other notables were on the scene to view the operations of the troops. After a trip to the front in a government-owned motor car, Doyle made his way around among the men by hopping rides in army trucks whenever he could. Through his agency, the *Gazette Times* was able to achieve two outstanding news scoops, both following the Armistice. On Christmas Day, 1918, Doyle happened in at Tonerre on a surprise dinner tendered the men of the 319th Regiment, western Pennsylvanians to a man. The reporter jotted their names in his pocket notebook and sent a story together with the names, through to the paper, in which it was published on the twenty-ninth. A tremendous impression was made by this first uncensored information of their boys that the parents had had in months.

Doyle returned to America on a slow fruit steamer, the "Santa Clara," with the Fifteenth Engineers, a contingent of about a thousand Pittsburgh men. Because of rudder trouble the transport was three days late arriving in New York, where the families of the soldiers were gathered to welcome them home. Anxiety for the fate of the "Santa Clara" was freely expressed. Somewhere in the fog were a thousand homesick doughboys, but where? Aboard the "Santa Clara" was a wireless sending apparatus that was limited to a range of approximately three hundred miles. As the steamer neared Sandy Hook late Saturday evening, April 26, a happy inspiration prompted Doyle to tap out a radiogram, which was picked up by a Long Island station and relayed to the *Gazette Times* in Pittsburgh. On Sunday morning Pittsburgh learned to its relief that the boys were safe. The mothers in New York knew it, too, and the *Gazette Times* received credit for another stroke of enterprising journalism.[10]

One of Doyle's most prized souvenirs of his wartime days was a letter from the commander-in-chief:

> It gives me great pleasure to express my appreciation of the services you have rendered to the Army and to the Pittsburgh public during your stay with the American Expeditionary Forces.
> You had good opportunities for observing the latter phase of the Meuse-Argonne Battle and you have written fully and intelligently on this operation for the benefit of the people of Western Pennsylvania.
> With sincere regards, believe me
> Very sincerely yours,
> JOHN J. PERSHING.[11]

Pittsburghers were transported with joy by the news that the war was ended. Luckily the *Gazette Times* escaped the embarrassment of spreading the false armistice rumor for which the United Press was unhappily responsible. When reliable information as to the signing of the Armistice reached Pittsburgh, many were still skeptical. Thousands telephoned in to the *Gazette Times* to assure themselves that this time no mistake had been made.

Realizing the avid interest of its readers in the actions of the peace conference that was to assemble in Paris, the paper watched the proceedings of the treaty-makers closely. Ever suspicious of Wilson, it grew more hostile toward him and his work as time went on. When the Versailles Treaty finally perished in the Senate on March 19, 1920, the *Gazette Times* placed the responsibility for the deed squarely on Wilson's shoulders. He had "strangled his own child." And so the newspaper turned its gaze away from the invalid president and labored for the success of his Republican opponents in the national election of 1920.

Probably the greatest mistake the *Gazette Times* made during the Oliver *régime* was occasioned by the death of Woodrow Wilson in 1924. In the absence of the chief editor one of the other members of the staff took it upon himself to write an editorial about Wilson that completely disregarded the editorial canon to say nothing but good of the dead. The editorial dwelt upon Wilson's personal egoism and his "excessive love of adulation," and it declared that he had been weighed in the balance as a statesman and found wanting. The storm of public disapproval that succeeded the editorial convinced the publishers that a false step had been made. Three days later the paper took a courageous action almost unprecedented in the history of American journalism. It publicly apologized for the editorial with the statement that it would never have been published had it been submitted to the publishers for approval. With "keenest regret" the paper disavowed the statements set forth in the editorial and expressed a desire to make all honorable amends.[12]

Both women's suffrage and the liquor question were political issues of the World War period that forced the *Gazette Times* to take a stand. The paper's support of women's suffrage was not actively enlisted until 1915, when the question became a live state issue; but its policy toward the liquor question had a long history. Beginning in 1907, George T. Oliver, through his newspapers, undertook to fight for local liquor option (i.e., the right of a locality to abolish the sale of liquor therein by a special referendum). In April, 1915, he presided over a great mass meeting held to urge passage of the local option bill before the current legislative session. There were just three ways of handling the liquor traffic in his estimation: regulation, restriction, and prohibition. The public was no longer in sympathy with the first, and so more drastic measures must be adopted or state-wide prohibition would be the inevitable end. Already in January, 1914, the Oliver papers had taken the step of refusing all further liquor advertisements. When the question of local option finally came before the Pennsylvania legislature in 1917 it was badly defeated, but by that time prohibition was on the way to supplanting local option as an issue. The eighteenth amendment to the federal constitution had been referred to the states by Congress. What would Pennsylvania do?

On the morning of February 15, 1918, the *Gazette Times* printed an editorial dictated by Senator Oliver, whose leadership was followed by scores of newspapers throughout the state. The editorial admitted that for a long time the *Gazette Times* had felt that prohibition was a local question to be handled by each state according to its own discretion. In fact, the tendency toward centralization of governmental authority was in general one to be curbed, but the growth of public sentiment in favor of prohibition had reached a point requiring special treatment. "The *Gazette Times* is, therefore, of the opinion the amendment should be ratified and the liquor traffic abolished." The paper proceeded to canvass the opinions of every Republican candidate for the Pennsylvania state legislature and place the information, together with the names of the candidates, at the disposal of the voter. After the advent of national prohibition the *Gazette Times* continued until 1927 to champion the cause.

The paper took a prominent part in Allegheny County in the election of Harding (1920) and Coolidge (1924). During the latter campaign the paper first suggested that another agency might some day displace it as a medium for the presentation of political issues to the public. The *Gazette Times* looked with some disgust upon the tumult and shouting at the party conventions and in its analysis of the radio in politics predicted:

> One almost certain result of the experiences of the past week will be the abandonment of the radio for broadcasting stump speeches during the coming presidential campaign. It is too faithful and impartial a reporter, and reveals in all its nakedness an empty mind.[13]

CHAPTER XXI

ONLY YESTERDAY

In 1900 the Boers of South Africa were surprising the world with the stubborn resistance that they offered to the loyal soldiers of the Queen; in far off China the Boxers were organizing to drive the "foreign devils" into the sea; in Europe fast crystallizing alliances were paving the road to war; and in Pittsburgh architects and contractors were building a city in the direction of the stars. The Pittsburgh of 1905 that was illustrated in the Sunday *Gazette* on New Year's Day was not remotely different from the Pittsburgh of today. A few skyscrapers have since been added. The transfer of the steel mills from the Point to the suburban districts has ensued gradually. From the sky, even then, the city must have been an impressive sight, its hills mantled with streets running athwart each other at crazy angles, its streams interlaced with bridges.

In 1908 Pittsburgh bestirred itself to note its sesqui-centennial anniversary. The *Gazette Times* brought out a special edition in honor of the occasion. Times were good; people did not talk about prosperity because they had come to take it for granted. Even a major catastrophe like the great flood of 1907 was quickly forgotten.

A few brave souls were cautiously traveling about in rickety contraptions known as automobiles. Some, less brave than foolhardy, were indulging in extravagant bursts of speed dangerous alike to themselves and their fellow men. Desiring to curb the mania, the director of public safety in 1904 prepared a city ordinance limiting the speed of automobiles in the built-up section of the city to eight miles per hour. On the boulevards the driver might, if he would, permit his speedometer to rise to the reckless level of twelve miles per hour! But let him venture into the country districts if he dared. A traveler who "made" Pittsburgh that year pronounced the roads of western Pennsylvania the worst of many that he had seen. The editor of the *Gazette* admitted that this was not saying too much. The expense of building paved surfaces and the failure to apply engineering skill in any degree to road construction had militated against material improvements. In 1907 Pittsburgh witnessed its first automobile show, seven years after the first spectacle of the kind, held in New York's Madison Square Garden. When in 1914 the Sunday *Gazette Times* featured a two-paged spread advertisement for the Maxwell automobile, one might have been pardoned for assuming that the automobile business had come to stay.

On the night of March 3, 1909, Walter Christy, the *Gazette Times* political editor, was on the way home from Harrisburg after having decided not to go on to Washington for the inauguration of President Taft. On the train Christy chanced to encounter the genial Andrew Carnegie, who readily consented to an interview. Leaning back in his chair, Carnegie confided to his reporter friend a circumstance that troubled him greatly, the opportunity that Pittsburgh had allowed to slip by when she permitted Detroit to become the cradle of the automobile industry. Every necessary element for an extensive automobile manufacturing plant was present in the steel city. Some day, and Carnegie sighed at the thought, Pittsburgh would regret her ill-judged indifference. By and large, pre-war Pittsburgh was still in the "horse and buggy" age. Save for strange factory noises, the city was industriously quiet, except when Billy Sunday came to town and drew thousands to his tabernacle to sample his brand of vocal Christianity.

The consternation evoked in the decorous city by the sound and fury of the Thaw murder case in 1906 can better be imagined than described. The scion of one of Pittsburgh's leading families involved in the shooting of America's leading architect—all for the wayward affection of a beautiful artist's model who had left Pittsburgh years before to seek her livelihood in the New York studios! It was "hot news." The stage was set for a newspaper sensation that would be the talk of many a year. The *Gazette Times* was not inclined, however, to exploit the story for mere effect. There were many reasons why it should not. The Thaw family had been highly respected in Pittsburgh ever since that day early in the century when William Thaw came from Philadelphia to enter the banking business in Pittsburgh. Furthermore Harry Thaw was a grandson of Josiah Copley, the *Gazette* editor of an earlier period. Most important of all, the general policy of the paper was to avoid needless sensationalism.

The *Gazette Times* followed closely the details of the trial when it opened. The "Trial by Journalism" that the yellow press was conducting disgusted the editor, as indeed it did many others. It was meet, said Gable, that the proceedings should be reported fully and fairly, but the family and friends of the family were being subjected to a kind of publicity that lay outside the bounds of public necessity.

> Picturesque or notorious "experts," women special writers charged with a hypodermic of hot mush—to borrow a term from Ade—high-priced phrase mongers, tinglers, thrillers, the dizzy, the dippy, the professional fit-throwers, the mawkish, the frenzied, the fanatic, many of the foolish and some of the fallen—and the maudlin, these all have been taken off the shelf and shoved to the front to make an American holiday through the medium of the press while the real jury system of our country is being put to a supreme test in vindication of the law.[1]

When at length a mistrial resulted, the *Gazette Times*, voicing the feelings of thousands of its readers, expressed definite regret that the outcome had proved so disappointing to the hopes of the Thaw family and its friends. A mistrial was better than a miscarriage of justice, however, and, with a wish that the sanity of the offender might soon be ascertained and final judgment rendered, the paper turned away from court rooms and trial lawyers and concerned itself with other aspects of community life.

Like the automobile, the aeroplane looked very much like a fresh painted toy in the first days of the century. Even so, when Orville Wright established at Fort Myer in 1908 a world's endurance flight record of sixty-two minutes and fifteen seconds the

Gazette Times took due notice of the accomplishment and hazarded the prediction that "we have indeed entered the age of aerial navigation." [2] It was to be ten years before Pittsburgh was to enjoy her first air-mail service and still two years more before the Pittsburgher intent on travel could step into scheduled "palatial parlor car planes" and fly daringly away to some point on a regular passenger itinerary.

Radio news found little place in the *Gazette Times* before 1920. Yet Pittsburgh became the home of the pioneer broadcasting station of the world KDKA, which ushered in the modern radio age when it transmitted the returns of the Harding-Cox election on the night of November 2, 1920. There was no reference to the event in the *Gazette Times* until five days later, and then "The Radio Amateur," C. E. Urban, said simply, "The returns by wireless telephone ... were exceptionally clear and distinct.... Between announcements of the returns radiophone music was transmitted which added much to the entertainment." Back in 1908 the editor of the *Gazette Times* had seen the phonograph, "which appears in some new rôle almost daily," threatening to do its share to drive the professional lecturer into retirement. Now the menace of the phonograph was obscured by a far more potent instrument. The radio concert became a source of delight to many. In 1922 the *Gazette Times* viewed Pittsburgh's first radio show, held in the William Penn Hotel and described it as "a fairyland of modern science." Already radio programs had become a daily *Gazette Times* feature. In 1924 the paper commented with interest on the first radio program broadcast from Europe and picked up by Pittsburgh radio fans.[3]

Many of the cultural trends that the *Gazette Times* indicated in those days were shaped by the philanthropies of Andrew Carnegie. Hardly a year passed without some new gift to Pittsburgh drawing its meed of editorial praise. The Carnegie Institute was rebuilt, enlarged, and richly endowed with treasures and facilities that the humblest mill-worker might enjoy in common with the child of the steel king. Founder's Day brought each year to Pittsburgh a speaker of high renown: Woodrow Wilson, James Bryce, William Howard Taft, Calvin Coolidge, and others. So it was that many of the activities that the *Gazette Times* reported—musical, artistic, educational—drew their strength from the open purse of the shrewd little Scotchman.

From time to time the *Gazette Times* devoted special efforts to making the community conscious of cultural interests. In 1900, for example, the paper ran a daily feature, "The *Commercial Gazette's* Self Culture Courses," which attempted to present in an understandable way topics of a literary, historical, or scientific nature. Again in 1910 another series of the kind explored the literary and artistic achievements of Pittsburgh so as to supplement a feature running in the Sunday edition at the time, "Pittsburgh, a City to be Proud Of."

One of the articles in this second series disclosed an able exposition of the musical facilities which the city possessed in 1910. The Pittsburgh Symphony Orchestra—sixty-six musicians strong under the spell of Emil Paur's potent baton, provided the city with from fifteen to twenty concerts a year, a liberal provision for excellent orchestral music offered in few cities at the time. In the realm of vocal music the Mozart Club stood out, well seconded by three able male chorus groups, the Apollo Club, the Pittsburgh Male Chorus, and the Mendelssohn Choir. To their concerts, customarily given at Carnegie Music Hall, large numbers of Pittsburgh's music lovers went. Pittsburgh had an annual season of from four to six performances of grand opera, usually the work of a company from Gotham's Metropolitan. The season of 1910, more brilliant than most, brought to Pittsburgh no less than three important opera companies. The masses of the people could also enjoy the orchestra and band concerts that were held for several weeks in the autumn at the old Pittsburgh Exposition. There for twenty-five cents the average citizen might listen to the Theodore Thomas Orchestra from Chicago or the New York Symphony Orchestra for three or four hours at a time. It was a special day in Pittsburgh in 1912 when Victor Herbert, "Our Own

Victor" as the *Gazette Times* called him, brought his magnificent symphony orchestra to the Point.[4] When the Pittsburgh Exposition of 1914 opened the *Gazette Times* noticed it with a special editorial testifying to the fact that

> This is essentially a music-loving city and the visits of distinguished artists and organizations under the auspices of the Exposition are invariably looked forward to eagerly by a large portion of the population. There are few auditoriums in the country on a par with the spacious music hall at the Point ... a fact which has evoked comment from world famous leaders of orchestras.[5]

From 1913 to 1925 Glendinning Keeble was music critic for the *Gazette Times*, probably the most scholarly and thorough that the paper had ever had. In accordance with its general policy the *Gazette Times* allowed its critic a free hand in his field. The only serious difference that Keeble had with his paper was the result of that sultry World War atmosphere that drove some men insane and made others act quite otherwise than normally. The effect of the war on music was very detrimental. Prejudice against all things German mounted to such a level that even renditions of the German classics were often forbidden. Regarding this as unreasonable, the *Gazette Times* lodged an editorial protest against dropping German songs from concert programs. Under these circumstances, Fritz Kreisler, the world famous violinist, was invited to Pittsburgh in 1917 for two concerts. After Kreisler's arrival the authorities decided to deny him a permit to play. So egregious an insult to an artist of Kreisler's superlative merit moved Keeble to write an article sternly rebuking the city for its folly. The editors decided that the article in its existing form was best left unprinted, whereupon Keeble picked up his hat and walked straight out of the office. Some months later, however, he was prevailed upon to overlook the grievance and return.

Keeble also covered the art exhibitions, most of which were held at the Carnegie Institute galleries. The artistic high points of those years were the autumn International Exhibitions and occasional Art Society Exhibitions. The latter's 1916 exhibition of American work was arranged so skillfully by Arthur Davies that "The Quiet Observer" agreed with Keeble that Pittsburgh was on the way to becoming a "reputable art center." To some extent the European war, which acted to restrain artistic expression abroad, was responsible, inasmuch as it gave American artists in general and Pittsburgh artists in particular a better opportunity to show their own talent.

In its drama department the *Gazette Times* was fortunate enough to have Charles M. Bregg, one of the most widely known theatrical writers in the United States and one who had an extensive acquaintance among the brotherhood of the buskin. So honest were his criticisms and so well did he reflect the best public opinion of the time that during his tenure with the *Gazette Times*, a score of years all told, Pittsburgh obtained more theater openings than any other city outside of New York. Bregg was Virginia-born and one of the Civil War generation upon whose shoulders fell the burden of building the New South. He did not remain there for long. After some preliminary journalistic experience in Virginia and a period with the *Louisville Courier-Journal*, he made his way to Philadelphia. There he worked with the *Record* and the *Ladies' Home Journal* previous to answering the summons of the *Call*, which wanted him for its managing editor. On the side he wrote dramatic critiques of such excellent timbre that the *Call* soon became a factor of considerable importance in the dramatic journalism of Philadelphia. Sometime during those years he met John Wanamaker, for ever after his fast friend and frequent correspondent. In 1900 Bregg shifted his activities to Pittsburgh; there he slipped into the post of dramatic editor with George T. Oliver's new *Gazette* organization. At first he wrote editorials for the *Gazette*, usually "sermon editorials," which won him a wide audience. Afterwards he gave up those duties and confined himself entirely to the province of the drama.

Knowing the history of the stage as did few other critics of his time, Bregg was not content with developing the purely technical side of his profession. Approving the high standards of the players' art as he did, it outraged his sense of propriety to see profits prevail before all else. The clean play, artistically presented, could count on an enthusiastic review from him, but woe betide the manager and actor who sought to exploit low public taste! Bregg never allowed himself to be deluded by such presentations under the guise of "art"; and with the fearlessness and independence that marked his individuality, he justified the confidence of many a Pittsburgh theater goer, who was often heard to say, "Oh, well, I'll wait and see what Bregg says." Withal the *Gazette Times* critic was a defender rather than a reformer. His frankness brought him the enmity of a few, but on the whole he was very popular, for his gracious personality and courtly manners, so typical of the Southland, bespoke a truly gentle heart.

Innumberable examples could be given of Bregg's insistence upon the highest quality of theatrical entertainment. Once in 1904, for instance, he took a fling at "the prurient play title" employed to advertise the emphasis of popular melodrama upon the sex problem. Such titles were the adornment of city bill-boards, meeting the eye of young and old alike. The *Gazette* at his suggestion asked the civil authorities, in behalf of public decency, to adopt measures limiting this practice and took the initial step itself of banishing the titles of one of the offending plays from its columns.

Another case of the kind brings to mind one of the most spectacular episodes in which Bregg's work as dramatic critic involved him. In January, 1908, Henry Vaughn Moody's play, *The Great Divide*, came to Pittsburgh from a long and successful run on Broadway. Anticipating its arrival, Bregg wrote an advance notice in the *Gazette*, which merits quotation:

> The return of the Moody play to Pittsburgh is doubly interesting for the reason that in this city it received its "trying out," having been brought here immediately after its premier in Washington.

This was in October, 1906. In reviewing the play at

that time this department very frankly dissented from the premise upon which Mr. Moody built his drama. I am still of the same mind....

"The Great Divide" is a remarkably clever piece of work and is presented with just the sort of appeal in the acting of Miss Anglin to give its unusualness full effect.

But that it is the long-looked for American play is putting it somewhat strongly. To evolve a situation requiring a Puritan woman to subsequently fall in love with a man who has won her in what is apparently a bestial raffle for the possession of her person has about it vast stage possibilities, but it prevents a shock to normal human minds that even Prof. Moody's adroit and compact skill does not wholly save....After the play went into New York and achieved a signal and sensational success, Mr. Miller [*the leading man*], in the warm glow of victory, had something to say of the dullness of "provincial critics."

If there was any malice in this, and I suppose there was, Mr. Miller is forgiven, for the very good reason that "provincial criticism" judged the play on its merits and turned to the consideration of new duties.

The prestige of a long New York run has been added to the inherent virtues and vices of the Moody play. This does not alter fundamental truths; and with all its excellent qualities I am still disposed to doubt the soundness of a play that transcends a fundamental law of psychic being.[6]

One of the large number who read the review was Henry Miller, the star, who had nursed for two years resentful feelings inspired by Bregg's unmerciful review of the play when it first opened in Pittsburgh. Chuckling in his sleeve because of the ovation that sophisticated Broadway had accorded his efforts, Miller had been confident that the Pittsburgh "Dogberry" could do no more than remain silent in the face of press and popular opinion. Still rankling with a sense of injustice, Miller strode onto the stage for the Monday night's opening performance and cast his eyes over the footlights to see if he might not catch a glimpse of his tormentor. Restraining his feelings, he slipped with accustomed ease into his part. All was proceeding smoothly, when a whispered warning to the effect that a fire had broken out in the adjoining building began to circulate. At this a part of the audience rose and made for the door. Observing the commotion, Miller lost his self-control and interrupted his lines with a strident denunciation of Bregg and others who, in his opinion, were unfriendly to the theater. Before he had concluded his remarks, the manager of the theater rushed out on the stage and explained to the angry actor that dislike of the play had nothing to do with the action of the audience. Somewhat mollified, Miller took up his lines again, but during his curtain call at the end of the performance he amplified what he had said before about the obnoxious critic. A *Leader* reporter, scenting a story posed a sympathetic ear; the next day the *Leader* "plugged" the story, not without a few malicious touches that lent flavor to the account. Miller was quoted as accusing "the *Gazette Times* poseur" of a determined effort to invest Professor Moody's masterpiece with the stigma of immorality. Moreover this "Black Hand" attack must be stopped; to that end Miller was resolved "never to appear again in this city until I am assured that the city is rid of the evil influence of this man." True to its policy of giving its dramatic critic a free rein in his own department, the *Gazette Times* made no move to discipline him. The city was thrown into an uproar immediately, but even those who thought Bregg's criticism too severe approved the moderate manner in which he answered the exaggerated charges hurled at him by the tempestuous Miller. After some time the excitement died down, and within a year the actor, all smiles, was ready to sit down at the dinner table with Bregg and forget all about his wrath.[7]

Bregg was accustomed to receiving many letters from stars on the theatrical horizon. David Belasco, whom he gently styled "The Knight Errant of the Naughty Ladies," was a frequent correspondent. So too were Mrs. Fiske, Richard Mansfield, David Warfield, and many other theatrical luminaries of the time. Booth Tarkington wrote to ask for suggestions in remodelling the play,

Poldekin, which had been remade to provide a vehicle for George Arliss. On another occasion, after hearing Bregg deliver an evening lecture in an East End church, a professor of English at one of the local institutions of higher learning penned an earnest appreciation well summed up in the words:

> It was what church men, live men, young men needed, and pardon me for saying it, you with your deep earnestness, high ideals, and sane view were just the man to give it....
>
> Let me add that there are many in Pittsburgh who are grateful to the Gazette Times for its free rein in dramatic criticism and for the wise dramatic editor, many more who appreciate your earnest and sound criticism. I am especially thankful for this opportunity to feel your personality through your voice.[8]

The old timers will probably recollect the feud which arose between the *Gazette Times* and the Nixon Theatre over a review of *The Girl in the Taxi*, thought by the Nixon management to be quite unwarrantable. The Nixon Theater was new at the time. On the day of its opening in 1903 (a big *Gazette* news story) it had been called the world's perfect theater. Henry Nixon, the proprietor, aiming a blow at the critic who had maligned the play, started the fracas by withdrawing all his advertising from the *Gazette Times* and issued an order barring Bregg from the playhouse. Backing its critic to the limit, the *Gazette Times* made a public statement explaining the reason for Nixon's action and promised that a Mary Roberts Rinehart play coming the next week would still be reviewed, just as any future productions would be, even if Bregg's way to the theater had to be paid by his employers. The paper was deservedly popular on account of its stand. One communicant congratulated the city on having "some really first class newspapers that will take up their readers' interest before an advertiser's when an advertiser arrogantly forces the issue." For nearly a year, the Nixon kept its advertising out of the *Gazette Times*. Then, because of the loss that this policy entailed, the management rescinded its action and resumed normal business relations with the paper.[9] Such tempests were the daily stock and trade of the theater critic.

Like most lovers of the legitimate drama, Bregg was disturbed from the very first by the vogue that the moving pictures were coming to have. It was back in June, 1905, that the first moving picture theater devoted exclusively to cinematic productions in the history of the world started up under the name of "The Nickelodeon" on Smithfield Street in the Triangle. There was no contemporary hint of the new form of entertainment in the *Gazette* but sometime later the editor commented with interest on the large numbers who were finding their way to the "nickle show." [10] The *Gazette Times* saw three indictments against the prevailing type of movie: perversion and debasement of the child's imagination, danger to the eye from constant exposure to the electric screen, and finally the dark narrow rooms, whose unwholesome ventilation and cooped up space were harmful to the young and old of both sexes. The force of these objections could hardly have been strongly felt, for moving picture houses sprang up in Pittsburgh in the miraculous way of filling stations in a later decade, and many of them were in the business section, where plentiful crowds offset the added expense of showing feature films. The war accelerated the increase in their numbers. In an attempt to forget their anxiety or sorrows people demanded more and more entertainment. Theaters of all kinds did a rushing business. One of the biggest "scoops" the *Gazette Times* made during the World War was a showing in February, 1915, of the first moving pictures direct from the battlefields of Europe. Bregg did not live to see the luxurious temples of the Loew and Warner circuits. For him the evil day when the legitimate stage was at last restricted to one theater in Pittsburgh was postponed. After his death others came along to keep up the high standards that his name signified in Pittsburgh's theater world.

PART VI—1927–1936

THE NEWSPAPER OF TODAY

CHAPTER XXII

THE LAST MERGER

In July of 1927, less than three months after Charles A. Lindbergh had proved that transatlantic flights in heavier-than-air machines were feasible, a major revolution occurred in the Pittsburgh newspaper world. Not that the local news field was unused to sudden changes. In 1923 the Pittsburgh newspapers had banded together to reduce the costs of publication by joint action; as a result, the moribund *Dispatch* and *Leader* had been shuttled into the hands of a combine of Pittsburgh newspaper owners, whose presiding spirit was Arthur E. Braun of the *Post*. These papers were dissolved upon their acquisition by the combine; their circulation and the good will that went along with it were divided among the *Post*, the *Sun*, the *Press*, the *Gazette Times*, and the *Chronicle Telegraph*. The arrangement was mutually satisfactory. That Pittsburgh had long been an "over papered" city was manifest. Both readers and advertisers were pleased. Then in 1924 came a fresh surprise. Colonel Hershman, a participant in the earlier agreement, decided to sell the *Press* to the Scripps-Howard syndicate, which was anxious to break into the Pittsburgh field now that it had become so attractive.

William Randolph Hearst had also negotiated at one time for the *Press* and never relinquished his purpose of entering the Pittsburgh field. In 1927 he approached the Olivers and arranged the purchase of the *Gazette Times* and the *Chronicle Telegraph*.

At about the same time Arthur E. Braun, representing the Given estate, which owned the morning *Post* and evening *Sun*, was negotiating with Paul Block, a prominent publisher, for the sale of those properties. Even before the deal was actually closed, Mr. Block arranged with Mr. Hearst to exchange the evening *Sun* for the morning *Gazette Times*, which by consolidation gave the former the *Post-Gazette*, being then and now Pittsburgh's only morning newspaper. On August 2, 1927, the *Post-Gazette* made its bow before the Pittsburgh public.

The merger was veritably a miracle of political journalism. The *Post* and the *Gazette* had for so long been ranged on opposite sides of the political fence that their combination must have seemed incredible to one familiar with their past. The *Post* had a history as honorable and only less venerable than that of the *Gazette*. On September 1, 1842, William H. Smith, editor of the weekly *Pittsburgh Mercury and Democrat*, and Thomas Phillips of the *American Manufacturer*, another weekly, joined forces and spun rosy plans for the issuance of a daily. Their equipment consisted of the typographical layout on hand and forty-four dollars cash capital to apply on the first week's wages. Ten days later the first edition of the *Daily Post*, some two thousand copies, was rolled out under the roof of the old Mansion House at the intersection of Wood and Fifth Streets. Surviving the great fire of 1845, of which it gave one of the best accounts printed, the *Post* pushed aggressively on. Almost simultaneously it secured telegraphic news service and a steam press. In honor of the event the *Post* originated a new department that bore the powerful name, "Received by Lightning; Printed by Steam."

After numerous changes of ownership the *Post* was sold in 1857 to James P. Barr, who had been with it ever since it started. During the Civil War the paper was handicapped by the stigma that had fallen upon the Democratic party in western Pennsylvania. There were muttered threats that if Barr did not mend his ways he would find himself strung up to a telegraph pole in front of his own office. There was talk of destroying his plant, too. Fearing that these menaces were a prelude to violence, Barr at length took his case to some of the most respected Republican leaders in the city and informed them that if his rights as an American citizen were disregarded the city must take the consequences, for he would resist to the end any interference with himself or his property. After that he was not molested.

Once the war was over, Barr associated with himself Edwin A. Myers, William Schoyer, and Joseph S. Lare as J. P. Barr & Co. This firm name was continued until 1886, when the title "The

Post Publishing Co." was substituted. The fiftieth anniversary of the paper's founding in 1892 was celebrated in an unusual way, for on that occasion, the Sunday *Post* emerged from its chrysalis and proved almost immediately successful. During the nineties the *Post* won many laurels. In 1896 it introduced a special cable and wire service that was the envy of its contemporaries. Chastened for the moment by a fire in 1897 that compelled it to take temporary lodgings with the *Leader*, the *Post* entered the Spanish American War days with such enterprise and skill in news gathering that it gained favorable notice everywhere.

In fact it was the Spanish American War that provided the *Post* with the opportunity for a journalistic coup that its staff could never forget—it scooped the country with an account of Dewey's victory at Manila Bay twenty-four hours in advance of any other American newspaper. The story, appearing under a Hong Kong dateline, was written in Pittsburgh. The "Hong Kong correspondent," G. Schlotterbeck, had never seen Hong Kong except in his mind's eye, and to him Dewey's fleet was as much a matter of curiosity as it was to any news-hungry Pittsburgher. The bulletins from across the Pacific had told just enough to be tantalizing. They indicated that a battle had been fought, even that Dewey had won, but otherwise they had been eloquently silent. All day Sunday and late Sunday night Joe Myers, the managing editor, sat in his office poring over the disappointing bulletins and waiting for the complete story. Suppose that the story were to arrive after the morning edition had gone to press. Then the evening papers, no friends of the *Post*, would proclaim their triumph. Again it might be that one of the other morning papers, the *Commercial Gazette* or the *Dispatch*, had the story in its possession at that very moment and was waiting to spring it in the last edition. What happened next is best related by Schlotterbeck himself:

> At 1:30 Monday morning, Joe Myers ... called me into his office and said, abruptly: "I appoint you our special correspondent at Hong Kong."

"You have a lively imagination," the managing editor
continued, "now weave these few bulletins into a connected story. We will set it in 10-point and triple-lead it,
so as to fill the entire front page."

I went to my task with high enthusiasm ... and
within an hour had the story complete.

Demand for the "Post" was so tremendous on Monday
morning that the presses were kept running until noon.
The old Pittsburgh "Dispatch," owned by the O'Neils,
was flabbergasted, and for months showed its grief at
being scooped out of its boots.

On Tuesday forenoon a letter from Uniontown arrived, reading as follows: "Your correspondent was so
accurate in his details that he must have been on both
flagships at the same time." [1]

Soon after the turn of the century Sidney Smith, the creator
of "The Gumps," came to work for the *Post* as political cartoonist.
As the *Post's* only "artist," it was his duty to fashion the cartoons,
turn out the illustrations for the Sunday magazine section, and
perform all the retouching on the photograph and line drawings
that were used in the paper. Sometimes work of a less routine
nature came his way. Once he kidnapped his small daughter in
violation of a court order that only permitted him to visit her at
intervals. Carrying her in his arms, he hopped a ride on a freight
train from Bloomington, Indiana, to Pittsburgh. With the sheriff
at his heels, he became a fugitive from justice, but he sent in his
daily cartoons to the *Post* editorial office from scattered points in
West Virginia, then Ohio, then New York, and finally Maryland.
The sheriff was especially exercised by the fact that the absconding
Smith's cartoons continued to appear daily in the *Post*, although
the man had vanished seemingly without a trace. At last the
governor of Pennsylvania came to Smith's rescue with a statement
to the effect that he would honor no extradition papers if the
cartoonist were caught.

In 1906 the *Post* started an afternoon paper, the *Sun*, which
became popular almost as quickly as its famous namesake. Over
118,000 copies were sold the first day. As a party journal the *Post*

now took it upon itself to conduct a vigorous campaign against factionalism. Much credit inhered to it for the harmony that was gradually restored to the councils of the Democratic party, county and state, during those years. All through his stormy term in the White House the *Post* gave President Wilson strong and continuous support. It was one of the first newspapers in the country to advise his renomination in 1916, and its influence was chiefly responsible for raising his 1916 vote total to twenty-one thousand votes above that of 1912. It is no less significant that, when in 1924 a story from the *Post* was honored by being included in a collection of the best news stories of that year, the theme was that of Wilson in his last illness silently receiving a succession of callers, old friends who had come to say a last farewell to their dying chief.[1]

The *Post* was by no means insensitive to the need for community betterment. It conducted several vigorous anti-vice crusades. One of them, undertaken in 1925 in coöperation with the Citizen's League, brought to light the glaring weaknesses of local prohibition enforcement and the swarms of speakeasies that thrived in the midst of the city of churches. The idea of the Sesquicentennial celebration of 1908 was conceived by an editorial writer on the *Post*, Burd S. Patterson. Repeated *Post* editorials urging the celebration of this paramount municipal event were probably the strongest factor in inspiring the community to lay plans for the commemorative exercises.

During the World War the *Post* laid claim to the distinction of being the war paper of Pittsburgh. It was entitled to no small share of the credit for the success of the local Liberty Loan drives. In one night $750,000 was raised as a result of the hysterical excitement engendered by an open-air entertainment held on a platform in front of the *Post* building and sponsored by the *Post*. Mayor Babcock was there to speak; special moving pictures of the soldier boys at Camp Lee were shown.

It is a matter of pride, as well, to the old *Post* organization that the first radio broadcast in the history of the world, referred to before as having taken place on election night, November 2, 1920, issued from a studio in the Post Building, where the Westinghouse station KDKA was housed until 1927.[3]

So much interested in aeronautics was the *Post* that it was called by many "the aviation paper of Pittsburgh." It was one of the first to have an aviation editor. In 1918 it undertook to amuse the town with an amazing airplane circus in Schenley Park. This was vastly entertaining for the children, some of whom were already enrolled in another activity of the paper that drew to itself national attention. At one time over 125,000 children were members of the Fair Play Club, whose "fair play" pledge was administered to them by the *Post's* Uncle Walt (Garett Geerlings). For a time the members of the club furnished the material unaided for a whole section of the Sunday edition reserved specifically for them. In these and other ways, the *Post* retained the loyalty of its following and built up its daily circulation, until in 1927 the figure was not far short of 150,000.

After the consolidation the *Post-Gazette* underwent a drastic change in makeup. The two papers had used a somewhat gaudy format with two or three banner headlines. At the wish of the new owner, a conservative dress was adopted, and the paper used a standard three- or four-column makeup for the lead story.

Strong emphasis was placed upon news coverage. At various times the paper made use of the facilities of the Associated Press, the United Press, the Consolidated Press, the Chicago Tribune Service, the New York World Service, the New York Times Service, and the Universal Service. The New York Times Service was dropped during the depression, but even so the *Post-Gazette* continued to possess more wire facilities than any other Pittsburgh paper, for a time more than any other newspaper in the country. Very recently the North American Newspaper Alliance Wire Service was added to its other facilities. News was emphasized, rather than features; from the start, the paper ran two to four more pages of news matter daily than either of its predecessors had done.

The *Post-Gazette* took leadership in the daily field almost

PAUL BLOCK, PUBLISHER OF THE POST-GAZETTE

RIVERS DROP; CREST 46 FEET
THOUSANDS AWAITING RELIEF

Johnstown Has 10,000 Homeless

Three Known Dead, Two Reported Drowned.

RUIN GENERAL

False Report of Dam Breaking Starts New Panic.

JOHNSTOWN, Pa. (By Telephone From Ebensburg, 13 Miles Away), March 18 (A. P.)—The suffering citizens of this flood-ravaged city were thrown into a panic a second time today by reports the great Quemahoning dam had broken but their latest fears apparently were unfounded.

State troopers reported more than 10,000 homeless in this city, 6,000 of whom live within the downtown devastated district. Three are known dead; two are reported drowned.

As a precautionary measure, however, the troopers diverted some 15,000 refugees who had been on an airstrip in to Nanty to more of the danger zone in the dark should give way.

(Continued on Page Eight)

Health Facilities Are Mustered To Fight Pestilence

Food, Shelter and Pure Water Supply Most Pressing Problems; Typhoid Danger Menacing.

Pestilence, the horrible aftermath of so many big floods, was the threat against which city and county authorities, medical groups, welfare organizations and businessmen had organized last night under direction of the Red Cross.

Dengue of Typhoid Epidemic Acute.

(Continued on Page Eight)

Relief Groups Speed Action

Police, Firemen, Red Cross and All Other Relief Agencies Swing Into Action; McNair Presides at Special Safety Conference.

Paralyzed Pittsburgh threw its greatest concentration of manpower into the prevention of public safety as dusk descended on the stricken city last night following an emergency meeting of all city officials in the City-County building late in the afternoon.

(Continued on Page Eight)

Reporter in Skiff Tours Flood Area

Scores Found Marooned and Hungry Amid Destruction in Vast, Swirling Lake Covering Triangle District.

*By Charles H. Allred,
Post-Gazette Staff Writer*

(Continued on Page Eight)

Explosions And Fires Add Peril

Oil Plant in Flames Under Liberty Bridge

SEVEN INJURED

Alarms Keep Fighters On Alert, Many On Rescue Work.

Following in the wake of the surging waters that swept over Pittsburgh, fires and explosions last night added new peril to flood-stricken residents of the city.

(Continued on Page Eight)

48 DEATHS FROM FLOODS IN COUNTRY

By the Associated Press.

Partly eight deaths were attributed to floods and correlated weather conditions in the eastern area at midnight. The deaths by states:

Pennsylvania	13
Vermont	7
New York	6
Maryland	4
New Hampshire	3

Rhine Peace Agreed Upon

Plan Is Adopted to Adjust German Occupation Of Territory

Copyright, 1936, by Associated Press

LONDON, Thursday, March 19.—A British agreement and partial solution of the German re-occupation of the Rhineland.

(Continued on Page Eight)

BIG AID FUND VOTED; TROOPS GUARD CITY; EIGHT KNOWN DEAD

Power Fails, Large Area Is in Darkness; Trolleys Stop; Food and Water Scarcity Add To Peril in Wake of Flood.

Pittsburgh's roaring flood waters began receding early this morning leaving a frightful toll of death and terror and property damage in their wake.

Even as the rolling yellow tide of the three rivers swept misery into new sections of the county, word came that their level at The Point had dropped a foot in the hour between 12:30 and 1:30 o'clock, after attaining a crest of 46 feet.

Darkness and hunger and thirst, and the threat of an imminent disease epidemic hung over the beleaguered city, despite the cheering words from observers.

Weather Observer W. S. Brotzman announced that he expected the fall of the flood to continue, with the stage about 42 feet at the Point by morning.

City and Federal Governments joined in the efforts to relieve the suffering caused by the flood, and to rehabilitate the district's inhabitants after the rivers drop.

President Roosevelt last night ordered $1,000,000 appropriation for relief of victims, according to a report from informed sources, and City council, meeting with the county commissioners, voted another million, after assigning the Red Cross to care for the thousand of sufferers.

20 FEET OF WATER IN SOME STREETS.

Six more persons were drowned while police scouted in boats through the submerged streets. Two had been drowned the previous day.

Great timbers, roofs of houses, trees — all spilled through the currents of the downtown district, crashing through plate-glass windows and spilling thousands of dollars worth of merchandise into the bulging flood.

Electric power went out in virtually every section of the city, with no chance of light until the rivers drop at least to the 12-foot stage.

Water was cut off in sewers of communities. The city was only enough in its reservoirs to last until Friday morning, at the latest. Gas lines were out in the early evening and most of the city was left without heat.

Street car service was abandoned in all but the East End and East Boroughs section, and there were no trains, except a few shuttles, anywhere within the vast metropolitan district, populated by nearly 2,000,000 people.

TROOPS ARRIVE, MAYOR PROCLAIMS EMERGENCY

National Guardsmen held to devices section under tight control amounting to virtual martial law, refusing entrance to any but those on urgent business.

(Continued on Page Eight)

INSPIRING SPIRIT SHOWN

Because of flood conditions and the complete failure of electric power, it was not possible for any newspaper to be printed in Pittsburgh today. We are greatly indebted to the New Castle News for the proffer of its facilities for the production of this edition.

Unfortunately many departments and most of our features were necessarily omitted today. We also regret that due to lack of engraving facilities we were unable to use a number of fine late flood pictures, but expect to print them tomorrow. Every effort is being made to restore operations on a basis approximating normal as quickly as possible.

The Post-Gazette takes this opportunity to thank the loyal men and women associated with us who have done such splendid work under the most trying circumstances. Their spirit has been a real inspiration; nothing could have been finer.

Of course, it is unnecessary to say that all co-workers, including union men, who would have been employed by us regularly under normal conditions will receive full salary during this period. Whether or not they have all been able to do their usual jobs is not important; there is no question of their eagerness to do everything in their power to assist in this emergency and to assure Pittsburgh of consistent and accurate newspaper service no matter what the difficulties of the moment may be.

PAUL BLOCK
Publisher

THE MORNING AFTER
THE SAINT PATRICK'S DAY FLOOD

immediately and has held it by a comfortable margin ever since. In general, the political complexion of the paper has been Independent Republican. It has regularly supported the Republican presidential candidates, even when it endorsed candidates of both parties in several local contests. In 1930 it endorsed John M. Hemphill, the Democratic candidate for governor, primarily because of his liberal stand on the liquor question. The *Post-Gazette* came out very early for repeal of the eighteenth amendment and campaigned for it actively while there was still strong prohibition sentiment in western Pennsylvania.

Although it was hardly to be classified as a crusading journal, the *Post-Gazette* conducted several spirited campaigns. One of the first was against slot machines. Likewise the paper directed a strong fight against discriminatory freight rates adversely affecting Pennsylvania coal and injuring both miners and operators. Of especial note in this connection was an editorial that appeared early in June, 1931, and drew favorable comment from all sides. It was the *Post-Gazette* that "broke" the first story indicating scandal in the Pittsburgh Department of Supplies and led the way to a thorough investigation and audit, which ended with the conviction of Director Bertram L. Succop and Mayor Charles Kline. More recently the paper has campaigned forcefully against abuses of the National Works Progress Administration in Pennsylvania.

In January, 1933, the *Post-Gazette* called to the attention of the community the attempts of certain self-interested individuals to bring the Pittsburgh public schools more directly under the control of the political bosses by making school boards elective instead of appointive. A series of articles, "When Ward Bosses Ran Our Schools," by James R. George, were very helpful in arousing the public to a sense of the danger of the projected change. The articles were clipped by the Board of Education and given a permanent place in their file records.

When an attempt was made by a group of politicians to remove Pittsburgh's picturesque mayor, William N. McNair, from office by "ripper" legislation, the *Post-Gazette* swung to his defense. It had been opposed to his election in the first place, but it felt that the method contrived for his removal represented unwarranted interference with local self-government. The *Post-Gazette* editorials, backed up by a popular poll of voters conducted by the paper, were considered by both McNair and the state assembly senate leaders to have largely influenced the defeat of the measure.

Perhaps one of the outstanding examples of reporting was a series written by Ray Sprigle during a mine strike. Dressed as a miner, he secured employment as a strike-breaker and lived for ten days behind one of the stockades in the midst of the strike zone. He wrote a fair, dispassionate story, which drew favorable comment from both miners and operators, of what was going on.

Another public service was performed in connection with the murder of a state highway policeman near New Castle, Pennsylvania. Following the case very closely, the newspaper office chanced to learn that the woman in the case, Irene Schroeder, had relatives in Osage, Oklahoma. A short wire story carried by the afternoon papers, with no suggestion of a local tie-up, concerning the kidnapping of a deputy sheriff in Arizona by a woman and man in a car was discounted by state police officers as having no connection with the local case. A telephone call from the *Post-Gazette* to the sheriff of Maricopa County, Arizona, succeeded in identifying the pair, however, and when they were trapped by a Posse in the desert and confronted with the Pennsylvania charge, they admitted their identity. The *Post-Gazette* sent a man by airplane to Arizona and covered all angles of their arrest.

A most amusing incident was associated with Inspector Charles Faulkner of the North Side, who had a great dislike for the old *Post* and later the *Post-Gazette* because of their constant battle with the police for permitting rackets to flourish in that part of the city virtually without interference. On the occasion of a fire in the old Cyclorama, Faulkner gave orders that the *Post-Gazette* should be prevented from taking any pictures and sent a photographer back in a taxi to the office with those instructions. At once the paper dispatched five men to the scene, two of them photographers. When one set up his camera and was pounced upon by the police, the other took a picture of the police jumping on him. The second man was arrested and lodged in the police station, but he managed to smuggle out the plate through the connivance of a friendly officer. A farcical hearing was conducted before a magistrate the following morning, but as a result of the intervention of the mayor, the case was dropped and the city council paid $75 for damage to the camera.

Following the tradition set up by the *Post*, the *Post-Gazette* evinced an alert interest in the promotion of aviation. In September, 1929, it sponsored a race from Cleveland to Pittsburgh for women flyers and soon afterwards brought out a special thirty-six page aviation edition to support a campaign for an adequate county airport. Repeatedly it alluded to the advantages of Pittsburgh as a great airplane manufacturing center.

Almost on the eve of its sesqui-centennial anniversary, the *Post-Gazette* was provided with a unique opportunity for community service. In the early morning hours of Saint Patrick's Day, 1936, the muddy waters of the Allegheny and the Monongahela rivers began to mount alarmingly above the standard twenty-five-foot flood level. Fed by melting snows and a general downpour of rain over western Pennsylvania, the rivers rapidly overflowed their banks and poured a torrent of destruction into the Golden Triangle. Stricken by a calamity that outran all forecast, the community was temporarily all but cut off from the outside world. The supply of power was shut down; the pure water reserve dropped dangerously; the threat of vandalism was narrowly averted by the prompt arrival of the national guard.

The paper quickly saw its function and performed it well. At first it extended hospitality to its unfortunate neighbor, the *Press*, but when the water came pouring into the *Post-Gazette* office there was no recourse but to make for the *Sun-Telegraph* office, fortunately situated on higher ground. But hardly had arrangements been completed for use of the presses that evening before high water put all power plants out of commission, and all three papers were forced to seek aid out of town. With perseverance, the *Post-Gazette* at once made arrangements to transfer its headquarters first to New Castle, Pennsylvania, and then to Youngstown, Ohio, where, in the offices of the *News* and the *Vindicator* respectively, it continued to print its editions until it could make arrangements to return to Pittsburgh.

One of the most difficult problems was to secure newsprint, since the out-of-town papers lacked supplies adequate to meet the demands of the *Post-Gazette's* 210,000 circulation. A large stock was on hand at the Duquesne warehouse, but, located as it was in the flooded area, it soon became inaccessible. Fearing this contingency, the management had arranged the previous night to have three cars hauled back to East Liberty, but this was of doubtful value for operations in New Castle, because the Pennsylvania Railroad line to that city was cut off. A trade was arranged with the *Sun-Telegraph* for a similar quantity of paper that had been held in Aliquippa because of the rising water. Forty men, including copy-readers, reporters, printers, stereotypers, and pressmen, as well as executives, were rushed by automobile to that steel town, where a special Pittsburgh and Lake Erie train carried men and paper to New Castle. In the meantime a corps of trucks was organized and with a crew of mailers dispatched to New Castle by way of Butler to handle the papers when printed and to take them back to the city. For the first three days of the flood emergency advertising was omitted to permit more comprehensive news coverage with the limited facilities available. After the first morning, however, when the supply of papers was gobbled up by news-hungry Pittsburghers within an hour after their arrival, regular delivery service was resumed to all readers of the paper.

The power shutdown cut off all telephone and telegraph service the first night, but press association wires from other points were hastily set up in the *New Castle News* office, and messengers relayed late developments from the flood-stricken area until three o'clock in the morning, when storage batteries permitted the first call from the Pittsburgh staff with final bulletins.

The damage inflicted by the high water on the newspaper plant was considerable. For days a crew of men was kept busy pumping water out of the basement of the *Post-Gazette* building at the rate of thirty thousand gallons per hour. Probably the loss ran into six figures. Nevertheless the paper exerted itself to keep the community apprised of all necessary announcements by the city authorities, and when the waters began to subside from the forty-six-foot stage, an all-time high, it was among the first to launch a campaign for immediate action on the part of the federal government in the construction of flood reservoirs to make impossible a repetition of the occurrence.

Throughout the years since 1927 the *Post-Gazette* has felt the steady influence of its owner, Paul Block, an Elmira, New York, lad who won outstanding success in the advertising business in New York City. His long experience as special representative for leading publishers brought him in constant and intimate contact with all phases of newspaper problems, and he entered the publishing field himself as co-owner of the *New York Mail* prior to its sale to Frank A. Munsey. His present group of papers had its beginning shortly after the World War when he purchased the *Newark Star-Eagle* and promptly proceeded to make it an effective force as well as a successful publishing enterprise in that city. He gradually extended his interests until today, in addition to the *Post-Gazette* and the Newark property, he owns the *Toledo Blade*, the *Toledo Times*, and the *Milwaukee Sentinel*. The *Memphis News Scimitar* was sold because he did not wish to be inconsistent politically, and the staff in Memphis insisted that it could only achieve real success as a Democratic paper. The *Lancaster New Era* and more recently the *Duluth Herald* and the *Duluth News-Tribune* were sold because he preferred to concentrate his interests in larger cities.

Many of the men who first started with him in the special representative business are now executives of Paul Block and Associates. Prizing friendship as one of the finest traits in human nature—his country home is known as "Friendship"—he has established a remarkable record of long tenure among those associated with him. There are many "twenty-five-year men" both in the "special" agency and on the staffs of all his newspapers, and there are many who have been employed for even longer periods.

Though independent politically, as evidenced by his support of Theodore Roosevelt's Bull Moose party in 1912 and his advocacy of many Democrats for local and state offices, Mr. Block has favored Republican administrations nationally. He knew well the late Calvin Coolidge and visited him at the White House on numerous occasions; his first announcement on assuming control of the *Post-Gazette* included an endorsement of Coolidge's administration and a pledge of hearty support.

Mr. Block maintains no elaborate central editorial or managing organization, but he keeps in extremely close personal touch at all times with each paper. He allows much latitude to executives on local issues and problems, but, of course, outlines major features of general policy for all the papers, and he frequently expresses his views on the most important national questions in signed page-one editorials.

The growth of the *Post-Gazette* has taxed the facilities that it acquired with the purchase of the *Post*, and plans have been outlined for a large investment in a new plant. The site at the corner of Grant Street and Second Avenue has been acquired for the purpose, but building plans were interrupted by the depression.

Sensing the potential importance of radio, the *Post-Gazette* publisher some years ago acquired station WWSW, which is operated by a separate corporation but in close coördination with the paper. While its development has been retarded by lack of adequate power, its facilities have been steadily improved. In the spring of 1936 the transmitter was moved to a new location close to the center of population, and a vertical antenna of the most modern type was erected.

Oliver Keller, the editor and vice president, assumed his

present position with the paper when the Block *régime* began. He is a native of Lancaster, Pennsylvania, where he had his first journalistic experience on the Lancaster *Examiner* and *New Era*. It was while on the latter that he first became associated with Mr. Block. Mention should be made as well of R. Kent Hanson, the business manager; Warren U. Christman, the managing editor; Ray Foudray, the circulation manager; Joseph Shuman, the city editor; William T. Martin, the chief editorial writer; and Cy Hungerford, the paper's ace cartoonist. The friends of Gifford Pinchot will not soon forget the Old Scout series, which Hungerford dedicated to the memory of Pennsylvania's effervescent governor. The King Charles the First series occasioned by Mayor Kline's European tour was also cleverly conceived. A special type of recognition was accorded to Hungerford in 1935, when a number of his drawings were placed on exhibition at the Gulf Galleries in Pittsburgh.

In 1936, its sesqui-centennial year, the *Post-Gazette* still preserves something of the uniqueness that is its inheritance from the past. It is a matter of record that the *Post-Gazette* carries more department store advertising than any other standard-sized morning newspaper in the United States not sold in combination.[4] In other respects the paper still gives indication that the *Gazette* tradition of leadership goes on. John Scull would probably view with approval the fact that the name *Gazette* is still carried at the masthead, and he would be constrained to admit that his successors have kept the paper in the line of its tradition by presenting a dignified brand of journalism and by consistently striving to advance the best interests of its community of readers.

NOTES

Chapter I—*The Press in the Wilderness*

¹ See further James Callahan, "An Account of the Resources and Industries of the Upper Monongahela Valley and the Tributary Region," in Bernard L. Butcher, *Genealogical and Personal History of the Upper Monongahela Valley, West Virginia*, 1:24 (New York, 1912).

On November 13, 1836, the *Gazette* printed an autograph letter from George Washington to Major Craig (February 13, 1796) inclosing an advertisement for the sale of some lands taken up by Washington in his surveying days. Washington requested particularly that the advertisement should be inserted three times in the *Pittsburgh Gazette* with an interval of two or three weeks between each appearance.

² *Pittsburgh Gazette*, September 2, 1786.

³ Neville B. Craig, *The History of Pittsburgh*, 214 (Pittsburgh, 1851). The letter was reprinted from the original in the *Gazette*, April 24, 1851. As late as 1800 Major Craig scrawled in his memorandum book opposite the date, September 17, 1800, "Lent John Scull twenty-seven quires of cartridge paper."

⁴ *Pittsburgh Gazette*, March 15, 1788.

⁵ *Ibid.*, February 24, 1798.

⁶ *Ibid.*, October 7, 1786.

⁷ A size of printing paper measuring 22" x 28".

⁸ *Pittsburgh Gazette*, January 29, 1813.

⁹ William G. Johnston, *Life and Reminiscences from Birth to Manhood of William G. Johnston*, 11 (Pittsburgh and New York, 1901).

Chapter II—*Newspaper Glimpses of Early Pittsburgh*

¹ Neville B. Craig, ed., "Extracts from the Journal of Arthur Lee," in *The Olden Time*, 2:339 (1847).

² This sketch is conveniently reprinted in Hugh H. Brackenridge, *Gazette Publications*, 7–19 (Carlisle, 1806).

³ *Pittsburgh Gazette*, June 13, 1789.

⁴ *Ibid.*, April 21, 1807.

⁵ *Ibid.*, June 13, 1787.

⁶ *Ibid.*, November 2, 1793.

⁷ The offspring of a white and a quadroon.

⁸ *Pittsburgh Gazette*, March 3, 1807.

⁹ *Ibid.*, April 20, 1799.

¹⁰ *Ibid.*, March 2, 1793.

¹¹ *Ibid.*, September 23, 1803.

¹² *Ibid.*, January 30, 1796.

¹³ *Ibid.*, December 26, 1789.

[14] *Ibid.*, March 9, 1816.
[15] *Ibid.*, August 25, 1787.
[16] *Ibid.*, November 11, 1815.
[17] *Ibid.*, October 10, 1808.
[18] *Ibid.*, February 20, 1790.

CHAPTER III—*Laying the Foundations of the New West*

[1] In September, 1800, George Cochran wrote to Colonel John Irwin expressing concern on account of the declining state of Mrs. Scull's health.
[2] *Pittsburgh Gazette*, March 26, 1813.
[3] *Ibid.*, August 26, 1806.
[4] *Ibid.*, February 7, 1812.
[5] *Ibid.*, November 2, 1793.
[6] *Ibid.*, January 21, 1803.
[7] *Ibid.*, July 22, 1803.
[8] *Ibid.*, April 25, 1789.
[9] *Ibid.*, August 19, 1803.

CHAPTER IV—*A Lone Outpost of Federalism*

[1] *Pittsburgh Gazette*, June 28, 1788.
[2] *Ibid.*, September 13, 1794.
[3] *Ibid.*, January 21, 1797.
[4] *Ibid.*, August 12, 1797.
[5] *Ibid.*, November 7, 1800.
[6] *Ibid.*, December 7, 1799.
[7] *Ibid.*, August 23, 1800. The *Gazette* reflected a latent anti-Semitic prejudice in the community directed against Israel's ancestry. Indeed he was usually referred to as "the Jew."
[8] *Pittsburgh Gazette*, August 29, 1800.
[9] *Tree of Liberty*, November 15, 1800.
[10] *Pittsburgh Gazette*, December 5, 1800.
[11] *Tree of Liberty*, October 2, 1802.
[12] *Pittsburgh Gazette*, October 8, 1813.
[13] *Ibid.*, May 7, 1813.
[14] *Ibid.*, August 26, 1815.
[15] *Ibid.*, March 30, 1816.

CHAPTER V—*New Pilots and Changing Winds*

[1] Holmes to John Irwin Scull, July 19, 1813.
[2] That is, the peace treaty that terminated the hostilities.
[3] *Pittsburgh Gazette*, August 9, 1816.

4 *Ibid.*, January 30, 1818.

5 John Irwin to John Irwin Scull, editor of the *Pittsburgh Gazette* (undated).

6 *Pittsburgh Gazette*, August 18, 1818.

7 W. H. Venable, *Beginnings of Literary Culture in the Ohio Valley, Historical and Biographical Sketches*, 375 (Cincinnati, 1891).

8 Mrs. Anne Royall, *Mrs. Royall's Pennsylvania or Travels Continued in the United States*, 2:81 (Washington, 1829).

9 *Pittsburgh Gazette*, July 2, 1819.

CHAPTER VI—*A Fighting Editor*

1 Reminiscences of the first carrier of the *Daily Gazette* in the *Pittsburgh Commercial Gazette*, July 29, 1886.

2 *Daily Pittsburgh Gazette*, January 1, 1838.

3 George T. Fleming, in his preface to the 1917 revised edition of Craig's *History of Pittsburgh*.

4 *Daily Pittsburgh Gazette*, January 25, 1834.

5 *Pittsburgh Mercury*, June 20, 1838.

6 *Daily Pittsburgher*, April 30, 1840.

7 *Daily Pittsburgh Gazette*, May 27, 1836.

8 Reprinted in Erasmus Wilson, *Standard History of Pittsburg, Pennsylvania* 849 (Chicago, 1898).

CHAPTER VII—*The Antimasonic Heresy*

1 Horace Greeley, *Recollections of a Busy Life*, 81 (New York and Boston, 1868)

2 See further the author's article, "The Antimasonic Movement in Western Pennsylvania," in *Western Pennsylvania Historical Magazine*, 18:255–266 (December, 1935).

3 *Pittsburgh Gazette*, July 16, 1830.

4 *Pittsburgh Daily Gazette*, August 11, 1841.

5 *Daily Pittsburgh Gazette*, January 19, 1836.

6 *Pittsburgh Mercury*, December 9, 1835.

7 A letter written by Van Buren (July 20, 1830) while secretary of state to the American Consul in Rome authorizing him to congratulate the Pope on his recent elevation to the Holy See.

8 *Daily Pittsburgh Gazette*, October 11, 1837.

9 *Pittsburgh Mercury*, October 18, 1837.

10 *Daily Pittsburgh Gazette*, September 13, 1838.

11 Reprinted in *ibid.*, January 29, 1840.

12 *Ibid.*, January 23, 1840. Later in the campaign, Craig remarked, "The singing of Tippecanoe songs at the corner of 4th and Market Streets last night would have awakened the drowsiest of Amos' children."

13 *Daily Advocate and Advertiser* (Pittsburgh), October 8, 1840.

14 *Daily Pittsburgh Gazette*, October 9, 1840.

CHAPTER VIII—*The Gazette Adopts the American System*

[1] *Pittsburgh Gazette*, September 29, 1818.

[2] *Pittsburgh Gazette and Manufacturing and Mercantile Advertiser*, November 20, 1820.

[3] *Daily Pittsburgh Gazette*, January 29, 1840.

[4] *Pittsburgh Gazette*, September 17, 1819.

[5] *Ibid.*, December 31, 1819.

[6] *Daily Pittsburgh Gazette*, March 26, 1834.

[7] *Ibid.*, July 14, 1836.

[8] *Pittsburgh Gazette*, November 26, 1813.

[9] *Daily Pittsburgh Gazette*, March 16, 1836.

[10] *Ibid.*, July 26, 1839.

[11] *Pittsburgh Gazette and Manufacturing and Mercantile Advertiser*, October 30, 1820.

[12] *Ibid.*, October 30, 1820.

[13] *Daily Pittsburgh Gazette*, July 11, 1837.

CHAPTER IX—*Smoke Stacks and Steeple Tops*

[1] *Daily Pittsburgh Gazette*, March 25, 1835.

[2] *Pittsburgh Gazette*, October 27, 1818.

[3] *Ibid.*, September 28, 1832.

[4] *Daily Pittsburgh Gazette*, April 16, 1836.

[5] *Ibid.*, February 11, 1840.

[6] *Ibid.*, March 13, 1834.

[7] *Pittsburgh Gazette*, January 21, 1820.

[8] *Pittsburgh Daily Gazette*, June 24, 1841.

[9] *Pittsburgh Gazette*, January 14, 1817.

[10] *Pittsburgh Gazette and Manufacturing and Mercantile Advertiser*, December 25, 1820.

[11] *Pittsburgh Gazette*, May 16, 1817.

[12] *Daily Pittsburgh Gazette*, April 27, 1840.

CHAPTER X—*A Deacon at the Helm*

[1] *Pittsburgh Daily Gazette and Advertiser*, December 11, 1844. In 1850, the distribution of the *Gazette* in Pittsburgh was still taken care of by one city carrier.

[2] *Daily Pittsburgh Gazette*, December 8, 1857.

[3] *Pittsburgh Daily Gazette*, August 24, 1849.

[4] *Daily Pittsburgh Gazette*, April 12, 1860.

[5] *Philadelphia North American*, January 5, 1847.

[6] *Pittsburgh Daily Gazette and Advertiser*, November 19, 1844.

[7] *Ibid.*, April 8, 1846.

8 A printing term signifying a space one column wide and of equivalent length.

9 *Daily Pittsburgh Gazette*, January 8, 1859.

10 *Ibid.*, January 1, 1853.

11 *Ibid.*, January 9, 1851.

12 *New York Daily Tribune*, November 25, 1853.

CHAPTER XI—*Political Cross-Currents*

1 *Pittsburgh Daily Gazette*, January 5, 1848.

2 *Pittsburgh Daily Gazette and Advertiser*, November 12, 1844.

3 *Ibid.*, July 8, 1845.

4 *Pittsburgh Daily Gazette*, April 24, 1847.

5 *Ibid.*, September 14, 1848.

6 *Ibid.*, October 10, 1848.

7 *Ibid.*, November 1, 1848.

8 *Daily Pittsburgh Gazette*, August 31, 1852.

9 *Ibid.*, March 6, 1854.

10 *Ibid.*, January 3, 1855.

11 *Ibid.*, March 30, 1855.

12 *Pittsburgh Commercial Gazette*, December 30, 1878.

13 *Daily Pittsburgh Gazette*, January 1, 1856.

14 *Ibid.*, May 24, 1856.

15 *Ibid.*, May 22, 1860.

16 *Ibid.*, March 9, 1861.

17 *Ibid.*, April 13, 1861.

CHAPTER XII—*The Battle Cry of Freedom*

1 The valuation of the entire newspaper industry in Pittsburgh in 1865 was estimated by the editor of the *Gazette* as being approximately a quarter of a million dollars.

2 *Daily Pittsburgh Gazette*, June 13, 1863.

3 *Ibid.*, July 17, 1863.

4 *Daily Pittsburgh Gazette and Commercial Journal*, October 28, 1861.

5 *Daily Pittsburgh Gazette*, June 18, 1863.

6 *Ibid.*, November 7, 1864.

7 *Ibid.*, April 16, 1865.

CHAPTER XIII—*Mid-Century Strivings*

1 *Pittsburgh Daily Gazette and Advertiser*, August 9, 1844.

2 *Ibid.*, August 9, 1844.

3 *Wheeling Daily Times*, August 20, 1846.

4 *Daily Pittsburgh Gazette*, May 5, 1864.

5 *Pittsburgh Daily Gazette*, August 5, 1848.

6 *Daily Pittsburgh Gazette*, January 1, 1853.

[7] *Ibid.*, January 1, 1853.

[8] *Pittsburgh Daily Gazette and Advertiser*, August 29, 1845.

[9] *Ibid.*, February 7, 1846.

[10] *Ibid.*, March 17, 1846.

[11] *Ibid.*, January 9, 1847.

[12] *Pittsburgh Daily Gazette*, May 26, 1848.

[13] *Daily Pittsburgh Gazette*, July 21, 1851.

[14] *Ibid.*, March 8, 1853.

[15] *Ibid.*, February 16, 1854.

[16] *Pittsburgh Daily Gazette and Advertiser*, April 11, 1845.

[17] *Ibid.*, April 23, 1845.

[18] *Ibid.*, February 25, 1846.

[19] *Pittsburgh Daily Gazette*, August 18, 1849.

[20] *Pittsburgh Daily Gazette and Advertiser*, February 4, 1846.

[21] *Daily Pittsburgh Gazette*, June 3, 1853.

[22] *Ibid.*, March 8, 1861.

[23] *Ibid.*, January 19, 1858.

[24] *Pittsburgh Daily Gazette and Advertiser*, October 14, 1846.

[25] *Pittsburgh Daily Gazette*, September 22, 1849.

[26] *Daily Pittsburgh Gazette*, August 1, 1860.

CHAPTER XIV—*The Reign of Reed*

[1] For further information about N. P. Reed's early life see the obituary account in the *Pittsburgh Commercial Gazette*, March 30, 1891.

[2] The *Pittsburgh Leader*.

[3] A good review of Ford's journalistic experience may be found in the *Dictionary of American Biography*, 6:515–16 (New York, 1928—date).

[4] The literature having to do with Erasmus Wilson's career is extensive. See in particular George I. Reed, *Century Cyclopedia of History and Biography of Pennsylvania*, 2:48–49 (Chicago, 1904); George T. Fleming, *History of Pittsburgh and Environs*, 3:869–870 (New York and Chicago, 1922), and various Pittsburgh newspapers bearing the dates January 14 and 15, 1922.

[5] This poem was read by Riley at the annual dinner of the Pittsburgh Press Club, January 29, 1891, in response to the toast, "Our Kind of A Man." It is reprinted in *The Poems and Prose Sketches of James Whitcomb Riley*, 1:41–45 (New York, 1915).

[6] *Dictionary of American Biography*, 16:533–534; *Pittsburgh Commercial Gazette*, January 25, 1890.

[7] Josiah Copley, *Kansas and the Country beyond on the Line of the Union Pacific Railway, Eastern Division, from the Missouri to the Pacific Ocean, Partly from Personal Observation and Partly from Information Drawn from Authentic Sources*, (Philadelphia, 1867).

⁸ These circulation figures were obtained from data compiled by George P. Rowell & Company, publishers, *American Newspaper Directory*, (New York, 1869–1910); and N. W. Ayer & Son, publishers, *Directory of Newspapers and Periodicals*, (Philadelphia, 1880– date).

CHAPTER XV—*Tales from the Headlines*

¹ Frank M. O'Brien, *The Story of the Sun*, 156 (New York and London, 1918)
² *Pittsburgh Commercial Gazette*, February 21, 1898.
³ *Ibid.*, June 18, 1898.
⁴ *Ibid.*, June 20, 1898.
⁵ *Ibid.*, September 21, 1881.
⁶ *Ibid.*, June 1, 1889.
⁷ See the *Daily Post* (Pittsburgh), July 26, 1877.
⁸ *Pittsburgh Commercial Gazette*, July 23, 1877.
⁹ For a fuller explanation of this curious affair see Donald L. McMurry, *Coxey's Army, a Study of the Industrial Army Movement of 1894* (Boston, 1929).
¹⁰ *Pittsburgh Commercial Gazette*, April 3, 1894.

CHAPTER XVI—*The Heritage of a War*

¹ *Pittsburgh Commercial Gazette*, February 26, 1877.
² *Gazette Times* (Pittsburgh), July 27, 1911.
³ *Daily Post* (Pittsburgh), September 2, 1880.
⁴ *Pittsburgh Commercial Gazette*, October 28, 1880.
⁵ Salt River was a current expression for party defeat. The allusion was to a river in Kentucky, very crooked and located near the retreat of a pirate band that was noted for never disgorging any goods falling into its hands.
⁶ *Pittsburgh Commercial Gazette*, September 17, 1884.
⁷ *Ibid.*, October 6, 1892.
⁸ *Ibid.*, May 5, 1886.
⁹ *Ibid.*, December 27, 1895.
¹⁰ *Ibid.*, October 28, 1896.
¹¹ *Ibid.*, November 4, 1896.
¹² Wayland F. Dunaway, *A History of Pennsylvania*, 524 (New York, 1935).
¹³ *Pittsburgh Gazette*, May 29, 1904.
¹⁴ *Pittsburgh Commercial Gazette*, February 22, 1893.

CHAPTER XVII—*The Quiet Observer*

¹ *Pittsburgh Gazette*, May 11, 1869.
² *Pittsburgh Commercial Gazette*, May 18, 1880.
³ *Ibid.*, July 23, 1896.
⁴ *Pittsburgh Gazette*, September 23, 1870.

[5] *Daily Pittsburgh Gazette*, June 11, 1866.

[6] *Pittsburgh Commercial Gazette*, September 5, 1877.

[7] *Ibid.*, September 5, 1889.

[8] *Ibid.*, July 17, 1893.

[9] *Pittsburgh Gazette*, February 8, 1873.

[10] *Pittsburgh Commercial Gazette*, August 27, 1884.

[11] *Ibid.*, May 29, 1879.

[12] *Pittsburgh Gazette*, January 31, 1871.

[13] *Pittsburgh Commercial Gazette*, December 26, 1881.

CHAPTER XVIII—*Enter—The Olivers*

[1] Designed by D. H. Burnham, one of the architects who drew the plans for the Columbian Exposition.

[2] *Gazette Times* (Pittsburgh), February 8, 1915.

[3] *Ibid.*, July 2, 1908.

[4] These and the above circulation figures were collated from the annual volumes of N. W. Ayer & Son, *Directory of Newspapers and Periodicals*.

CHAPTER XIX—*Faces and Features*

[1] *Gazette Times* (Pittsburgh), July 29, 1911.

[2] *Dictionary of American Biography*, 6:515.

[3] So George Seibel relates the story.

[4] According to some oral recollections of McCready Huston, who was acquainted with Connelly at the time.

[5] The substance of this account of Baglin was related to the author by Pierce Egan, Baglin's friend and helper for some years.

[6] See *Gazette Times* (Pittsburgh), March 26, April 8, 1911; *Pittsburgh Press*, March 26, 1911; *Pittsburgh Chronicle Telegraph*, March 28, 1911.

[7] The occasion was a gathering of the press humorists on the Rockefeller estate in Cleveland.

[8] *Gazette Times* (Pittsburgh), October 30, 1906.

[9] *Pittsburgh Gazette*, November 9, 1902.

[10] Grant Overton, *The Women Who Make Our Novels*, 228 (New York, 1922).

CHAPTER XX—*The Editor's World*

[1] *Pittsburgh Commercial Gazette*, June 1, 1900.

[2] *Gazette Times* (Pittsburgh), May 4, 1906.

[3] A newspaper man in Zanesville, Ohio, was so impressed by one of the editorials that he wrote to the *Gazette Times* congratulating it for the best editorial on the subject that had come to his attention.

[4] *Pittsburgh Gazette*, November 4, 1904; *Gazette Times* (Pittsburgh), October 12, 1908.

5 *Ibid.*, November 6, 1916.

6 *Ibid.*, July 28, 1914.

7 See issues from May 9 to May 15, 1915.

8 *Gazette Times* (Pittsburgh), September 19, 1916.

9 *Ibid.*, May 15, 1918.

10 *Ibid.*, April 27, 1919.

11 From papers in the possession of Charles J. Doyle.

12 *Gazette Times* (Pittsburgh), February 7, 1924.

13 *Ibid.*, June 28, 1924.

CHAPTER XXI—*Only Yesterday*

1 *Gazette Times* (Pittsburgh), January 31, 1907.

2 *Ibid.*, September 10, 1908.

3 *Ibid.*, March 14, 1924.

4 Victor Herbert was conductor of the Pittsburgh Symphony Orchestra, 1898–1904.

5 *Gazette Times* (Pittsburgh), August 28, 1914.

6 *Ibid.*, January 12, 1908.

7 The episode is amply described in clippings preserved in the Bregg scrap books.

8 George W. Putnam to Charles M. Bregg (undated).

9 Bregg scrap books.

10 *Gazette Times* (Pittsburgh), October 11, 1908.

CHAPTER XXII—*The Last Merger*

1 *Pittsburgh Post-Gazette*, August 21, 1934.

2 Joseph Anthony and Woodman Morrison, eds., *The Best News Stories of 1924*, 296–299 (Boston, 1925).

3 As related by Arthur Braun, the *Post* publisher, who was present on that occasion.

4 Consult *Media Records* for 1934 and 1935.

INDEX